Going Global

GOING GLOBAL

An Information Sourcebook for Small and Medium-Sized Businesses

Susan C. Awe

LIBRARIES UNLIMITED
An Imprint of ABC-CLIO, LLC

A B C 🌐 C L I O

Santa Barbara, California • Denver, Colorado • Oxford, England

Copyright 2009 by Susan C. Awe

All rights reserved. No part of this publication may be reproduced, stored in a retrieval system, or transmitted, in any form or by any means, electronic, mechanical, photocopying, recording, or otherwise, except for the inclusion of brief quotations in a review, without prior permission in writing from the publisher.

Library of Congress Cataloging-in-Publication Data

Awe, Susan C., 1948–
  Going global : an information sourcebook for small and medium-sized businesses / Susan C. Awe.
    p. cm.
  Includes bibliographical references and index.
  ISBN 978–1–59158–651–7 (hard copy : alk. paper)
1. Small business. 2. International trade. 3. Globalization. I. Title.
HD2341.A94   2009
658.8'4—dc22 2009020615

13 12 11 10 9   1 2 3 4 5

This book is also available on the World Wide Web as an eBook.
Visit www.abc-clio.com for details.

ABC-CLIO, LLC
130 Cremona Drive, P.O. Box 1911
Santa Barbara, California 93116-1911

This book is printed on acid-free paper ∞

Manufactured in the United States of America

Contents

Illustrations

Acknowledgments

I'd like to thank the University of New Mexico University Libraries for providing time to research and write this book and the InterLibrary Loan services and staff. And, of course, I thank the staff of UNM's Parish Memorial Library for Business and Economics for their support.

I want to thank my husband Steven Maddock for all his love and support throughout my library career and while working on this book! Chaco, Gretta, and Poudre, my feline assistants, once again provided moral support, diversion, and companionship.

And, I am grateful for the help and assistance of Barbara Ittner, Acquisitions Editor at ABC-CLIO, for keeping me on track and giving me lots of virtual pats on the back when I experienced technical difficulties, and in general to Libraries Unlimited/ABC-CLIO for support and encouragement during the process.

Introduction

Even though it now houses over 6 billion people, the world continues to shrink thanks to the Internet, cheaper and faster air travel, and a general business bent toward globalization. The average travel time from Chicago, Illinois, to Beijing, China, is 13 hours and 40 minutes, and Internet travelers can get there in a few clicks. The Internet is dramatically altering the way customers and businesses interact, raising service levels to customers, and generating more sales. Global communication networks, next-day airfreight deliveries worldwide and even CNN make international business quicker, easier, and more logical. All types of barriers to international trade are coming down and user-friendly systems are the norm. Today's business world is one of unprecedented change, and the former business practices are just not good enough. The digital economy helps all businesses increase customer communications and generate sales through more frequent customer interactions.

When goods and/or services are exchanged across national borders, it is called international trade. Exports are the goods and services sold by individuals or nations; and imports are the goods and services purchased. Small and medium-sized enterprises (companies with fewer than 500 employees or SMEs) accounted for 97 percent of all U.S. exporters in 2004 per the current U.S. Census Bureau's *Profile of U.S. Exporting Companies, 2003–2004*, and 59 percent of all SME exporters posted sales to only one foreign market. SMEs could sharply boost sales by entering new markets. About 90 percent of SMEs are doing business from a single U.S. location, and they often do not have offshore business affiliations that can help circumvent trade barriers and gain market access. In the *Profile of U.S. Exporting Companies, 2004–2005*, the number of identified exporting companies increased by 6,266 or nearly 3 percent, and nearly all of those were small and medium-sized businesses. China remains the fourth-largest market for U.S. merchandise exports from SMEs after Canada, Mexico, and Japan.

Many U.S. companies that are currently involved in the international marketplace started out when their interest was piqued by an international inquiry generated from a Web site, attendance at a trade fair, or an ad placed in a U.S. publication. If this happens to you or your company, how you decide to proceed in developing your international market or not will likely set the tone of your company's fortunes for years to come. Learn here how to develop a strategy and approach to exporting or importing that will increase your chances of success.

ORGANIZATION

Going Global will provide SMEs with the print and Web resources necessary to discover advantages and disadvantages of international business, information gathering, the importance of business, export, and marketing plans, ins and outs of international selling, using the Internet, and more. Taking your business international is a long-term project that involves many steps and requires careful planning. Chapters are organized around functional areas such as how to do a business plan, how to analyze the competition and the market, how to find foreign customers, how to set up an international business, and how to manage a global business.

One of the top reasons that SMEs fail in attempts to sell to another country is inadequate planning, and poor planning and management results in poor market analysis and failure. Remember, though, that 90 percent of the means by which your company conducts domestic operations are directly transferable to the international marketplace. Chapter 1 looks at why a company goes global, if your company is ready and what factors need to be in place. Chapter 2 leads you to many sources of statistics and information that will help you get ready to export and/or import. Chapters 3, 4, and 5 tackle the topics of market analysis, competition, finding customers, different approaches to exporting or importing, and setting up to do business. Chapter 6 will help you learn about different cultures and how they do business as well as discuss international franchising as a way to enter the global market. Chapter 7 illustrates the necessity of good management skills and the use of technology and the Internet to succeed in business today. Finally, Chapter 8 is all about e-commerce and the global market. A lengthy Appendix leads you to regional and country-specific resources for help when you have decided on which markets to enter.

Going Global gathers together in one source a vast amount of information to help new international businesses locate and use data from a wide range of resources. It is imperative that small and medium-sized businesses understand the concepts covered and use current, accurate information for their plans. When we as consumers enjoy fresh flowers from Latin America or foreign cars from Europe, we are participating in and benefiting from international trade, so it is a game where everyone wins.

SMEs are vitally important to our nation and helping them succeed helps us all. Selling our products/services elsewhere in the world or bringing new products to U.S. consumers also benefits everyone. Learning how and when to use knowledgeable experts to assist in generating and managing international growth is a key to success. Also learning and understanding who your experts are and what they do may generate additional revenue for your company. Use *Going Global* to ready your company to proceed into international business from a well-organized, strategic base.

Why Get into International Trade

Chapter Highlights:

Opportunities
Potential Problems: Risks and/or Disadvantages
When Is the Right Time to Enter the Global Market?
Are You and Your Company Ready to Export?
Why Good Exporters/Importers Fail

First, can a small business with less than a million dollars in annual sales succeed as an exporter in today's highly competitive global market, and does your business have good reasons for doing business outside of the United States? According to Howard Lewis III and J. David Richardson in their book *Why Global Commitment Really Matters!* (Institute for International Economics, 2000), "yes, absolutely!" is the only answer for both questions. Companies that export continually grow faster and fail far less often than companies that do not. According to Lewis and Richardson, U.S. exporting firms experience 2–4 percent *higher annual growth in employment than their nonexporting competitors*. In addition, the decision may have partially been taken out of your hands if you discover that your company is competing internationally because foreign-owned companies are becoming involved in your domestic market. What are the advantages of getting into international business?

OPPORTUNITIES

1. *Business expansion.* Increasing sales and profits are always incentives for business expansion. According to the World Trade Organization, 95 percent of the world's consumers live outside the United States, so U.S. businesses selling

exclusively to a domestic market are reaching a very small number of their potential customers. Exporting allows companies to grow, to become more competitive, and to diversify their portfolios to weather changes in the domestic economy. Exporting helps to ensure survival and generate additional income.

2. *Increased sales.* Increasing sales is important. The potential for expanding into exporting is enormous and will provide your company with information in relation to your competition, new product development, and emerging opportunities. If most consumers live outside the United States, there is a huge market for all types of goods and services. The information a company gathers to expand by doing a market analysis as explained in Chapter 3 will prove useful for many types of decisions. According to the Small Business Administration, small and medium-sized companies account for almost 97 percent of U.S. exporters but still represent only about 30 percent of the total export value of U.S. goods.

3. *Market diversification.* Diversifying your business's markets is essential today. Joining the export market will reduce your dependence on existing markets. After developing an export relationship with one country, it is easier to move forward to reach other countries in that region, further expanding your market. The U.S. Commercial Service on the Export.gov Web site (http://www.export.gov/) states that nearly two-thirds of small and medium-sized exporters only sell to one foreign market; many of these firms could boost exports by expanding the number of countries they sell to and gaining a larger global market share.

4. *Enhanced domestic competitiveness.* Being competitive is essential. The development of a strategic alliance with a foreign partner may help your company save money on development costs of new technology, giving your business a competitive edge in the industry. While your company may want to stay the same size and focus on quality, the competitive environment creates situations where your competition continues to grow and offer lower prices and more selection because they sourced components internationally and can now offer economy of scale.

5. *Stability.* Exporting will stabilize seasonal market fluctuations and help sell excess production capacity. Many businesses are affected adversely by changes caused by the climate, storms, droughts, and so forth, and selling into more markets will help a company shorten or bypass seasonal fluctuations. By tapping global markets, firms are no longer held captive to economic changes, varying consumer demand, and seasonal fluctuations in the domestic economy. Agriculture, tourism, construction, and manufacturing —especially toy and apparel sectors—industries are most affected by seasonal fluctuations. Inventory does not produce income until it is sold and often costs a company dollars needed for expansion.

POTENTIAL PROBLEMS: RISKS AND/OR DISADVANTAGES

In doing business of any kind, uncertainty and risk are always present, but they can be managed and controlled. All the major exporting countries make provisions for payment risks and losses in goods or services to protect exporters and the bankers who provided financial support for these ventures. In general, the four major areas of risk include commercial, foreign exchange, political, and shipping or transportation.

1. Commercial concerns involve not being paid, goods not delivered, default by the buyer, changes in competition, and disputes over the product or service and its warranty.

2. Foreign exchange fluctuations are always part of the picture for international trade. A market-based exchange rate changes whenever the values of either of the two component currencies change. A currency tends to become more valuable whenever demand for it is greater than the available supply.

3. Political issues include a coup d'état, revolution, expulsion, revocation of license, and similar incidents that can occur at any time.

4. Shipping or transportation issues arise in domestic business as well and must always be dealt with on an individual basis. Insurance can be expensive but is wonderful to have when something is damaged or lost in transit.

Additionally, disadvantages for exporters and importers may include having to subordinate short-term profits to long-term gains, hire additional staff and assign some personnel to travel abroad, incur more administrative and travel costs, modify your product or package as well as modify or develop new promotional materials, wait longer for payments, endure fluctuations in foreign currency exchange, and obtain additional financing and import or export licenses. The company may want to pursue exporting or importing through an intermediary if the decision is to forego direct exporting right now because the disadvantages are difficult or impossible to overcome. However, proper planning can overcome these obstacles and help avoid critical mistakes.

WHEN IS THE RIGHT TIME TO ENTER THE GLOBAL MARKET?

The economies of the world are interdependent. And, as uschamber.com magazine (http://www.uschambermagazine.com/content/default) states, free trade creates more jobs for everyone. Called the age of interdependence, now is a time of increasing expectations brought about by worldwide distribution, the Internet, satellite communications, and speedy transportation systems. Globalization is no longer a buzzword but a reality. As Ben Bernanke, chairman of the Federal Reserve System, stated in a speech at the Montana Development Summit 2007, "At the most basic level, trade is beneficial because it allows people to specialize in the goods and services they produce best and most efficiently." International trade is not a static process, so businesses must constantly adjust. Regardless of national deficits or surpluses, fluctuating exchange rates, and political problems in individual countries, the time is always right for an import or export business to make a profit. Experienced entrepreneurs and business owners know that they have to swing with the continuous political and economic changes over which they have no control. To succeed in international markets, you do not have to be a big-name firm with lavish resources and an entire department devoted to exporting or importing. The next chapter provides many resources to explore opportunities in international trade.

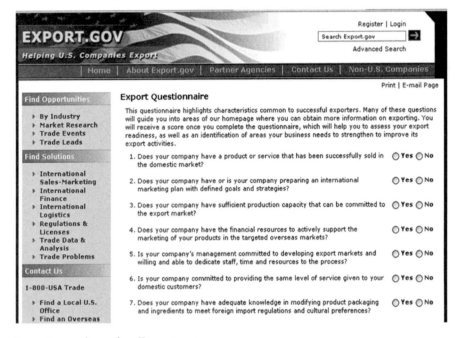

Export questionnaire. Export.gov.

ARE YOU AND YOUR COMPANY READY TO EXPORT?

If you are feeling unsure about whether exporting is too big a jump for your business, the Export.gov Web site sponsored by the U.S. government has a questionnaire at http://hq-intranet04.ita.doc.gov/bid/export _questionnaire.asp that may help you decide what to do and determine what you do or do not know about exporting.

This questionnaire will help you assess your readiness to export, reminding you to think about your product or service, production if necessary, marketing, market selection and research, pricing, management, financing, and other parts of an export plan. A useful book from the U.S. Department of Commerce (10th ed. 2007), published online, is *A Basic Guide to Exporting*.

This practical guide is divided into sections on "The Vision," "Technical," and "Conducting Business Abroad." It suggests you ask yourself the following questions:

- What knowledge of the foreign market that you want to enter do you already have or have available?
- What is the company's capacity to produce, distribute, and sell in a foreign market?
- Is your company flexible enough to meet the changing needs of the domestic and foreign market? Be clear and develop achievable export objectives and be open to new ways of doing business.
- What staffing, management, and other skills are available in your company to support foreign expansion? Are you committed to exporting and can you develop efficient ways of responding quickly to customer inquiries and of dealing with the language barriers?
- Can you obtain enough capital or lines of credit to produce necessary products or services? Can you locate people to advise you on the legal and tax implications of exporting and dealing effectively with different monetary systems?

An additional very useful resource is the Centers for International Trade Development Web site, created by the State of California. Find its practical information on export readiness, exporting basics, and export FAQs at http://www.citd.org/StartupKit/index.cfm (see page 6).

The State of California's Trade Information Database includes U.S. and world trade and economic data, trade contacts and leads, trade reference tools, foreign market research, trade and investment regulations, trade documentation, and finance and insurance sections. A trade resources director provides information on numerous trade associations and organizations. A trade show calendar is also available.

WHY GOOD EXPORTERS/IMPORTERS FAIL

Primary reasons for failure include inefficient control over costs and cash flow, underpricing goods, poor or nonexistent customer service, poor relationships with suppliers, indecisive management, and reluctance to select and pay professional help. These factors of failure are included to help in your planning for international expansion. The U.S. government promotes increasing our exports and will help new exporters or importers in many ways; take advantage of resources provided by tax dollars. By developing your knowledge of the intricacies of international trade and increasing your networks of contacts, your chances of success will be greatly increased.

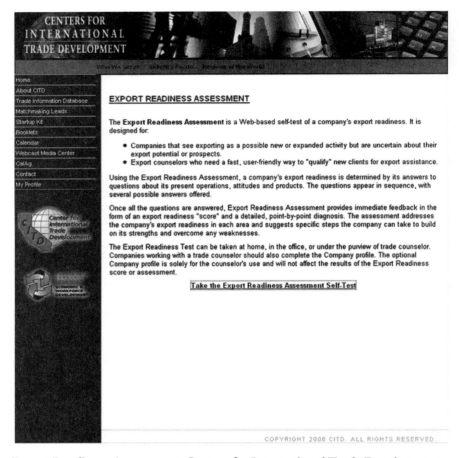

Export Readiness Assessment. Centers for International Trade Development.

Source: California Community Colleges,
Economic and Workforce Development Program

REFERENCES

(Starred titles discussed in the chapter)

Print Resources

A Basic Guide to Exporting: Official Government Resource for Small and Medium-sized Businesses. 10th ed. U.S. Department of Commerce, 2007. 190p. ISBN 0-16079-20-4-5. $19.95. Also available online (1998 edition) at www.unzco.com/basicguide/index.html.

Conventional wisdom once held that U.S. businesses should be content selling in their domestic market as international markets were too difficult and too expensive to penetrate. However, in the past decade, barriers to trade have been lowered and advances in communications technology have been and are tremendous. Now exporting is seen as a prime growth area, and this title describes the costs and risks associated with exporting, how to develop a strategy for success, where to get the knowledge to enter exporting, and how to find contacts and leads. This comprehensive guide is full of nuts-and-bolts information necessary to meet the challenges of globalization. Find out how to identify markets for a company's products, finance international transactions, handle orders and shipping, as well as locate professional export advice. Sample letters and forms plus very detailed information on government programs and contact information in many different countries are included. Assistance from the federal and state government is also discussed.

Capela, John J. *Import/Export for Dummies*. Wiley Publishing, Inc., 2008. ISBN 978-0-470-26094-4. 338p. $19.99.

Capela is an international business consultant, and this practical guide covers how to evaluate import/export opportunities, expand your global operations, identify target markets, find customers, follow the rules and regulations of different countries, and develop a marketing strategy. The introductory discussion of what environmental forces make international business different is essential reading before you start your international adventure. Another important section discusses the selection of products and suppliers. Learn about the various approaches to exporting and importing and some of the qualities you need to possess to be successful.

Cyr, Donald, and Gray, Douglas. *Marketing Your Product*. 4th ed. Self-Counsel Press, Inc., 2004. 200p. ISBN 1-55180-394-1. $18.95.

Covering all the essentials of marketing, this expanded edition of a marketing classic demonstrates how your business can carve a niche for its products or services. Learn about market researching, market positioning, marketing strategy planning, product launching, and competitor awareness. Cyr and Gray answer readers' questions, such as what you should know about global marketing and why people choose one product over another. One highlight in this edition is a chapter on the value of the Internet as a marketing tool in the global marketplace. Good worksheets help entrepreneurs and new small-business owners develop individualized marketing plans.

Dorsey, Jennifer. *Start Your Own Import/Export Business*. 2nd ed. Entrepreneur Press, 2007. 252p. ISBN 1-59918-108-8. $15.95.

This book contains insights and practical advice for entering global markets. It covers aspects of the start-up process, including collecting money from overseas transactions, using the Internet to simplify your transactions, accessing trade law information to keep your business in compliance, how to find contacts in the United States and abroad, and choosing a customs broker. Chapters on market research, working online, employees, pricing, and insurance will help run a business efficiently and effectively. A brief appendix on international trade resources may also prove useful. Interviews with successful importers and exporters and an updated resource list will help show the way to success.

Exporters' Encyclopaedia. Annual. Dun & Bradstreet.

A comprehensive world reference guide, this encyclopedia is divided into 220 country-specific sections; firms specializing in international business, laws, and legislation; international trade associations; government agencies; shipping practice; and reference data on weights and measures for overseas ports. Find key contacts, trade and safety regulations, and information on required documentation. Marketing data include legal requirements for importer/agents, procurement standards, environmental protection and pollution control, marking, and labeling. The encyclopedia also provides passport regulations and business etiquette guidelines.

Foley, James F. *The Global Entrepreneur.* Jamric Press International, 2004. 424p. ISBN 0-975-3153-07. $19.95.

Using simple language, Foley explains the world of international trade. He uses personal experiences to explain the technical fundamentals of creating a competitive international strategy, avoiding financial and legal hassles, and participating in a trade mission for the first time. Foley explains how to use the Internet to expand a small business overseas. An appendix provides sample forms and instructions for nine basic export documents.

Hinkelman, Edward, et al. *Importers Manual.* Annual. World Trade Press. 960p.

Information on how to import virtually any commodity into the United States can be found in this practical reference. It is precisely organized for ease of use and is divided into the major sections of Commodity Index; U.S. Customs Entry and Clearance; International Banking; Legal Considerations of Importing; and Packing, Shipping, and Insurance. The heart of the work, the Commodity Index, contains entry procedures, documentation, restrictions, and prohibitions; marking and labeling requirements; and contact information for regulatory agencies for all products that can be imported into the United States.

Jagoe, John R. *Export Sales and Marketing Manual 2008: The Bible of Exporting.* Export Institute of the United States. 520p. ISBN 0-943677-66-1. $295.

Having been updated annually for 21 consecutive years, this international trade publication has achieved longevity and global reach. This manual covers all the steps involved in selling products in world markets. Over 120 illustrations, 85 graphs, 40 flow charts, and 60 sample international trade documents lead the user through the process. Jagoe helps users conduct market research through 1,200 Web site addresses providing information on various markets and products and services, and he provides a lengthy glossary of export terms and a detailed index for quick access to important information. This professional and practical resource will help you effectively enter and succeed in the global market.

**Lewis, Howard III, and Richardson, J. David. *Why Global Commitment Really Matters!* Institution for International Economics, 2001. 69p. ISBN 0-88132-298-9. $15.00.

In this study, Lewis and Richardson explore new gains from deep international integration. A growing body of research literature demonstrates that globally engaged firms and their workers enjoy numerous performance benefits over local counterparts that are identical with respect to size, industry, and location. Conscious decisions to export, import, invest abroad, or partner with foreign investors or technology seem to be a catalyst for added benefits, especially rapid and stable job growth. Gradually, globally engaged firms rejuvenate whole industries as their market share rises and that of more insular firms shrinks.

Any, many, or all types of global commitments reward firms, workers, and local communities. The study supplements its research survey with real-life profiles of representative U.S. exporters, importers (often businesses importing machines and components), investors abroad, foreign affiliates, and technology partners. It also weighs criticisms and alternative interpretations of the research, and it discusses the problems of those left on the margins of global engagement.

Nelson, Carl A. *Import/Export: How to Take Your Business Across Borders*. 4th ed. McGraw-Hill Companies, 2008. 352p. ISBN 0-07-148255-5. $21.95.

As in previous editions, Nelson demystifies international trade, including basics like writing the business plan, choosing a product or service, making samples for customs and duties, financing international transactions, and more. He uses examples and success stories to illustrate his points. Hot-button issues such as the World Trade Organization (WTO), doing business with North American Free Trade Agreement (NAFTA), Africa, India, China, and the European Union (EU), and the changing world of e-commerce are explored. His step-by-step guidance will help you succeed in international ventures and use the Internet to your advantage.

Seyoum, Belay. *Export-Import Theory, Practices and Procedures*. 2nd ed. International Business Press, 2008. 677p. ISBN 0-789-0056-8-7. $49.95.

More on the theoretical side, but written in a straightforward, concise manner, Seyoum provides historical overviews of international trade practices, legal necessities, and promotion and marketing strategies, while explaining the importance of international trade and the reasons behind the extensive documentation requirements. The reader is also provided with numerous references, case studies, and international perspectives on the subject matter covered within the chapter. There are even review questions for further self-study. The chapters on import regulations are very valuable, and the section on export licensing and regulations of the Commerce Department is a boon to any new or seasoned export manager. Seyoum's useful presentations of typical import and export transactions as well as samples of distributor agreements and business plans are practical and very useful.

Small Business Sourcebook. 2v. Thomson Gale. Annual. $405.00.

This directory provides a wealth of information for the small business owner or manager. The small business profiles cover 340 different small businesses. Businesses profiled include catering, cooking schools, fish farms, antique shops, bookstores, and car washes, for example. Entries contain as many as 17 subheadings, such as start-up information, educational programs, reference works, sources of supply, statistical sources, trade periodicals, trade shows and conventions, consultants, and franchises and business opportunities. The chapter on import/and export services will prove useful along with the section on trade shows and exhibiting, which lists publications to help you get more out of exhibiting. The small business topics section covers general ideas like budgets or budgeting, retailing, service industry, franchising, insurance, and seasonal business. Like the small business profiles, these entries have the same 17 subheadings and lead users to many resources related to the topics. The state listings and federal government assistance sections list programs and offices that provide information and support to businesses. Check your library for this practical, well-organized source.

Travis, Tom. *Doing Business Anywhere: The Essential Guide to Going Global*. John Wiley & Sons, Inc., 2007. 202p. ISBN 0-470-14961-2. $24.95.

Travis presents his six tenets of global trade and illustrates them in the context of real stories of global trade. He emphasizes the importance of international trade to the economic prosperity of all the world's nations. If you want to start a new venture or expand your present one, Travis helps you to organize, plan, operate, and execute with a global mind-set. Learn how to navigate conflicting and confusing laws, deal with different cultures, and operate in different countries. He also explains how to leverage the benefits of free trade agreements to set up and operate a competitive and profitable business, and he highlights how to protect your brand through patents, copyrights, and trademarks. Security concerns and measures are also discussed. Travis will convince readers that embracing his six tenets is key to "doing business anywhere."

Weiss, Kenneth D. *Building an Import/Export Business*. 4th ed. John Wiley & Sons, Inc., 2008. 320p. ISBN 0-470-18577-5. $19.95.

Weiss, an entrepreneur and international trade consultant, offers tips and instructions for every aspect of an import or export business. Learn how to get started in the post-9/11 import or export landscape. He explains how to take advantage of WTO, Central American Free Trade Agreement (CAFTA), NAFTA, and other trade agreements. Weiss covers all new and updated regulations, laws, and customs and shipping procedures to help ensure that businesses are in compliance with the Transportation Security Administration (TSA), U.S. Customs and Border Protection (CBP), and U.S. Immigration and Customs Enforcement (ICE). Besides helping importers and exporters plan their business expansion, Weiss describes how to research a raw idea and then successfully launch a stable, profitable business operation. Learn from the real-life examples presented here.

Zodl, Joseph A. *Export Import: Everything You and Your Company Need to Know to Compete in World Markets*. 4th ed. IIEI Press, 2005. 174p. ISBN 0-9773098-0-0. $39.95.

In easy-to-understand language and writing style, Zodl leads the reader into the world of international business, dispels the myths, simplifies tasks and processes, and illustrates important points with real-world examples. Zodl defines the vocabulary and terminology needed to understand the world of international business and points out sources for expert advice. This title provides the information the exporter needs to take a U.S.-manufactured product, sell it to a foreign buyer, make the shipment correctly, and get paid in U.S. dollars. It shows a middleman how to buy a product made by someone else and resell it at a profit to an overseas customer. Chapters on getting paid and the terms of sale will help new exporters avoid many mistakes. Zodl also has a Web site users may be interested in checking out at http://www.zodl.net/firstpage.htm.

Online Resources

BEOnline: Business and Economics Online: http://www.loc.gov/rr/business/ beonline/ (accessed Spring 2009).

Compiled by the Library of Congress Business Reference Services for researchers, this site has, under Subject Lists, a lengthy list of business topics such as associations, business plans (forms), companies by industry, data sets, e-commerce, economic indicators, international trade, legal resources, and more. If you click on Associations, you will find a short list of associations. Clicking on an association takes you to its Web site. Under the International Trade listing, you will find Foreign Trade Statistics and the Trade Compliance Center, for example.

Business Owners Idea Café: http://www.businessownersideacafe.com (accessed Spring 2009).

Developed by successful entrepreneurs and authors of published guides on starting a business, this large site presents short articles on all aspects of small business or entrepreneurial life. The main divisions include CyberSchmooz, Starting your Biz, Running Your Biz, Take Out Info, Classifieds, The "You" in your Biz, De-Stress and Have Fun, About Idea Café, and Join Idea Café. The large Running Your Biz: eCommerce section has excellent coverage on all things e-commerce plus links to outside information on e-commerce. Here you can find experts to answer your questions or discuss your current business crisis. You will find sample business plans, financing help, business forms, and business news.

Buyusa.gov: http://www.buyusa.gov/home/export.html (accessed Spring 2009).

This simple-to-use government Web site offers to help businesses get into international sales through market research, trade events, introductions to buyers and distributors, and counseling for any and every step of the export process. One part of the Web site helps importers to the United States, and another helps exporters from the United States. Both parts cover products and services. When you click on a country, you get the Country Commercial Guide (CCG), a calendar of events, employment opportunities, market information, and services for U.S. exporters and suppliers. Also part of this site is the *Commercial News USA*, the "official export promotion magazine of the U.S. Department of Commerce." This online publication also contains a wealth of information, including franchising, trade shows, and a company index.

**Centers for International Trade Development: http://www.citd.org/StartupKit/index.cfm (accessed Spring 2009).

This very useful site has a guide for new exporters, an export readiness assessment tool, and an excellent Export FAQ for companies just getting into international trade. Their trade information database includes U.S. and world trade and economic data and sections dedicated to trade contacts and leads, trade reference tools, foreign market research, trade and investment regulations, trade documentation, and finance and insurance. A trade resources directory provides information on numerous trade associations and organizations. A trade show calendar is also available, as are booklets on the best markets for various U.S. industries. Start gathering import and export information here.

Entrepreneur.com: http://www.entrepreneur.com. (accessed Spring 2009).

Entrepreneur Magazine provides a wealth of information and assistance to the new entrepreneur. A thorough understanding of the need for the right type of marketing plan to fit your business and your style of planning and working is very important; and this site guides you through the process of discovering the right type for you. Learn how to determine your marketing goals and objectives and how a plan will help you to achieve them. Under Marketing & Sales, you will find tips on building buzz, branding, word-of-mouth advertising, and marketing materials. Learn about the "9 Tools for Building Customer Loyalty," for example. Discover how to create an ad budget and create great ads and direct-mail pieces. The E-business section explains legal issues, setting up an e-commerce site, e-mail marketing, Internet security, and more. International marketing research is well covered in the Marketing section. Use this outstanding site often during the planning and opening of your global business.

Entrepreneurs.About.com: http://entrepreneurs.about.com/ (accessed Spring 2009).

This large site has many different parts and is at times a bit difficult to navigate. Use the search feature if you have trouble. On the left side of this main page, you will find Choosing a Business, Business Ideas, Business Plan Outline, Business Legal Organizational Structure, and a "How to" Library. Further down on the page, topics such as Financing, Case Studies and Interviews, and Resources also provide more links to information. The About.com large Web site also covers the biotech/ biomedical, composites/plastics, metal, insurance, and retail industries. The retail industry (http://retailindustry.about.com/), for which it is notoriously difficult to locate information, is especially well done; articles provide information on current retail trends, retail statistics, retail industry profile, apparel trends, consumer trends, and more. The entire site is fully searchable, so put in keywords and find information. Under Business and Finance, you will also find articles on, for example, various industries, selling to the government, store operations, retail trends, advertising costs, and branding. International information on global trade shows and industry trends is also available through a simple search.

**Export.gov: http://www.export.gov (accessed Spring 2009).

Export.gov's goal is to help U.S. companies succeed globally. In this government portal, you will find resources from across the U.S. Government to help in planning international sales strategies and to succeed in today's global marketplace. Look for market research and trade leads from the U.S. Department of Commerce's Commercial Service to export finance information from the Export-Import Bank and the Small Business Administration. The National Trade Data Bank (NTDB) provides access to Country Commercial Guides, market research reports, best market reports, and other programs. You will also find global business opportunity leads as well as market and country research. FedBizOpps, formerly known as Commerce Business Daily, is linked here too. Also linked is the TradeStats Express page for national and state export data. Export.gov is fully searchable and allows you to search globally the contents of all of its contributing entities. Export.gov helps exporters avoid pitfalls such as nonpayment and intellectual property misappropriation.

GlobalEDGE: http://globaledge.msu.edu/ (accessed Spring 2009).

Managed by Michigan State University's Center for International Business Education and Research (MSU_CIBER), this site links to a broad selection of international trade data, including economic trends, statistical data sources, government resources, trade portals, journals, and mailing lists. Its Global Resources section provides access to more than 2,000 online resources. MSU_CIBER has also contributed its own resources including an interactive forum for business professionals and portions of the information contained in the Knowledge Room, GlobalEDGE's section on the latest issues and trends affecting international business.

International Expansion: http://www.entrepreneur.com/grow/international/ index.html (accessed Spring 2009).

The main section of the Entrepreneur.com site, "How to Start an Import/Export Business," contains a wealth of information on ways to get involved and target market identification, and types of costs, procedures, and more. Other articles cover finding customers, international etiquette, attending and working international trade shows, and much, much more. Also find more information under other sections of the Web site, for example, marketing, e-business, and technology. Links to trade journals, classifieds, special offers, and products and services may also be helpful.

Market Entry Assistance: http://faculty.philau.edu/russowl/market.html (accessed Spring 2009).

Professor Lloyd C. Russow at Philadelphia University has organized a large number of Web resources useful for new exporters and importers. You will find country information, product classification systems, and international organizations as well as market entry resources. The section titled Are You Ready to Go International is very useful as is the Documentation section. Refer to this useful site often.

New York Public Library, International Trade Research Guide: http://www.nypl .org/research/sibl/trade/trade.html (accessed Spring 2009).

This wonderful guide produced by the Science, Industry and Business Library (SIBL) will provide invaluable information in learning how to conduct business between the United States and another country. Guides, business directories, periodicals, and trade statistic sources can be located through this large and practical site. The site is well organized and easy to navigate; you will find information grouped under market research, trade leads, shipping and logistics, and cross-cultural business communication.

Quick MBA: http://www.quickmba.com/entre/bplan/ (accessed Spring 2009).

For those new to business plans and SWOT (strengths, weaknesses, opportunities, threats) analysis, this site is thorough and practical. Learn the basics of both these concepts and many more here. Management and Marketing articles are useful and helpful to new owners and managers as well as experienced ones. Discussed is a political, economic, social, technical (PEST) analysis, why to use it, and how it relates to SWOT. Often articles include recommended readings.

Small Business Administration: http://www.sba.gov (accessed Spring 2009).

This official government site offers a wealth of resources and programs for starting and growing a small business. Under Startup Basics, check out the areas you need help with while doing your business planning. Other major sections cover business planning, financing, international trade, managing, marketing, employees, taxes, legal aspects, and business opportunities. Find here online forms, sample business plans, loan information, and many publications. The Export Library contains titles like Breaking into the Trade Games, Export Working Capital Program, Export Financing for Small Businesses, and SBA & Ex-Im Bank Co-Guarantee Program. Some content is available in Spanish. Trade Mission Online is also found on the SBA site and is useful to businesses that want to export their products for use by foreign firms and U.S. businesses seeking U.S. partners or suppliers for trade-related activities. The Small Business Development Centers (SBDCs) at http://www.sba.gov/sbdc are also part of the SBA. SBDCs are located in every state and deliver counseling and training for small businesses in the areas of management, marketing, financing, and feasibility studies.

USA.gov: http://www.usa.gov (accessed Spring 2009).

Information by Topic will interest and amaze first-time visitors. Topics include Defense and International, Environment, Energy and Agriculture, Money and Taxes, Reference and General Government, and Science and Technology. Tabs at the top of the page include Businesses and Nonprofits, which has a section on International Trade. Clicking on Data and Statistics brings up an alphabetical list of links to resources chock-full of statistics. Economic Indicators is the Web site of the Economics and Statistics Administration, part of the U.S. Department of Commerce (http://www.economicindicators.gov), and it provides timely access to the daily releases of key economic indicators from the Bureau of Economic Analysis (BEA) and the Census Bureau. In addition, a section titled Foreign Businesses Doing Business in the U.S. is under Businesses and Nonprofits. Under Frequently Asked Foreign Business Questions you can find a section called Doing Business Abroad. Spanish translation of the site is also available. You can e-mail questions about the site and the statistics or telephone for help too. Your taxes pay for the collection, compiling, and publishing of these statistics, and they are available for your use.

U.S. Trade and Development Agency (USTDA): http://www.ustda.gov (accessed Spring 2009).

The USTDA's mission is to promote economic growth in developing and middle-income countries (MICs). MICs are a large and diverse group of countries that are of considerable importance globally and to the World Bank. Egypt, China, and Peru are examples of MICs. The USTDA also aims to assist U.S. businesses to export their products and services to create U.S. jobs. It is an independent U.S. Government foreign-assistance agency funded by the U.S. Congress. Find business opportunities here as well as grant funding for overseas projects that support the development of modern infrastructure and open trading systems. The Library contains completed USTDA-funded studies in various regions or countries as well as feasibility studies.

VIBES: Virtual International Business and Economic Sources: http:// library .uncc.edu/display/?dept=reference&format=open&page=68 (accessed Spring 2009).

This site offers more than 3,000 links to free sources of information on topics related to international business and economics. The table of contents breaks the sites into three groups: comprehensive, regional, and national. The comprehensive section organizes its links by categories such as banking and finance, business practices and company information, emerging markets, and international trade law. The regional section allows searching devoted to a single region or continent such as Europe or the Middle East. The national section links to sites devoted to one particular country. Research and statistical tables and graphs are highlights of this site.

2

Research, Statistics, and Information Gathering

Chapter Highlights:

U.S. Government Information and Statistics
The U.S. Census Bureau Foreign Trade Data
The North America Industrial Classification System (NAICS)
Federal Interagency Council on Statistical Policy
State Government Agency Help for Exporters/Importers
Commercial Publishers
    Entrepreneurs.About.com
    Market Research, Industry Research, Business Research
Basic Statistical Concepts
    Sampling and Probability
    Forecasts, Projections, and Estimates

When starting a new phase of business such as entering the world of international trade, it is impossible to have too much information. Statistics—the classification, tabulation, and study of numerical data—are necessary to make good decisions. The field of statistics relates to both the systematic collection of numerical data and the interpretation of these data. Details on customers, competition, the industry, industry trends, licensing, markets and potential markets, the national and global economy, and more are necessities. Decision-making based on intuition and expertise with a thorough (statistical) understanding of the facts available is important to gaining and maintaining a competitive edge.

Because the cost of collecting and analyzing primary statistical data is great, most businesses depend on secondary statistical data generated by a variety of sources including government agencies, trade associations, commercial publishers, and, less often, private research firms. Generally, you will be able to find the online and print resources listed here at local libraries or free on the Internet. Some of the sites have free information but are commercial and will try to sell you their products. Please note that this guide does not endorse any of these products.

U.S. GOVERNMENT INFORMATION AND STATISTICS

The U.S. government is probably the largest single compiler and publisher of statistics pertaining to U.S. businesses; therefore it is a good source to begin searching for markets, export or import advice and help, trade leads, and more. Many U.S. agencies that produce statistics of interest to the public and other countries also have agencies devoted to export or import information. Many of these agencies have Web sites with statistics free to all Internet

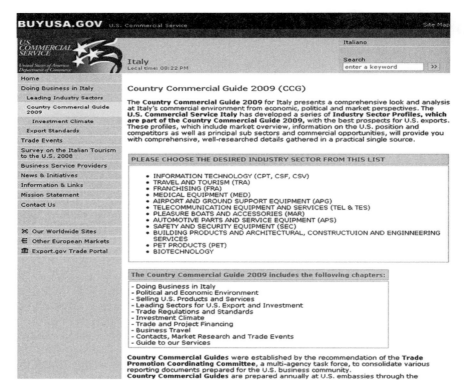

Country Commercial Guide 2009. Buyusa.gov (U.S. Dept. of Commerce).

users, and the various search engines like Google, Yahoo, and AltaVista have crawled these sites and indexed some of the data. If you search for "export Italy," you will find a wealth of sites, free government ones and, of course, many dot-com sites wanting to sell you a variety of things. For example, in this search the Italy Country Commercial Guide 2007 (CCG) from http://www.buyusa.gov/italy/en/countrycommercialguide.html is one of the first sites to be indexed.

U.S. embassies and numerous other U.S. government agencies prepare the Country Commercial Guides annually. Other CCGs for numerous other countries are available at http://www.export.gov through the National Trade Data Bank (NTDB). These guides help find trade partners and provide market information, business service providers, industry sector profiles, links to law and regulations sites, and EU information (when appropriate), and more. Export.gov is the U.S. government's portal to exporting and trade services. You will find lots of useful information and help here.

A Basic Guide to Exporting. Export.gov.

This chapter's online resources include many useful free and fee sites to use in your research. The information and sites are presented in as linear fashion as possible, but there is a lot of interconnectivity and crossover. URLs are included whenever confusion seems possible.

After checking Export.gov, another large site to explore is the International Trade Administration (ITA), part of the U.S. Department of Commerce, http://trade.gov/index.asp. The goal of the ITA is to assist exporters and develop trade agreements. Here you will find the U.S. trade agreements and learn about import duty retaliations and industry trade policy. You will find trade data and forecasting and trends, as well as analysis from U.S. and foreign sources. You will also be able to locate information on how trade data are collected and measured. Industry analysis is another important aspect of the ITA, and industry information is also available here. For example, if you are thinking of exporting to Colombia, here is a report on U.S. exports to that country that describes major U.S. states exporting to Colombia as well as an agreement between the two countries made in 2006.

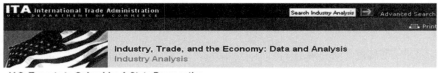

U.S. Exports to Colombia: A State Perspective
June 2007

- **Read more** about the U.S.–Colombia Trade Promotion Agreement.

- For HTML display of CAFTA-DR export data by state, start on the **TradeStats Express** state export data page; specify any state and choose Colombia as the trade partner.

- This report may be made available later in PDF format. **Let us know** if you would find this useful.

- Return to the list of OTII trade agreement reports.

Overview

The United States exported $6.7 billion in merchandise to Colombia in 2006, up from $3.6 billion in 2002. That was an 87 percent increase over the 2002–06 period, well above the 50 percent increase in U.S. exports to the world. Colombia was the 29th largest market for U.S goods in 2006, out of a total of 230 markets.

Eighteen states exported more than $50 million in goods to Colombia in 2006. Thirteen of these states exported goods worth more than $100 million, and two exported merchandise worth more than $1 billion.

Texas and Florida were the top state exporters to Colombia in 2006. Texas recorded merchandise exports of $1.7 billion to Colombia, while Florida recorded shipments of $1.6 billion. Together, these two states accounted for 49 percent of total U.S. goods exported to Colombia in 2006.

Other states that posted significant export totals to Colombia in 2006 were Louisiana ($630 million), Illinois ($214 million), Alabama ($206 million), California ($200 million), North Carolina ($154 million), New Jersey ($144 million), Pennsylvania ($127 million), and Georgia ($126 million).

Forty-three of the states increased their merchandise exports to Colombia from 2002 to 2006. Texas recorded the largest dollar increase, boosting shipments to Colombia by $994 million—from $690 million in 2002 to $1.7 billion in 2006. Other states with noteworthy increases in export value to Colombia over the 2002–06 period were Florida (up $613 million), Louisiana (up $214 million), Alabama (up $163 million), and Illinois (up $123 million).

Manufactured goods made up 86 percent of U.S. merchandise exports to Colombia in 2006. Basic chemicals were the largest manufactured export category, with $928 million, or 14 percent of total U.S. shipments of merchandise. Other significant manufactured export categories were computer equipment ($562 million); agricultural and construction machinery ($512 million); resin, synthetic rubber, and synthetic fibers and filaments ($351 million); and general purpose machinery ($226 million).

Charts and Tables

U.S. Exports to Colombia Have Increased 87 Percent Since 2002

Basic Chemicals Is the Largest Category of Exports to Colombia

Texas Recorded the Biggest Growth in Exports to Colombia from 2002 to 2006

27 States Exported $25 Million or More to Colombia in 2006

State Merchandise Export Totals to Colombia, 2002–06, Ranked by 2006 Export Value

U.S. Exports to Colombia: A State Perspective (June 2007). ITA (International Trade Administration).

The federal government collects and publishes a great deal of data and information. If at any time you decide you would like to see what paper publications the government has produced, visit a Regional Government

Depository at your State Library or a large University library in your state.

The Bureau of Economic Analysis (BEA) Web site (http://www.bea.gov) produces a wealth of statistical information on the U.S. economy and International Accounts data. The mission of the BEA is to produce and circulate accurate, timely, relevant, and cost-effective statistics and to provide a comprehensive, up-to-date description of U.S. economic activity. The ups and downs of the U.S. economy, regional economic development, and continued globalization affect every business in some way. The cost of a barrel of oil goes up, and it costs more to get supplies to your door or to ship overseas; consumers pay more for gas and have less to spend on clothes, food, or whatever. As a business person, you want to keep a close eye on what is happening in the U.S. economy and any countries to which you are marketing and selling your goods or services. The BEA's Overview of the Economy section will help you do just that. The BEA also produces the *Survey of Current Business*, a monthly publication that provides data on personal income, state and regional economic statistics, cross-border trade statistics, and more. Research articles and forecasting provide additional necessary information for exporters and importers.

The U.S. Department of Labor's Bureau of Labor Statistics (http://www.bls.gov) presents the latest numbers on areas such as inflation and consumer spending, wages, earnings, and benefits, and demographics in general. Explore their site to find the Inflation Calculator; understanding inflation and how it affects business and prices is essential for any company. Also find here the International Price Program (IPP). The IPP produces Import Price Indexes (MPI) and Export Price Indexes (XPI) containing data on changes in the prices of nonmilitary goods and services traded between the United States and the rest of the world. Other import and export price statistics are also available by country, and foreign labor statistics such as hourly compensation rates are available. When you hire employees to help you expand your business into the international arena, you will want to visit this site for information on compensation and working conditions and to review publications like the *Occupational Outlook Handbook* (http://www.bls.gov/oco/) for help with job titles and descriptions, training needed, and pay or earnings.

THE U.S. CENSUS BUREAU FOREIGN TRADE DATA

The largest statistical agency of the government is the Census Bureau (http://www.census.gov), and it collects, compiles, and publishes, as mentioned above, economic as well as population statistics. On the home page of the Census Bureau, you will find links in the center of the page to information on business and industry topics. These topics include foreign trade, economic census, and e-stats. Under foreign trade, you will find articles on exporting to specific countries and information about the seminars the

Census Bureau offers for tasks such as filing a Shipper's Export Declaration online. Also learn about Schedule-B codes, which are used to classify all U.S. exports and the difference between the Schedule-B codes (for exports) and the Harmonized Tariff Schedule (HTS) codes (for imports). More about these codes can be found in Chapter 4.

Another important part of the Census Bureau's Web page is the International Data Base (IDB) at http://www.census.gov/ipc/www/idb/. The IDB presents estimates and projections of basic demographic measures for countries and regions of the world. Country summaries, country rankings, and population pyramids all provide useful data. U.S. export and import statistics by commodity, country, customs district, and method of transportation provide value and quantity on a monthly, year-to-date, and annual history basis. U.S. state export data and port statistics for imports and exports are also available. Use this site frequently to help start and grow your business.

Further down the Business and Industry page are the Current Industrial Reports (CIR). Since 1904, the CIR program has provided monthly, quarterly, and annual measures of industrial activity. The program's surveys measure manufacturing activity in commodities such as textiles and apparel, computer and electronic components, consumer goods, and more. Reports can be accessed by subject or North American Industrial Code System (NAICS) subsectors.

New measures of the way the United States does business are always being added. In the 2002 reports, the Census Bureau included information on the e-commerce sales for most industries. Data for e-commerce sales, while formerly just a part of the industry reports, now have their own page at http://www.census.gov/eos/www/ebusiness614.htm. In May 2007, a lengthy report on how e-commerce grew in 2005 with statistics was provided, and an archive presents reports on e-stats back to 1999 with explanations of both how the statistics were collected and how what was counted as e-commerce has evolved and continues to evolve. Since 2005, Quarterly Retail E-Commerce Sales are compiled and posted also. You will find many more sources of information on e-commerce in Chapter 8.

THE NORTH AMERICA INDUSTRIAL CLASSIFICATION SYSTEM (NAICS)

Many of the U.S. government's statistics are gathered and presented by the North America Industrial Classification System or NAICS. Each business, when filing taxes, must identify itself by a NAICS number. NAICS has replaced the U.S. Standard Industrial Classification (SIC) system. NAICS was developed jointly with the United States, Canada, and Mexico to provide new comparability in statistics on business activities throughout North America. The NAICS also introduced a number of new industries including residential remodelers, electronic shopping and auctions, Internet publishing and broadcasting, and Web search portals. On the Census Bureau site you will find a link to NAICS where you can look up the code for your industry. Many statistical sources present industry ratios and trends by NAICS code.

Another great statistical resource, often called the nation's databook, is produced by the Census Bureau, the *Statistical Abstract of the United States*. It provides foreign trade statistics like trade balance with individual countries, agricultural exports and selected commodity import and export numbers, and exports and imports by NAICS in over 1,400 tables and charts. An Appendix, titled "Guide to Foreign Statistical Abstracts," presents abstracts and sponsoring agencies for the member nations of the Organisation for Economic Co-operation and Development (OECD) and Russia. Find this information at: http://www.census.gov/compendia/statab.

FEDERAL INTERAGENCY COUNCIL ON STATISTICAL POLICY

FedStats (http://www.fedstats.gov) is the official Web site of the Federal Interagency Council on Statistical Policy. This gateway to statistics from over 100 U.S. federal agencies is well organized and easy to use. You can find statistics and information using the links to statistics, with such subheads as Topic Links A–Z, MapStats, and Statistics by Geography from U.S. Agencies. By linking to Statistics by Geography from U.S. Agencies, you will see international comparisons, country analysis briefs and profiles, and demographic indicators for countries. The Statistical Reference Shelf subhead, a bit further down on the home page, is a large collection of online reference sources like the *Statistical Abstract of the United States*, which I have already discussed. Here are a variety of other sources such as the *State and Metropolitan Area Data Book* and *Digest of Education Statistics* (comparisons with other G8 countries), which will provide statistics on many topics of interest to many businesses. On the other half of the home page you can find links to statistical agencies, including the subhead Agencies by Subject; click on Economic on the drop-down menu there to find the BEA's International Trade statistics.

Other links and descriptions will lead you to the U.S. Census Bureau, Customs Service, Directorate for Information Operations and Reports (DIOR), Economics and Statistics Administration (ESA), International Trade Administration, Small Business Administration (SBA), and Statistics of Income (SOI). The ITA collects and disseminates data on imports, exports, production, prices, and foreign direct investment in the United States, as well as other economic data to analyze domestic and foreign market situations. The ITA also tracks data on tourism industries and international travel to and from the United States for many private sector firms. The Office of

Travel and Tourism Industries within the ITA provides a Web site with current statistical data on international travel to and from the United States; gives projections of international arrivals to the United States; and conducts the *Survey of International Air Travelers*, partially funded by states, cities, and the private sector.

Part of the Economics and Statistics Administration is known as STAT-USA; this subscription service is available through many university and depository libraries throughout the United States at http://www.stat-usa.gov/. The State of the Nation section of STAT-USA covers current and historical economic and financial releases and economic data. Look at Today's Hot Releases or Daily Releases for up-to-date economic data. On the lower left of the home page, you will find the most recently added State of the Nation (SOTN) files. Find here interest rates and new state and regional tables. Check out the State of the Nation Library (SOTN Library button at top of page) for a collection of over 3,000 files of U.S. economic information, including Industry Statistics, Economic Indicators, and the Survey of Current Business. Another part of STAT-USA is the GLOBUS & National Trade Data Bank (NTDB) database; the NTDB is chock full of useful trade statistics.

Learning to use the many and varied statistical resources of our federal government is no easy task. The Internet continues to improve visibility and searchability, but the enormity of available information is still daunting. When you start your search, have a clear idea of what you need but be flexible in the vocabulary you use to describe it. Also, ask a librarian to help you get started. Remember that you will probably have to use the data you find to extrapolate, which means you will estimate by projecting from known information or data.

STATE GOVERNMENT AGENCY HELP FOR EXPORTERS/ IMPORTERS

Statistical sources for state data from the states vary greatly. Many state and local government organizations collect the data and then submit those data to the federal government for compilation and publication—for instance, through the Census Bureau's State Data Centers. Most states do publish some information on the state's economy, economic or industrial development, and employment and unemployment statistics. Once again you can easily find a state Web site by searching Google, Yahoo, AltaVista, and other online search engines. Another resource is the State and Local Government on the Net Web site at http://www.statelocalgov.net/, a site that provides convenient access to all state and local government sites by listing the states alphabetically. Frequently updated, this directory of official state, county, and city government Web sites also provides a list of topics to choose from plus listings of government grants, with applications. Some states rely on the federal government to provide businesses with export or import help but some states like Colorado fund the Colorado International Trade Office, (http://www.colorado.gov/cs/Satellite?c=Page &cid=1165009699722&pagename=OEDIT%2FO), for example, which helps promote Colorado businesses and services in foreign countries and promotes foreign investment in the state. Check for sources of help when starting to export or import from your state or regional government offices.

COMMERCIAL PUBLISHERS

Staying with the statistics theme, many commercial publishers produce detailed and high-quality statistical sources. Industry research and averages are an important component of a business plan and when beginning a new phase of business, such as getting involved in importing or exporting, a revised business plan is a must to succeed. Three key resources for operating and financial ratios for many industries are Leo Troy's *Almanac of Business and Industrial Financial Ratios*, Dun & Bradstreet's *Industry Norms & Key Business Ratios*, and Risk Management Association's *RMA Annual Statement Studies*; check your local library to see if they purchase these resources. While available on the Web, the subscription costs for these services can be substantial. RMA Universe at http://www.rmahq.org/RMA/ allows users to purchase single industry data online for a reasonable price. Standard and Poor's *Industry Surveys* only cover about 50 industries in a three-volume set, but the overview, ratios, and trends data are invaluable. Specific company ratio and balance sheet comparisons are provided under the Basic Analysis section. The financial ratios in the resources listed above are organized by either SIC or the new NAICS. *Value Line Investment Survey Standard Edition* (Value Line, weekly) is another place to check for industry analysis and company data. Organized by industry, each of the 93 industry reviews contain current and future business environment descriptions and are followed by pages describing and evaluating individual companies. With the financial ratios in those resources, you can compare your projections with companies that are already established in your industry.

Due to the growth in small and franchised businesses in the United States, the market for popular statistics continues to grow and develop. An outstanding Web site for financial ratios, business statistics, and benchmarks called BizStats.com, at http://www.bizstats.com/. This once all-free Web site now charges for some statistics but is still worth a visit. Here you can find profitability and operating ratios for S corporations, partnerships, and sole proprietorships for industries such as furniture stores, electronics, gas stations, and sporting goods. You can find retail industry financial ratios for corporations, S corporations, and sole proprietorships. You can find current ratios and balance sheet ratios by industry, and industry profitability for sole proprietorships, for example. This site has financial and operating ratios for about 15,000 industry segments. Even if your industry is not found here, this site will show you how to do a financial and industry analysis using the figures you have gathered.

A wide range of industry directories can provide you with information on industries and specific companies, i.e., your competitors. You can also use existing firms' actual performance to validate your projections in your business plan. Listed here are two Web sites to check for industry information.

Entrepreneurs.About.com

Entrepreneurs.About.com is found at http://entrepreneurs.about.com/.

This large site has many different parts. Use the search feature if you do not see what you need. On the left side of this main page, you will find links to specific topics with titles such as Business Ideas, Business Plans, Business Plan Outline, Buying a Business, Business Legal Organizational Structures, the "How to" Library, Financing, Running a Business, and Sales and Marketing. The Resources heading also provides more links to information. The About.com Business and Finance pages also cover the biotech/biomedical, composites/plastics, metal, insurance, and retail industries. The Retail Industry (http://retailindustry.about.com/), for which it is notoriously difficult to locate information, is especially well done; articles provide information on current retail trends, retail statistics, retail industry profile, apparel trends, consumer trends, and more. You will find import help at this site by just searching on "import." The entire site is fully searchable, so put in your keywords and find information. Under Business and Finance, you will also find articles on, for example, selling to the government, store operations, retail trends, advertising costs, branding and more. International information on global trade shows and industry trends is also available through a simple search.

Market Research, Industry Research, Business Research

Market Research, Industry Research, Business Research is found at http://www.virtualpet.com/industry.

This major portal for researching companies and industries presents a step-by-step process to begin researching an industry. Find sources to help you learn about legal issues, regulatory issues, competition, markets, and even a history of the industry for your expanded business ventures. Additional links to industry portals are also available, and international trade associations are linked here. A section on the international market will prove useful in researching exports and imports. Three other linked sites offer help on How to Learn about a Company by Examining its Products, How to Review, Evaluate, Critique a Web Site, and How to Conduct a Patent Search. The many links this site provides are extremely useful.

BASIC STATISTICAL CONCEPTS

Every business person needs to be familiar with some key statistical concepts in order to use them in business planning and projections. Earlier in this chapter, we have seen that the government and commercial publishers present us with both "descriptive statistics," which utilize numerical and graphical methods to look for patterns, summarize and present that information in a set of data, and "inferential statistics," which utilize sample data to make estimates or predictions about a larger set of data as an aid to decision-making. In this section, I briefly define some of the concepts relevant to business statistics in general.

Sampling and Probability

Sampling is the process of selecting units (e.g., people, organizations) from a population of interest so that by studying the sample we may fairly generalize our results back to the population from which they were chosen. A sample is anything less than a survey of the full population. Population statistics are important to business owners and researchers, and while it would be best to collect information from each person in the population being studied, surveying each individual is usually not possible. Therefore, sampling is used to select a small but representative group and make inferences or conclusions about the entire population. A good source to learn more about sampling, especially in relation to market research, is Paul Hague's *Market Research in Practice: A Guide to the Basics*. A descriptive citation follows:

Hague, Paul, et al. *Market Research in Practice: A Guide to the Basics.* Kogan Page, 2004. 226p. ISBN 0-7494-4180-1. $32.50.

Hague uses real-life case studies to present his views on the topic of market research. With a decidedly British tone, tools and techniques used by market researchers are described and explained, such as desk research, focus groups, data analysis, and report findings. Learn how to use a sample to see trends in your business, your local area, or foreign markets. Even if you hire someone or a company to do market research for you, you will want to understand what they will be doing and how they obtain the information you receive, and this title will provide that level of basic knowledge.

Based on the theory of probability, sampling can only be thoroughly understood in those terms. Probability is the basis of sampling; it shows the likelihood or chances for each of various potential outcomes based on a set of assumptions about how the world works generally. Using the data from a random sample, you can infer knowledge or probability about the population from which the sample was drawn. The objective of sampling is to select a part that is representative of the whole. For example, the TV rating service Nielsen tracks TV watching behavior of a sample of viewers and makes inferences about the popularity of shows to the majority of TV viewers.

Earlier in this chapter we looked at statistical sources produced by the Census Bureau. The Census Bureau uses sampling extensively to produce many of its publications. To be aware of when and how sampling is used to produce statistics, careful readers always check the introductory matter and/or the footnotes to ascertain what methods were used for the statistics presented. When checking the source of statistics also ask yourself: (1) are the statistics self-serving, and (2) is the source biased? Obviously, the government does not have any vested interest in presenting the population statistics, but when you use other sources for statistics, forecasts, or ratios, remember to keep the above questions in mind. Statistics work best when you combine them with your own expert judgment and common sense.

Forecasts, Projections, and Estimates

Forecasting is the use of known measurements to predict the value of unknown measurements that will occur at a later date generally no more than two years into the future. Forecasting always applies to the future but is based on information about the ways in which variables have behaved in the past. In forecasting it is assumed that the behavioral patterns traced in the past will continue in the future. Business forecasting is a process that seeks to answer a variety of forward-looking questions about the operations of a company and the demands that will be placed upon it. Business forecasting cannot deliver absolutely accurate, error-free forecasts, but they can have a reasonably small margin of error and will reduce future uncertainty to a manageable level. For international interests, the Economist.com (http://www.economist.com/) is worth a visit. You will find country-specific forecasts in the areas of politics and the economy. If you are thinking of exporting to Argentina, for example, *The Economist* will project the trend for import spending, currency strength or weakness, any changes in government or government policy in regard to foreign trade, and more.

Statistical projections do not always yield accurate forecasts because any analysis of trends depends on the assumption of stable political, economic, and social conditions. Projections are predictions made about the distant future so are more speculative and prone to error than forecasts. Projections cannot always take into account the effect of technological advances and man-made and natural disasters. You need to understand forecasting and projections as they are important elements in planning and control in any business. Management decisions must often be based on what is likely to happen in the future, which may be tomorrow, next week, or next year. To arrive at a sales forecast, the owner may start with an economic forecast, which considers trends in the whole global economy. If your are thinking of moving into a country, many aspects of that country will need to be examined.

An estimate is an approximation of an unknown value based on an extrapolation from a known value. Estimates may apply to any time—past, present, or future measurements. Statistical estimation finds a statistical measure of a population from the corresponding statistics of the sample. It is an estimate because it is not certain that the sample is an exact reflection of the entire population. An estimate draws a conclusion from the study of representative cases.

This quick overview of research sources and definitions will help you gather the information you need to decide whether to expand your business or not, which foreign market to enter, how much money it will cost to expand, how to begin researching international trade statistics, and more. The following resources will help you understand business concepts more and find needed statistical sources.

REFERENCES

(Starred titles discussed in the chapter)

Print Resources

Berger, Suzanne. *How We Compete: What Companies Around the World Are Doing to Make It in Today's Global Economy.* Currency Doubleday, 2006. 334p. ISBN 0385513593.

> Berger and the MIT Industrial Performance Center looked at over 500 international companies to discover which practices are working in today's global economy. They compared strategies and successes of companies in various industries. For example, in electronics and software, they compared Intel and Sony, who make their own products, to Cisco and Dell, who rely on outsourcing. You will find their conclusions fascinating, instructive, and surprising, and will learn the many ways to win in the global economy.

Berinstein, Paula. *Business Statistics on the Web.* CyberAge Books, 2003. 244p. ISBN 0-910965-65-X. $29.95.

> Berinstein illustrates how to search the Internet to find statistics about companies, markets, and industries in this handy reference guide. Chapters are organized under broad topic areas such as statistics basics, U.S. industry sources, non-U.S. industry sources, market research sources, and company information. Dispersed among the chapters are sometimes lengthy case studies that illustrate the breadth and depth of information you can find on the Web. Additionally, Berinstein discusses and identifies international associations and governments with their URLs, describing the basic information provided. The last chapter, which covers estimating company numbers you cannot get, will be especially useful for small businesses.

**Dun & Bradstreet. *Industry Norms & Key Business Ratios.* Annual.

> This annual resource is very expensive, but some libraries still purchase for their business collections. D&B analyzes nearly 800 business lines and can help small businesses make financial projections. If you have not been able to find financial norms for your industry, try this resource.

Europa World Year Book. Annual. Routledge, Taylor & Francis. 2 v.

This well-respected annual provides a great deal of detailed information on the political, economic, and commercial institutions of the world. Each country is covered by an individual chapter composed of an introductory survey that includes recent history, economic affairs, government, and defense; followed by data on social welfare, finance, telecommunications, trade and industry, utilities, and education. Now also an online product, a free trial electronic subscription is available from the Europa World Web site at http://www .europaworld.com

Exporters' Encyclopaedia. Annual. Dun & Bradstreet.

A comprehensive world reference guide, this encyclopedia is divided into 220 country-specific sections; firms specializing in international business, laws, and legislation; international trade associations; government agencies; shipping practice; and reference data on weights and measures for overseas ports. Find key contacts, trade and safety regulations, and information on documentation needed. Marketing data include legal requirements for importer or agents, procurement standards, environmental protection or pollution control, marking, and labeling. The encyclopedia also provides passport regulations and business etiquette guidelines.

**Hague, Paul, Hague, Nick, and Morgan, Carol-Ann. *Market Research in Practice: A Guide to the Basics (Market Research in Practice Series)*. Kogan Page, 2004. 226p. ISBN 0-7494-4180-1. $32.50.

Hague presents clear, concise advice with real-life case studies on the topic of market research. Fully international in scope, this book offers comparative examples and case studies from Europe, the United States, and the rest of the world. Tools and techniques used by market researchers are described and explained. With a decidedly British tone, the authors detail qualitative market research, questionnaire design, administered interviews, response bands, telephone interviewing, conjoint analysis, quota samples, and more. The Sampling and Statistics chapter is particularly useful and succinct. As a refresher or as an introduction, this title is outstanding.

Hinkelman, Edward, et al. *Importers Manual.* Annual. World Trade Press. 960p.

Information on how to import virtually any commodity into the United States can be found in this practical reference. It is precisely organized for ease of use and is divided into the major sections of Commodity Index; U.S. Customs Entry and Clearance; International Banking; Legal Considerations of Importing; and Packing, Shipping, and Insurance. The heart of the work, the Commodity Index, contains entry procedures, documentation, restrictions, and prohibitions; marking and labeling requirements; and contact information for regulatory agencies for all products that can be imported into the United States.

International Marketing Data and Statistics. Annual. Euromonitor Publications Ltd.

This data handbook provides marketing and business information spanning 24 years and covers 161 non-European countries. International organizations such as the International Monetary Fund (IMF) and United Nations and 1,000 information sources in total are contacted for this information. Data are presented in easy-to-use and -understand tables. You can find current statistics on socioeconomic trends, consumer market sizes, expenditure patterns, number of telephone lines, and more here.

International Trade Center. *Export Quality Management: An Answer Book for Small and Medium-Sized Exporters.* International Trade Centre, 2005. 252p. ISBN 978-92-9137-214-0.

The International Trade Center is sponsored jointly by the World Trade Organization and the UN Conference on Trade and Development. The Question-Answer format covers how exporters can navigate the world of international standards, mandatory technical regulations, sanitary and phytosanitary measures, and conformity assessment procedures. Sections provide answers on product certification, product testing, metrology, quality managements, ISO 9000, accreditation, and the agreements on Technical Barriers to Trade (TBT) and Sanitary and PhytoSanitary measures (SPS). Although this site is aimed at helping small and medium-sized enterprises (SMEs) in developing and transition economies, U.S. SMEs will also want to consult.

Jagoe, John R. *Export Sales & Marketing Manual 2008: The Bible of Exporting.* Annual. Export Institute of the United States. 520p. ISBN 0-943677-66-1. $295.

Having been updated annually for 21 consecutive years, this international trade publication has achieved longevity and global reach. This manual covers all the steps involved in selling products in world markets. Over 120 illustrations, 85 graphs, 40 flow charts, and 60 sample international trade documents lead the user through the process. Jagoe helps users conduct market research through 1,200 Web site addresses providing information on various markets and products or services, and he provides a lengthy glossary of export terms and detailed index for quick access to important information.

Morrison, Terri and Conaway, Wayne A. *Kiss, Bow, or Shake Hands: The Bestselling Guide to Doing Business in More than 60 Countries.* Adams Media Corp., 2006. 592p. ISBN 1593373686.

This encyclopedic resource presents information for each country on the country history, type of government, languages, religions, business practices, titles and forms of address for 60 countries. A cultural orientation for each country with negotiation strategies and value systems is included. Well-organized and concise, this newly revised guide will make learning to do business in a foreign country easier.

Moss, Rita. *Strauss's Handbook of Business Information.* 2nd ed. Libraries Unlimited, 2004. 453p. ISBN 1-56308-520-8. $85.00.

Business information has experienced a revolution in the past few years, i.e., user-friendly and sometimes free access to online databases filled with company, industry, association, and government information. The basic organization of the first edition has been followed here, dividing the *Handbook* into two main sections: Formats and Fields of Business Information. Additionally, with the globalization of business and economies, international resources are featured in each chapter. The Format section includes guides, directories, periodicals, loose-leaf services, and electronics. Fields covered include marketing, accounting and taxation, banking, stocks and bonds, futures, insurance, and real estate. Appendices cover acronyms, federal government agencies, state agencies, and selected Web sites. A title and a subject index complete the volume.

Plunkett, Jack W. *Plunkett's E-Commerce and Internet Business Almanac 2010.* Annual. Plunkett Research, Limited, 2010. 623p. ISBN 1-59392-163-2 $299.99.

Over 400 in-depth profiles of e-commerce and Internet companies are provided. This edition includes overviews through easy-to-use tables on all facets of business on the Internet, including e-commerce revenues, access and usage trends, and global Internet user data in the industry analysis section. Find data on Internet growth companies, online services and markets, online retailing strategies, emerging e-commerce technologies, manufacturers of software and equipment for Internet communications, and much more. Information is indexed and cross-referenced. Use *Plunkett's* to plan your global expansion.

Rivoli, Pietra. *The Travels of a T-Shirt in the Global Economy: An Economist Examines the Markets, Power, and Politics of World Trade.* Wiley, 2005. 254p. ISBN 0-4716-4849-3.

In order to understand how the global economy really works, readers will follow with Professor Rivoli a T-shirt from Texas cotton-growers to Chinese textile sweatshops, and, finally, to an African used-clothing bazaar. Learn how U.S. farmers teamed with government-sponsored researchers and, using subsidies and trade barriers, have come to dominate the world's cotton production. Explore with Rivoli the history, economics, and politics of world trade.

**RMA *Annual Statement Studies.* Risk Management Association, annual.

After 85 years in the business, Robert Morris Associates no longer produces the RMA Annual Statement Studies. The name of the association is now Risk Management Association. These studies collect and compile current and historical financial data for almost 350 industries by company asset and sales size. An annual volume is expensive so check your library or their Web site for information on buying one industry (http://www.rmahq.org/RMA/). The Web site is also described below in online resources. Banks use this information for analyzing business loan applications. Libraries have traditionally purchased these data for their business collections, but subscription costs keep rising.

Salacuse, Jeswald W. *The Global Negotiator: Making, Managing, and Mending Deals Around the World in the Twenty-First Century.* Palgrave Macmillan, 2003. 312p. ISBN 0-312-29339-9. $39.95.

This unique, outstanding guidebook breaks down the intricacies of international negotiations into understandable segments and provides the tools to ensure success in the creation, management, and remediation of international deals. Salacuse even explains how to deal with negotiations that go wrong, illustrating how deals may falter and methods to save them. Managers, lawyers, executives, and government officials will use this comprehensive guide to understand the transformations global business has experienced in the last decade.

Small Business Sourcebook. 2v. Thomson Gale, annual. $405.00.

This directory provides a wealth of information for the small business owner or manager. The Small Business Profiles cover 340 different small businesses. Businesses profiled include catering, cooking schools, fish farms, antique shops, bookstores, and car washes. Entries contain as many as 17 subheadings, such as start-up information, educational programs, reference works, sources of supply, statistical sources, trade periodicals, trade shows and conventions, consultants, and franchises and business opportunities. The chapter on import/export services will prove very useful along with the section on trade shows and exhibiting, which lists publications to help you get more out of exhibiting. The Small Business Topics section covers general ideas such as budgets and budgeting, retailing, service industry, franchising, insurance, and seasonal business. Like the small business profiles, these entries have the same 17 subheadings and lead users to many resources relating to the topics. The state listings and federal government assistance sections list programs and offices that provide information and support to businesses. Check your library for this practical, well-organized source.

Strawser, Cornelia J. *Business Statistics of the United States.* 13th ed. Bernan Associates, 2008. 633p. ISBN 1-59888-182-5. $154.

This comprehensive, classic business resource contains all kinds of data relevant to the economic performance of the U.S. economy. Historical data, including statistics on production, manufacturers' stocks, exports, and prices are provided for a variety of U.S. industries. Over 3,000 economic time series, mainly from federal government sources, are included. This huge compilation of data enables users to observe past trends and provides the basis for projecting trends in the future. Part B presents a general description of NAICS and its differences from SIC before presenting detailed industry data on the NAICS basis as far back as possible, usually the early 1990s. Part D includes State and Regional Data on personal income and employment back to 1972.

Travis, Tom. *Doing Business Anywhere: The Essential Guide to Going Global.* John Wiley & Sons, Inc., 2007. 202p. ISBN 0-470-14961-2. $24.95.

Travis presents his six tenets of global trade and illustrates them in the context of real stories of global trade. He emphasizes the importance of international trade to the economic prosperity of all the world's nations. If you want to start a new venture or expand your present one, Travis helps you organize, plan, operate, and execute with a global mind-set. Learn how to navigate conflicting and confusing laws, deal with different cultures, and operate in different countries. He also explains how to leverage the benefits of free trade agreements to set up and operate a competitive and profitable business and highlights how to protect your brand through patents, copyrights, and trademarks. Security concerns and measures are also discussed. Travis will convince you that embracing his six tenets is key to "doing business anywhere."

**Troy, Leo. *Almanac of Business and Industrial Financial Ratios*. Aspen Publishers, Inc., 2004. 801p. ISBN 0-7355-4319-4. $139.

This updated business reference standard covers 50 operating and financial factors in 192 industries and derives its data from IRS figures on U.S. and international companies. Data for each industry are subdivided into thirteen categories based on company size. Troy presents a variety of factors relating to operations, operating costs, financial performance, and an array of financial factors in percentages including debt ratio, return on assets, return on equity, and profit margins. Tables are divided into thirteen asset sizes to help with making comparisons.

**U.S. Department of Commerce. Census Bureau. *Statistical Abstract of the United States*. Government Printing Office, annual. Web version at: http://www.census.gov/compendia/statab/ (also available on CD ROM).

This collection of statistics on U.S. social, political, and economic conditions provides statistics on things like the number of cell phones in the United States, average cost of a home in different areas of the United States, educational level in various parts of the country, fastest growing jobs, where population growth is happening, and more in over 1,400 tables and charts. First published in 1878, the data are collected from over 220 difference government and private agencies. Each chapter begins with a description of the data being presented and definitions of terms and concepts. The International Statistics section presents statistics for the world as a whole and for many countries on a comparative basis with the United States. Data are shown for population, births and deaths, social and industrial indicators, the economy, agriculture, and communication. Use the subject index to quickly locate the statistical tables you need. Most tables present information for the past 5 to 10 years. Footnotes under the tables provide source information.

Walsh, Ciaran. *Key Management Ratios: Master the Management Metrics that Drive and Control Your Business*. 3rd ed. Financial Times/Prentice Hall, 2003. 400p. ISBN 0-273-66345-3. $24.95.

Business ratios are the standards and targets that help owners or managers work toward achieving their goals in running a successful business. Fully international, using companies in the United Kingdom, United States, European Union, and Japan, Walsh proceeds to teach readers everything needed to know about key business ratios, linking them to day-to-day operations. He also covers financial statements, balance sheets, cash flow, liquidity, and cost, volume and price relationships. You will take some knowledge away from studying this thorough and well-organized book.

Weiss, Kenneth D. *Building an Import/Export Business*. 4th ed. John Wiley & Sons, Inc., 2008. 320p. ISBN 0-470-18577-5. $19.95.

Weiss, an entrepreneur and international trade consultant, offers tips and instructions for every aspect of an import/export business. Learn how to get started in the post-9/11 import/export landscape. He explains how to take advantage of the General Agreement on Tariffs and Trade (GATT), the WTO, CAFTA, NAFTA, and other trade agreements. Weiss covers all new and updated regulations, laws, and customs and shipping procedures to help ensure that businesses are in compliance with the Transportation Security Administration (TSA), U.S. Customs and Border Protection (CBP), and U.S. Immigration and Customs Enforcement (ICE). Besides helping importers and exporters plan their business expansion, Weiss describes how to research a raw idea and then successfully launch a stable, profitable business operation. Learn from the real-life examples presented here.

World Directory of Trade and Business Journals 2007. 3rd ed. Euromonitor International PLC (Gale), 2007. 628p. ISBN 1-84264-416-5.

If you can find this huge directory in a library, it will provide you with a powerful business research tool. All major industries are represented and are indexed by sector and country for an easy-to-use, well-organized approach. An index of the journals listed by country adds another access point. Countries from Algeria and Belarus through Guyana and Mali to Yemen are covered, with industries ranging from confectionery, domestic electrical appliances, media, pet food and pet care products, to vegetables. Entries include language, frequency, content summary, country coverage, format, and publisher with contact information including e-mail, fax, and URL.

Zodl, Joseph A. *Export-Import: Everything You and Your Company Need to Know to Compete in World Markets.* 4th ed. IIEI Press, 2005. 174p. ISBN 0-9773098-0-0. $39.95.

In easy-to-understand language and writing style, Zodl leads you into the world of international business, dispels the myths, simplifies tasks and processes, and illustrates important points with real-world examples. Zodl defines the vocabulary and terminology needed to understand the world of international business and points out sources to turn to for expert advice. This title provides the information the exporter needs to take a U.S.-manufactured product, sell it to a foreign buyer, make the shipment correctly, and get paid in U.S. dollars. It shows a middleman how to buy a product made by someone else and resell it at a profit to an overseas customer. Zodl also has a Web site users may be interested in checking out at http://www.zodl.net/firstpage.htm.

Online Resources

American Association of Exporters and Importers (AAEI): http://www.aaei.org/ accessed Spring 2009).

Begun in 1921, this organization "has been the national voice of American business in support of fair and open trade among nations" with its expertise in custom matters and global trade issues. Members include manufacturers, distributors, and retailers as well as organizations serving carriers, banks, freight forwarders, and brokers. The association works with many U.S. government agencies. Access to news and press releases along with additional information is provided at the Web site.

American FactFinder: http://factfinder.census.gov/home/saff/main.html?_lang=en (accessed Spring 2009).

This federal government source for information on population, housing, economic, and geographic data is easy to use and well designed. You can get a Fact

Sheet for your community by just entering town, county, or zip code. A quick link gets you to the Decennial Census of Housing and Population, American Community Survey, the Economic Census, or the Population Estimates program. A couple clicks will get you to *County Business Patterns*, information on the NAICS code, statistics about small business from the Census Bureau, the characteristics of business owners' database, and more. A glossary, FAQs, and search will also help you use this great, free resource.

BBC News (Country Profiles): http://news.bbc.co.uk/2/hi/country_profiles/ default.stm (accessed Spring 2009).

The BBC's full country profiles include a complete guide to history, politics, and economic background for many countries divided into six major regions of the world. Nineteen international organizations are also profiled, many including sections on facts, leaders, and issues. The Country Profiles also are divided into Overview, Facts, Leaders, and Media. Related Internet links as well as related BBC links are also useful. The timeline of important events for each country provides practical, relevant information.

**BEOnline: Business and Economics Online: http://www.loc.gov/rr/business/ beonline/ (accessed Spring 2009).

Compiled by the Library of Congress Business Reference Services for researchers, this site has, under Subject Lists, a lengthy list of business topics such as associations, business plans (forms), companies by industry, data sets, e-commerce, franchises, economic indicators, and legal resources. If you click on Associations, you are taken to an associations database that includes contacts, descriptions, addresses, and events data for the organizations listed. Over 10,000 business organizations in the United States are listed. Find here a link to the Herb Growing and Marketing Network or the Association of Bridal Consultants. Under the Title listing, you will find Airlines of the Web, America's Business Funding Directory, American Chambers of Commerce Abroad, American City Business Journals, and more.

BizMove.com: http://www.bizmove.com (accessed Spring 2009).

The wealth of information on this site covers a variety of topics including general management, small business marketing, Internet business, and international trade. Worksheets and sample plans will help guide you. Check the International Business section for information on exporting and importing. International trade centers on exporting but covers many diverse topics including how to export a service and how to sell overseas.

**BizStats.com: http://www.bizstats.com (accessed Spring 2009).

Find profitability and operating ratios for S corporations, partnerships, and sole proprietorships for industries such as furniture stores, electronics, gas stations, and sporting goods. You can find retail industry benchmarks such as sales per foot (SPF), average sales per foot in malls, and SPF for a three-year trend. This site has Financial and Operating Ratios for 30,000 Industry Segments. Use the free financial calculators for start-up costs, financial ratios, and balance sheets. This well-organized site for small business statistics is easy to use and frequently updated but is no longer free. Check with them to see if statistics you need are available and how costly they are.

Bureau of Labor Statistics (BLS): http://stats.bls.gov/oco (accessed Spring 2009).

The BLS maintains the International Price Program (IPP) including the Import Price Indexes and Export Price Indexes. In addition, find here publications such as the *Dictionary of Occupational Titles* and the *Occupational Outlook Handbook* online. The *Handbook* provides training and education needed, earnings, and expected job prospects for a wide range of jobs. Here is help to write job ads, job descriptions, foreign labor statistics, and more. You will also learn about current government regulations and legislation in regard to employees.

Business.gov: http://www.business.gov (accessed Spring 2009).

This is another government site developed to help businesses find the information they need and want. The Market Research section of this site is especially noteworthy. Links to information on major industries, population and demographic resources, plus Rural America Facts provide users with a multitude of useful resources. International trade connections are useful for global or Internet businesses too. Major categories include laws & regulations, buying & selling, financial assistance, and taxes. Also find workplace issue information on interviewing, working environments, training, hiring procedures, and employing minors. The site map works like a table of contents and gets you where you want to go quickly and easily.

Buyusa.gov: http://www.buyusa.gov/home/export.html (accessed Spring 2009).

This simple-to-use government Web site offers to help businesses get into international sales through market research, trade events, introductions to buyers and distributors, and counseling for every/any step of the export process. One part of the Web site helps importers to the United States and another helps exporters from the United States and both parts cover products and services. When you click on a country, you get the Country Commercial Guide (CCG), a calendar of events, employment opportunities, market information, and services for U.S. exporters or suppliers. Also part of this site is the *Commercial News USA*, the "official export promotion magazine of the U.S. Department of Commerce." This online publication also contains a wealth of information, including franchising, trade shows, and a company index.

Centers for International Trade Development: http://www.citd.org/StartupKit/index.cfm (accessed Spring 2009).

This very useful site has a guide for new exporters, an export readiness assessment tool, and an excellent Export FAQ for companies just getting into international trade. Their Trade Information Database includes U.S. and world trade and economic data, trade contacts and leads, trade reference tools, foreign market research, trade/investment regulations, trade documentation, finance & insurance sections and more. A trade resources directory provides information on numerous trade associations and organizations. A trade show calendar is also available, along with booklets on best markets for various U.S. industries. Start gathering import/export information here.

CIA World Factbook https://www.cia.gov/cia/publications/factbook/index.html (accessed Spring 2009).

Prepared by the U.S. Central Intelligence Agency (CIA), this resource is a great beginning research point, with its concise country information such as economic, social, and political profiles. It is continually updated with demographics, gross domestic product statistics, membership in international organizations, and diplomatic, communication, and transportation information.

Country Studies: http://lcweb2.loc.gov/frd/cs/ (accessed Spring 2009).

These in-depth country studies and handbooks were prepared by a team of scholars under the direction of the Federal Research Division of the Library of Congress, as sponsored by the U.S. Army. At present, 102 countries and regions are covered, primarily focusing on lesser-known areas of the world or regions in which U.S. forces might be deployed. One word of warning, however: because funding for the country studies was cancelled in 1999, the studies range in date of preparation from 1988 to 1998. However, some Country Profiles also accessible from this site are being updated. Highlights of the individual studies include photographs, historical and economic backgrounds, tables, glossaries, and bibliographies. The site is searchable by topic.

Department of the Treasury Internal Revenue Service: http://www.irs.gov (accessed Spring 2009).

The IRS's Market Segment Specialization Program focuses on particular market segments—which may be an industry like auto body and repair, a profession like ministers, or an issue like aviation tax. Their guides discuss common and unique industry issues, business practices, and industry terminology. They are produced and updated on an as-needed basis, so some are quite old. Despite their age, however, you may find that, like the overview of the Bars and Restaurants industry from April 2003, the information presented is still very useful for your business.

Economic Research Service, U.S. Department of Agriculture: http://www.ers .usda.gov (accessed Spring 2009).

The Economic Research Service (ERS) is a primary source of economic information and research that provides economic analyses on agricultural economies, trade policies of various foreign countries, information on world agricultural trade and development issues, and links to information on the U.S. food and fiber economy. With 450 employees, ERS conducts a research program to inform public and private decision-making on economic and policy issues involving food, farming, natural resources, and rural development. ERS's highly trained economists and social scientists conduct research, analyze food and commodity markets, produce policy studies, and develop economic and statistical indicators. The ERS analyzes how factors influencing demand, production variables, governmental policies and programs, macroeconomic conditions, and major events affect a country's agricultural production, consumption and trade, international food and fiber prices, and U.S. food and fiber competitiveness. The ERS also produces an outstanding magazine, *Amber Waves*, available online at: http://www.ers.usda.gov/AmberWaves/AllIssues/.

**Economist.com http://www.economist.com (accessed Spring 2009).

Providing excellent coverage of world news, the Economist.com also contains information on world markets, the latest exchange rates, and country and city guides geared to the business traveler. It is the companion site to the print journal *The Economist*. Although much of the site is free and fully searchable, the Economist.com does charge to view archived articles. Other portions of the site are considered to be premium content viewable by subscription only.

**Entrepreneurs.About.com: http://entrepreneurs.about.com/ (accessed Spring 2009).

This large site has many different parts and is at times a bit difficult to navigate. Use the search feature if you have trouble. On the left side of this main page, you will find Business Ideas on a Budget, Choosing a Business to Start, Business Plan Outline, Business Legal Organizational Structures, and the "How to" Library. Further down on the page, topics such as Financing, Case Studies and Interviews, and Resources also provide more links to information. The About.com large Web site also covers the biotech/biomedical, composites/plastics, metal, insurance, and retail industries. The retail industry (http://retailindustry .about.com/), for which it is notoriously difficult to locate information, is especially well done; articles provide information on current retail trends, retail statistics, retail industry profile, apparel trends, consumer trends, and more. The entire site is fully searchable, so put in keywords and find information. Under Business and Finance, you will also find articles on, for example, various industries, store operations, retail trends, advertising costs, and branding. International information on global trade shows and industry trends is also available through a simple search.

Entrepreneurship: http://www.entrepreneurship.org (accessed Spring 2009).

The Ewing Marion Kauffman Foundation is the entrepreneur's trusted guide to high growth. This large site is filled with relevant, practical, and timely information on how to manage and expand your business. Included are original articles written for the site by entrepreneurs drawing on their own experiences and an aggregation of the "best of the best" existing articles and tools to guide you on the path to high growth. Topics are arranged around eight key subject areas: Accounting and Finance, Human Resources, Marketing and Sales, Products and Services, Business Operations, The Entrepreneur, Public Policy, and Entrepreneurship Law. The Sales and Marketing section includes a section on Global Markets. Search on Global and find articles like Eleven Pitfalls to Avoid in Going Global and Entrepreneurs, Manage Your Global Growth.

Euromonitor International: http://www.euromonitor.com/ (accessed Spring 2009).

Euromonitor International offers quality international market intelligence on industries, countries, and consumers. They have some 30 years of experience publishing market reports, business reference books, online information systems, and bespoke consulting projects. Their Web site has a huge article archive with short articles on topics like trends in retail, food prices, and brand growth, in various parts of the world. Many articles are on a specific company, country, or product. Complete company profiles and industry reports can be purchased.

Eurostat: http://epp.eurostat.ec.europa.eu/portal/page/portal/eurostat/home/ (accessed Spring 2009).

This large portal is sponsored by the European Commission. Listed are the general themes: General and Regional Statistics; Economy and Finance; Population and Social Conditions; Industry, Trade, and Services; Agriculture and Fisheries; External Trade; Transport; Environment and Energy; and Science and Technology. Under the Statistics tab, you will find tables on employment, demographic changes, environment, economic reform, and much more. Business and consumer surveys and consumer prices are also available. Much of the information is available free in PDF file downloads. This site is a good place to start for anyone looking to trade with Europe.

Export America. **U.S. Department of Commerce: http://www.trade.gov/exportamerica/** (accessed Spring 2009).

The official magazine of the International Trade Administration of the U.S. Department of Commerce, this publication offers practical export advice and is very valuable to small and mid-sized exporters. It includes country- and industry-specific opportunities, trade events, online marketing tips, and export statistics. Articles cover such topics as export documentation, market research, U.S. customs, and success stories, and selected articles from current journal issues can be viewed here. Although not globally searchable, full text of past journal issues from November 1999 through the most current completed year are also available.

The Exporter: http://www.exporter.com (accessed Spring 2009).

The focus of this publication is to provide information on exporting services and resources for businesspeople involved in international trade who need to understand and meet foreign import and U.S. export requirements. The Web site provides this and more, including a very current news feed and supplemental commentary and white papers focusing on international trade issues. Additional information can be accessed through free membership subscription.

**Export.gov: http://www.export.gov (accessed Spring 2009).

Created as a government-to-business initiative, Export.gov is the government's portal to exporting and trade services. It is designed to simplify the exporting process by being a single point of access to export-related services and thus reducing the need to view multiple government sources. Over 19 U.S. departments and agencies contribute the information it provides, including the U.S. International Trade Administration, the U.S. Commercial Service, the Department of Commerce, the Export-Import Bank, the Agency for International Development, and the U.S. Trade and Development Agency. Companies new to exporting will find step-by-step help through the export process. To facilitate international trade, companies can also find references on foreign tariff and tax information, search foreign and domestic trade events, and subscribe to receive trade leads and industry specific market intelligence, as well as gain access to federal export assistance and financing. Export.gov is fully searchable and allows you to search globally the contents of all of its contributing entities.

Export-Import Bank of the United States (Ex-Im Bank): http://www.exim.gov (accessed Spring 2009).

Begun 65 years ago, the bank's mission is to match officially supported foreign competition and fill financing gaps to support U.S. exports and contribute to the promotion and maintenance of U.S. jobs. Ex-Im Bank offers working capital guarantees to U.S. companies, export credit insurance, and direct loans or guarantees of commercial loans to foreign buyers of U.S. goods and services. Find Economic Impact Notices, credit reviews and compliance, forms and publications, handbooks, statistics, seminars, and related links here.

EXPORT911.com: http://www.export911.com/ (accessed Spring 2009).

This business and educational Web site focuses on international business. It provides in-depth information on export/import marketing, management, letters of credit, export cargo insurance, shipping, logistics, manufacturing, purchasing, bar codes, and more. Major sections include Gateways to Global Markets, Purchasing Department, Production Department, and Product Coding (bar codes). Business Tool titles include Conversion Tables, Abbreviations, Acronyms, and Symbols, and General References. Case studies and samples are also provided. This large site provides a plethora of educational and informational articles and data.

Federal Trade Commission (FTC) http://www.ftc.gov/bcp/business.shtm (accessed Spring 2009).

The FTC provides business information for consumers and businesses. One section is entitled E-Commerce and the Internet and provides you with rules and information about Internet advertising and marketing, a code of online business practices, online privacy needs, regulations of Internet auctions, securing your server, selling on the Internet, and more. Economic and legislation information related to the Internet is also provided.

Federation of International Trade Associations (FITA): http://www.fita.org (accessed Spring 2009).

Founded in 1984, FITA has more than 450 affiliates, which are independent international associations that fall into one of the following categories: world trade clubs, associations or chambers of commerce with regional/bilateral interests, associations focused on international logistics, associations supporting international trade, associations supporting exporters, or professional associations. More than 400,000 groups are linked here. Neither individuals nor companies can become members but can join the member organizations. FITA provides an outstanding linking site, which is searchable, has annotated links, and is available in languages other than English. The organization also publishes the e-mail newsletter *Really Useful Sites for International Trade Professionals*.

**FedStats: http://www.fedstats.gov (accessed Spring 2009).

The official Web site of the Federal Interagency Council on Statistical Policy is a gateway to statistics from over 100 U.S. federal agencies and is well organized and easy to use. You can find helpful information under the titles Links to Statistics, Topic Links A–Z, MapStats, and Statistics By Geography from

U.S. Agencies. MapStats provides statistical profiles of states, counties, cities, congressional districts, and federal judicial districts. The Statistical Reference Shelf, a bit further down on the home page, is a large collection of online reference sources like the *Statistical Abstract of the United States*. You will find a variety of other sources such as the *State and Metropolitan Area Data Book* and *Digest of Education Statistics*, which will provide statistics on many topics of interest to entrepreneurs. On the other half of the page, Links to Statistical Agencies, under Agencies by Subject, click Economic on the drop-down arrow to go to a list of Periodic Economic Censuses. Below this area, you will find Data Access Tools, which link users to agency online databases.

Free Management Library: http://www.managementhelp.org/ (accessed Spring 2009).

The Library provides easy-to-access, clutter-free, comprehensive resources regarding the leadership and management of yourself, other individuals, groups, and organizations. Content is relevant to most small and medium-sized organizations. Over the past 10 years, the Library has grown to be one of the world's largest well-organized collections of these types of resources. Approximately 650 topics are included here, spanning 5,000 links. Topics include the most important practices to start, develop, operate, evaluate, and resolve problems in for-profit and nonprofit organizations. Each topic has additionally recommended books and related articles. Grouped alphabetically by subject, the E-Commerce collection is particularly noteworthy.

The Global Connector: http://www.globalconnector.org (accessed Spring 2009).

Part of Indiana University's Center for International Business Education and Research (CIBER), this gateway leads to thousands of international trade sites. The Global Connector allows searching by either country or by industry. Country data include links to data on government, domestic economy, news and media, entry requirements, transportation, and international trade. Industry specific information can be searched by the type or source of information including trade shows, trade publications, trends/analysis, and regulatory matters.

GlobalEDGE: http://globaledge.msu.edu/ (accessed Spring 2009).

Managed by State University's Center for International Business Education and Research (MSU_CIBER), this site links to a broad selection of international trade data including economic trends, statistical data sources, government resources, trade portals, journals, and mailing lists. Its Global Resources section provides access to more than 2,000 online resources. MSU_CIBER has also contributed its own resources including an interactive forum for business professionals and portions of the information contained in the Knowledge Room, GlobalEDGE's section on the latest issues and trends effecting international business.

International Monetary Fund (IMF): http://www.imf.org/external/index.htm (accessed Spring 2009).

The IMF database contains approximately 32,000 time series covering more than 200 countries and areas and includes all series appearing on the International Financial Statistics (IFS) Country Pages, exchange rate series for all Fund member countries, plus Aruba and the Netherlands Antilles, and most other world, area, and country series from the IFS World Tables. Find here the *Export and Import*

Price Index Manual. Under the Country Info tab, users will find detailed, current information about the economic situation in the country. The site is fully search-able and easy to use. The complete text of the *World Economic Outlook* is also available online; learn how the economic slowdown in the United States in 2007 affected other areas of the world and continues to affect the global economy.

**International Trade Administration (ITA): http://trade.gov/index.asp (accessed Spring 2009).

Part of the Department of Commerce, the ITA has set up this site to try to strengthen the U.S.'s competitiveness, promote trade and investment, and encourage fair trade and compliance with trade laws and agreements. Find sta-tistics through its TradeStats Express and some PDFs of free publications, though many are only available for purchase. *A Basic Guide to Exporting* is probably the most thorough and useful publication as it provides practical help for exporters/importers. Find trade events and missions and get export counsel-ing through this site. The FAQ section has many links to more information for exporters and importers. The ITA conducts analytical studies of individual industries and of foreign countries, and this huge site has many industry and gross domestic products statistics. All of the agency and related Web sites com-prising the large DOC organization are globally searchable from the DOC site including the Economic and Statistics Administration. Besides national trade and industry statistics, find state and local trade data and links to key foreign country data sources. A Spanish version of the site is also available.

KnowThis.com: Marketing Virtual Library http://www.knowthis.com (accessed Spring 2009).

This large site is a smorgasbord of data and guidance on marketing, including how to conduct market research, promotion versus advertising, using current technologies, and a large section on Internet marketing, divided into methods and strategies and research. Find guidance on creating marketing plans as well as sample plans. New topics include selling virtual clothes for avatars and reviews of software to enhance small e-commerce sites. Tutorials on managing customers, personal selling, targeting markets, and more are available.

Market Entry Assistance: http://faculty.philau.edu/russowl/market.html (accessed Spring 2009).

Professor Lloyd C. Russow at Philadelphia University has organized a large number of Web resources useful for new exporters and importers. You will find country information, product classification systems, international organi-zations as well as market entry resources. The section titled Are You Ready to Go International is very useful as is the Documentation section. Refer to this useful site often.

**Market Research, Industry Research, Business Research: http://www.virtualpet .com/industry (accessed Spring 2009).

This major portal for researching companies and industries presents a step-by-step process to begin researching an industry. Here you can find sources to help you learn about legal issues, regulatory issues, competition, markets, and even history of the industry for your new business. Additional links to industry portals are also available. Three other linked sites offer help on How to Learn about a Company by Examining its Products, How to Review, Evaluate, Critique a Web Site, and How to Conduct a Patent Search.

National Association of Export Companies (NEXCO): http://www.nexco.org (accessed Spring 2009).

Dedicated to empowering small to mid-sized companies to build their global commerce efficiently and effectively, this group was founded in 1965. It is a forum for networking, business solutions, and advocacy through its Global Business Roundtable program and sponsors online conferences and an annual trade mission. Its Web site links directly to a comprehensive searchable database maintained by the Federation of International Trade Associations (FITA).

National Foreign Trade Council (NFTC): http://www.nftc.org (accessed Spring 2009).

Founded in 1914, the 300-plus member companies that comprise this organization advocate a rules-based world economy. Dedicated to advocacy in trade policy, export finance, international taxes, and human resources issues, the council works to advance open markets, fights protectionism, and advocates for the Export-Import Bank, IMF, and more. The Council's site provides links to current news and information related to NFTC activities and Positions. The Web site also provides full-text white papers produced by the organization.

New York Public Library, International Trade Research Guide: http://www .nypl.org/research/sibl/trade/trade.html (accessed Spring 2009).

This wonderful guide produced by the Science, Industry and Business Library (SIBL) will provide invaluable information in learning how to conduct business between the United States and another country. Guides, business directories, periodicals, and trade statistic sources can be located through this large and practical site. It is well organized and easy to navigate; find information grouped under market research, trade leads, shipping and logistics, and cross-cultural business communication.

Office of the U.S. Trade Representative: http://www.ustr.gov (accessed Spring 2009).

As the principal trade policy advisor to the president, the U.S. trade representative and office staffs are responsible for developing and implementing U.S. international trade, commodity, and direct investment polity. The agency's Web site includes information regarding issues of importance to the World Trade Organization including trade and environment, monitoring and enforcement, trade and development, and outreach.

Organisation for Economic Co-operation and Development (OECD): http:// www.oecd.org (accessed Spring 2009).

The 30 member countries of this organization produce two-thirds of the world's goods and services as well as collect data, monitor trends, analyze and forecast economic developments, and research social changes and trade patterns. The OECD seeks to stimulate economic cooperation among its members, expand world trade, and coordinate assistance for less-developed countries of the world.

The Web site offers information concerning a myriad of topics in the subject area. Some of the publications and statistics are available by subscription only, so check with your local library for access.

Quick MBA: http://www.quickmba.com/entre/bplan/ (accessed Spring 2009).

For those new to business plans and SWOT analysis, this site is thorough and practical. Learn the basics of both these concepts and many more here. Management and marketing articles are useful and helpful to new owner and managers as well as experienced ones. A political, economic, social, technical (PEST) analysis is presented, why to use it, and how it relates to SWOT. Often articles include recommended readings.

**RMA Universe: http://www.rmahq.org/RMA/ (accessed Spring 2009).

After 85 years in the business, Risk Management Association's *RMA Annual Statement Studies* are one of the standards in business ratios. This resource will help you show investors that you understand your business and are prepared to compete. Financial ratio benchmarks are included for over 700 industries, now using the NAICS codes. Trend data are available for five years. Using this data, you can make more informed decisions for your new business.

SBDCNET: http://sbdcnet.utsa.edu (accessed Spring 2009).

The Small Business Development Center National Information Clearinghouse provides timely, Web-based information to entrepreneurs. Small Business Development Centers (SBDCs) are located in all 50 states. SBDCs offer free, confidential business counseling. This Web site provides information on business start-up, international trade, e-commerce, industry research, marketing, trends, and more. The International Trade section has many links to more information and more help in moving into exporting or importing. Templates for business plans and marketing tools are also available. A free newsletter will help you keep up on trends in small business. Entrepreneurs will find plenty of links and information here to help plan, expand, and run a new business.

Small Business Administration: http://www.sba.gov (accessed Spring 2009).

This official government site offers a wealth of resources and programs for starting and growing a small business. Under Startup Basics, check out the areas you need help with while doing your business planning. Other major sections cover business planning, financing, international trade, managing, marketing, employees, taxes, legal aspects, and business opportunities. Find here online forms, sample business plans, loan information, and many publications. The Export Library contains titles like Breaking into the Trade Game, Export Working Capital Program, Export Financing for Small Businesses, and SBA & Ex-Im Bank Co-Guarantee Program. Some content is available in Spanish. Trade Mission Online is also found on the SBA site and is useful both to businesses that want to export their products for use by foreign firms and to U.S. businesses seeking U.S. partners or suppliers for trade-related activities. Also part of the SBA program are the Small Business Development Centers (SBDC) at http://www.sba.gov/sbdc. SBDCs are located in every state and deliver counseling and training for small businesses in the areas of management, marketing, financing, and feasibility studies. (see SBDCNET for more information.)

**State and Local Government on the Net: http://www.statelocalgov.net (accessed Spring 2009).

This site provides convenient access to all state and local government sites by listing the states alphabetically. Frequently updated, this directory of official state, county, and city government Web sites also provides a list of topics to choose from plus listings of government grants, with applications. Links are provided to even the smallest counties or state agencies in the nation if they have a Web presence. The directory lists 10,792 Web sites and can be searched by state, topic, or local government name.

**STAT-USA/Internet: http://www.stat-usa.gov/ (accessed Spring 2009).

This service of the U.S. Department of Commerce is a single point of access to authoritative business, trade, and economic information from across the federal government. An important part of this resource is www.stat-usa.gov/tradtest.nsf . Obtain here current and historical trade-related releases, international market research, trade opportunities, country analysis, and the trade library, the National Trade Data Bank (NTDB). The NTDB provides access to Country Commercial Guides, market research reports, best market reports, and other programs. USA Trade *Online* provides current and historical import and export statistics for over 18,000 commodities traded worldwide as well as the most current merchandise trade statistics available in a spreadsheet format. The International Trade Library is a comprehensive collection of over 40,000 documents related to international trade. All are full-text searchable, as well as keyword searchable by country or product.

USA.gov: http://www.usa.gov (accessed Spring 2009).

Information by Topic will interest and amaze first-timers. Topics include Defense and International, Environment, Energy and Agriculture, Money and Taxes, Reference and General Government, and Science and Technology. Tabs at the top of the page include one for Businesses and Nonprofits, which has a section on International Trade. Clicking on Data and Statistics brings up an alphabetical list of links to resources chock full of statistics. Economic Indicators is the Web site of the Economics and Statistics Administration, part of the U.S. Department of Commerce (http://www.economicindicators.gov), and it provides timely access to the daily releases of key economic indicators from the Bureau of Economic Analysis (BEA) and the Census Bureau. In addition, a section called Foreign Businesses Doing Business in the U.S. is under Businesses and Nonprofits. Under Frequently Asked Foreign Business Questions you can find a section titled Doing Business Abroad. Spanish translation of the site is also available. You can e-mail questions about the site and the statistics or telephone for help too. Your taxes pay for the collection, compiling, and publishing of these statistics, and they are available for your use.

**U.S. Bureau of Economic Analysis (BEA): http://www.bea.gov (accessed Spring 2009).

Part of the Department of Commerce, the BEA presents a wealth of statistical information here. Look on this site for international economic accounts data, industry data, and GDP by state and metropolitan area plus personal income statistics. Many types of international trade of goods and services statistics are also easily available. The Survey of Current Business provides current Export and Import statistics.

**U.S. Census Bureau: http://www.census.gov (accessed Spring 2009).

This Web page is the best place to start searching for the multitude of data produced by census programs, publications, and statistics. The home page groups the data under Census 2000, People, Business, Geography, Newsroom, At the Bureau, and Special Topics. Under Business, you can click on the Foreign Trade, Economic Census, NAICS, E-Stats, and Survey of Business Owners. Under Foreign Trade, learn directly from the Census Bureau how to properly classify your products for export and how to file your Shipper's Export Declaration online. The Bureau also processes, tabulates, and releases the data collected by the Bureau of Customs and Border Protection on exports and imports of goods in their International Data Base. Here you will find U.S. export and import statistics by commodity, country, customs district, and method of transportation providing value and quantity on a monthly, year-to-date, and annual history basis. U.S. state export data and port statistics for imports and exports are also available. The catalog, a search feature, and links to related sites are also accessible on the left side of the home page. Use this site frequently to help start and grow your business.

U.S. Customs and Border Protection (CBP): http://www.cbp.gov/ (accessed Spring 2009).

Under the Department of Homeland Security, the CBP unifies and integrates the work of several separate government entities including functions of the U.S. Customs Service, the Immigration and Naturalization Service, and the Agricultural Department's Animal and Plant Health Protection Service. It provides protection, advice, and control of merchandise shipped into the country as well as enforcement and compliance with many diverse regulations concerning homeland security, the flow of trade, inspections at ports of entry, and seizures of illegal drugs and contraband. The Importing and Exporting sections of the CBP Web site contain a wealth of information on current trade issues, export licenses and fees, news on specific products, the Harmonized Tariff Schedule, pertinent statutes and regulations, and other publications, forms, and videos.

U.S. Department of State (DOS): http://www.state.gov/ (accessed Spring 2009).

Containing a wealth of country information, including an online version of Background Notes, this site presents basic demographic and economic statistics as well as short narrative descriptions about the people, history, government, and foreign relations. In addition, there is U.S. Embassies and Consulate information as well as a diplomatic list. Listings on the left bar of the home page link to topical information including a series of publications that contain factual information on all countries with which the United States has relations. Country Commercial Guides can also be accessed through the site.

U.S. International Trade Commission (USITC): http://www.usitc.gov (accessed Spring 2009).

This nonpartisan, quasi-judicial federal agency provides trade expertise, determines the impact of imports on U.S. industries, and directs actions against certain unfair trade practices. Publications available through this Web site include the Harmonized Tariff Schedule, general fact-finding reports, economic effects reports, and the International Economic Review. The USITC *Interactive Tariff and Trade DataWeb* provides international trade statistics and U.S. tariff data to the public full-time and free of charge, including import and export statistics, U.S. tariffs, U.S. future tariffs, and U.S. tariff preference information. The Industry & Economic Analysis section contains Working and Research Staff Papers on a variety of topics available to the public in PDF format.

U.S. Trade and Development Agency (USTDA): http://www.ustda.gov (accessed Spring 2009).

The USTDA's mission is to promote economic growth in developing and middle income countries and to assist simultaneously U.S. businesses to export their products and services to create U.S. jobs. It is an independent U.S. Government foreign assistance agency funded by the U.S. Congress. Find business opportunities here as well as grant funding for overseas projects that support the development of modern infrastructure and open trading systems. The library contains completed USTDA-funded studies in various regions or countries as well as feasibility studies.

Valuation Resources.com: http://www.valuationresources.com (accessed Spring 2009).

This commercial site provides links to many industry information resources for over 250 industries. It pulls together industry resources from trade associations, industry publications, and research firms. Topics also included are industry outlook, financial ratios, salary surveys, economic data, and public market data. Check here to see what information is available on your industry. Also find trade association directories and information here.

VIBES: Virtual International Business and Economic Sources: http://library .uncc.edu/display/?dept=reference&format=open&page=68 (accessed Spring 2009).

The more than 1,600 links to free sources of information at this site were selected by Jeanie Welch of the University of North Carolina Charlotte. The table of contents breaks the sites into three groups: comprehensive, regional, and national. The comprehensive section organizes its links by category, including banking and finance, business practices and company information, emerging markets, and international trade law. Research and tables and graphs are highlights of this site. The regional section allows searching devoted to a single region or continent such as Europe or the Middle East. The national section links to sites devoted to a particular country.

World Bank. http://www.worldbank.org (accessed Spring 2009).

Established in 1944, the World Bank is comprised of five separate organizations all with distinct but related missions: the International Bank for

Reconstruction and Development (IBRD) and the International Development Association (IDA), the International Finance Corporation (IFC), Multilateral Investment Guaranty Agency (MIGA), and the International Centre for Settlement of Investment Disputes (ICSID). Resources provided from its business center include World Bank project and program summaries, documents, and reports. The side bar provides links to data and statistics on countries and regions, evaluations, news, and more. Arranged hierarchically, each of these categories allows you to drill down to even more specific information. In addition to providing access to its own collection of resources, the World Bank provides access to each member organization's site. Doing Business (http://www.doingbusiness.org) is a database that provides objective measures of business regulations and enforcement for 175 countries.

World Trade Magazine: http://www.worldtrademag.com/ (accessed Spring 2009).

This large site is a treasure trove of information for individuals and companies either involved in international trade or wanting to enter the global market and understand supply chains. Besides print information, you can find Webinars on supply chains, buyers and suppliers, financial supply chains, and more. Find a global supply chain buyers guide, currency calculator, white papers, eNews letter, and more. Industry news, such as the articles FedEx Post First Loss in 11 Years and Logistics Costs Higher in Russia, is also provided.

World Trade Organization (WTO): http://www.wto.org (accessed Spring 2009).

Established in 1995, the WTO is comprised of more than 140 countries that cooperate on global economic policymaking and provides the ground rules for international commerce. The organization's world-renown annual report *International Trade Statistics* is available on its Web site via the Resources link. Also available are documents published by the WTO, information on trade topics, and links to publications of many member countries, news, and international trade resources.

World Wide Chamber of Commerce Guide: http://www.chamberfind.com (accessed Spring 2009).

The local chamber of commerce has long been the best source for community data, local businesses, attractions, festivals, relocation data, tourist information and more. This site can be searched for U.S. chambers by state, World chambers by regions, or keywords. Local businesses that are chamber members can also be located here. Chamber sites vary, but most can be very useful before visiting an area. Many of the foreign sites provide at least some information in English by clicking on a U.S. or British flag.

Yahoo! Directory, National Governments: http://dir.yahoo.com/government/ (accessed Spring 2009).

This site is a quick way to find links to governments around the world. Countries ranging from Brunei, Burkina Faso, Moldova, and Oman to Vanuatu are listed. Some countries have few links under their category at this time, but many, like Australia, are a gateway to departments, documents, local governments, research labs, statistics, taxes, and more. Links are often briefly annotated.

3

Market Analysis/
Competitive Strategy

Chapter Highlights:

Where to Begin?
Screening Potential Markets for Exporting
Identify Your Competitors and Research Their Export/Import Efforts
Data Gathering
Choosing the Right Market
Develop Your Export Marketing Plan
Accidental Exporting

Economies all over the world are developing or just changing, and market development takes time. Flexibility and political astuteness are important. Remember that if you plan your export venture thoroughly and with care, you have a better chance of success in your target market and elsewhere. Many small and medium-sized enterprises (SMEs) start export ventures with inadequate market studies or none at all. Yet a market study is almost the only way to support your income (sales) projects and your marketing plan. In addition, a solid market study looks very good to potential investors and lenders.

Your international market research may take different forms as there are many ways to study a market. Remember that the more detailed your research, the less likely you are to overlook something important. To be successful, assess your potential markets to identify your marketing opportunities and constraints within individual foreign markets and also to identify and find prospective buyers and customers through market research.

In markets that are vastly different from the domestic market, some products or services will have limited potential. Differences may stem from social and cultural factors, climate and environmental factors, availability of raw materials or product alternatives, lower purchasing power, government import controls, and the like. Look at why your product or service sells well in the domestic market and then select similar markets abroad.

The main two types of market research are primary and secondary. Primary data, original information collected specifically for a particular requirement, are generally more accurate, relevant, and timely compared to secondary data, which are based on information that already exists from third parties. Primary data, of course, are also more costly and time-consuming to gather, especially for foreign markets. Primary research involves collecting data directly from the marketplace through interviews, surveys, and other direct contacts. Obstacles in the collection of primary international data include language, infrastructure, and cultural differences.

WHERE TO BEGIN?

Typically, a company begins an international market research project using as much secondary data as possible before resorting to costly primary data. Secondary data are collected from compiled sources such as trade statistics for a country or product or service. (In the future, products will be mentioned more than services, but this discussion applies to both). Working with secondary sources helps a company focus its marketing efforts and budget. International trade statistics available from many local libraries or online can give you a preliminary indication of overseas markets for a particular product by demonstrating where related products are already being sold. If your product is unique or has features that are difficult to duplicate abroad, it is likely that a good export market exists. Demand may be high for a unique product and competition very slight. In addition, countries that are less developed may not need state-of-the-art technology but may show a healthy demand for older products that are being replaced by more technically advanced products in the domestic market. Results of your market research should show the largest markets for the product or service, the fastest growing markets, market trends and outlook, market conditions and best practices, as well as competitive firms and products or services.

First you should be aware of a few caveats when collecting secondary data:

- *Comparability*: It is often very difficult to find the same data for several different countries or markets in order to identify market potential. The original data are collected for different purposes by different organizations. Statistics on services are often unavailable.

- *Lack of Current Data*: For many foreign markets, especially rapidly emerging markets, the frequency of surveys and data collection is much less often, sometimes only every five or ten years, or maybe it is not collected at all. The most recent statistics are often two years old during which time the market could have changed dramatically.

- *Costs of International Secondary Data*: In markets where government spending on statistical reporting is low and the burden falls on private industry, information is often difficult to collect due to problems and issues in the infrastructure. Companies who manage to collect data charge a premium price for their products. Incomplete data-gathering techniques are also often used.

SMEs use three standard methods of conducting secondary market research:

1. Being aware of world events that influence the international marketplace, watching for press releases of specific projects, or simply visiting likely markets. For instance, thawing of political rhetoric or even hostilities often leads to more or easier economic channels between countries.

2. Often collecting trade statistics by product category and by country so entrepreneurs and businesses can analyze them. A U.S. firm can learn about shipments of products over a specified period of time. Market potential for a company's product or service can be indicated by demographic and general economic statistics like population numbers and makeup, per capital income, and production levels by industry.

3. Expert advice obtained through government agencies and trade associations, attending seminars and trade shows, networking with successful importers or exporters, and hiring an international trade and marketing consultant will provide guidance on making the export or import decision.

SCREENING POTENTIAL MARKETS FOR EXPORTING

First obtain export statistics that show product exports to various countries. Due to their proximity, Canada and Mexico are often good first choices for companies new to exporting. All products and services use import and export codes classified by the Harmonized Tariff System (HTS). The HTS assigns six-digit codes in general categories. Participating countries that use the HTS may define commodities at a more detailed level than six digits, but all products and services must at least be defined in the six-digit framework. Export codes that the U.S. calls Schedule-B codes are administered by the U.S. Census Bureau and use a 10-digit HTS code. For a complete explanation and identification of Schedule-B codes, check out the Census Bureau at http://www.census.gov/foreign-trade/schedules/b/. For import codes, read and search the USITC Web pages at: http://dataweb.usitc.gov/. For complete descriptions of these agencies and their

Web pages, check the Online Resource list at the end of this chapter. Another source to check for the product or service's HTS code is the National Trade Data Bank (NTDB).

The NTDB is a Web-based subscription service of the Department of Commerce's STAT-USA, a trade library of over 200,000 documents on export promotion and international economic information from more than 20 federal sources. You can conduct searches on markets, tariffs and non-tariff barriers, importers, and logistics and product information, and learn about the NTDB at any of 1,000 federal depository libraries through the United States.

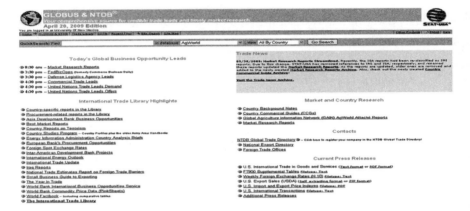

Today's Global Business Opportunity Leads. GLOBUS and NTDB—STAT-USA (4/20/09 Edition).

Next identify eight to ten large and fast-growing markets for your firm's product or service. Start a file for each potential market. Look at the market statistics for the past three to five years and see if growth has been consistent. Did the import growth remain or hold steady even during periods of economic recession? If not, did growth resume with economic recovery? Looking at past sales or competitor sales as a method for choosing markets is a reactive market selection strategy. But you should also use a proactive strategy and search for and identify fast-emerging but smaller markets that may provide ground-floor opportunities where there may be fewer competitors than in established markets. Each potential market profile should include:

- Market type (specify fast-paced and competitive, relationship-based and relatively affluent, or emerging or changing)
- Political highlights (describe the government, who's who, agreement with United States, other major political themes)

- Economic description (identify domestic economy, trends, general imports or exports and U.S. imports or exports)
- Business information (list currency, language, business regulations and differences in legal framework, government procurement practices, office hours)
- Support for market-entry strategies (locate industry associations, trade shows, trade media, research facilities, market research sources of information)
- Cultural considerations (describe forms of address, do's and don'ts, cultural differences, attitude toward Americans)

For more information on regions of the world and individual countries, please check out the Appendix at the end of this book.

IDENTIFY YOUR COMPETITORS AND RESEARCH THEIR EXPORT/IMPORT EFFORTS

Businesses usually have a good idea of who their competitors are domestically, but now think about finding a profitable niche outside the United States and explore which, if any, of your competitors have already started a similar effort. After you have identified eight or ten markets, find out if any of your competitors have penetrated these markets. List your answers to the following questions as a way to begin:

1. Who are your three or five nearest direct competitors?
2. Do you have any and, if so, who are your indirect competitors?
3. How does your product or service differ from your direct competitors and any indirect ones?
4. What do you know about their operations or advertising in international markets or on the Internet?
5. List your strengths and weaknesses and their strengths and weaknesses.

Answering the above questions will lead you into a SWOT (strengths, weaknesses, opportunities, and threats) analysis of your own company to discover its core competencies or what you do best. Export markets are competitive, and companies need to concentrate their efforts in areas of greatest strength to maximize the chances for success. Having a clear vision of the company's strengths and weaknesses is an initial step to matching successfully your product with the right export market. Strengths describe the activities that an organization does well and sets it apart from competitors. Examples of strengths might include a highly productive factory, easy access to financing, or a creative design team. Weaknesses are the areas in which a company needs to improve. Weaknesses might include poor quality control, poor customer service, or insufficient staff. You will learn more on SWOT analysis later in this chapter. However, if you are unfamiliar with a SWOT analysis, several books and Web sites mentioned in the resources list at the end of the chapter will go into further detail.

By knowing what your competitors are doing, you will gain a better understanding of what products or services you could be offering to an international market, how to market your products or services in another country, and how you can position your business in the marketplace. Sometimes businesses devote too much attention to the current large market-share competitors and overlook smaller and potential competitors. Critical insight can be gained in customers' buying behaviors by analyzing smaller rivals or the "substitute" rivals. Businesses with products or services that could be alternatives are substitute rivals. If you are having difficulty locating companies in your industry and targeting markets that are successfully exporting, contact your industry association for help. Another place to search is the U.S. Department of Commerce's *Commercial News USA* at http://www .thinkglobal.us/.

Commercial News USA is one of many export promotion tools available to U.S. businesses through the Commerce Department's Commercial Service

Commercial News USA **30th Anniversary.** *Commercial News USA*—U.S. Dept. of Commerce.

and showcases U.S.-made products and services. You will find lists of companies already exporting grouped in about 15 different industries. Trade show opportunities are highlighted and described often letting businesses know who attends and who should attend. This magazine is also an excellent source for trade leads and for advertising your products or services to find customers or partners. You can subscribe online or by mail. Since its start in 1978, *CNUSA* has proven to be an excellent cost-effective means of promoting U.S. products and services globally.

DATA GATHERING

Start a file on each of those three or five competitors you named and a similar one for your company. Research your own company right along with all your competitors. Competitive analysis can help you reflect on and learn about your own business and its vulnerabilities, limitations, and capabilities in relation to the competition before you start a new phase of development in your business. Develop a list of items it would be helpful to know about each competitor. This list might include how each is structured; the area of specialty or niche; the level of service or quality of product; values and practices; financial strength; domestic and overseas market share; and what each is likely to do next. Increase your awareness of the market and industry in general. Watch your competitors and market for customers' perceptions and loyalty, promotional campaigns, product quality and service levels, and changes in products or services. Understand how your competitors provide value to the customer. The following resource will help you use the Internet to begin gathering data:

Vibert, Conor. *Competitive Intelligence: A Framework for Web-based Analysis and Decision Making.* South-Western, 2003. 264p. ISBN 0-324-20325-X. $39.95

In Vibert's book you will find out how to conduct competitive research using the Internet. Managers constantly face difficulty as they try to make decisions in today's complex and competitive environment. In Part I of his book, Vibert presents a chapter "Strategically Searching the Web" and one called "Differentiating Good Online Information from Bad." Part II has chapters called "Analysis: Why It is Important" and "Web-Based Research Mission—Incorporating the Internet into Analysis." Part III's best chapter is "Using Web CI to Understand the Online Music Business, A Case Example." Vibert's contributors all focus on free, publicly available information sources rather than expensive commercial databases. Using these research suggestions, Internet search and analysis tools, and the analytical framework, you will have all you need to run an effective knowledge management program in your organization. Use these practical suggestions to learn about Internet research on competitors and how to use it to help your business.

CHOOSING THE RIGHT MARKET

At this point, narrow down the broad list of possible markets to three to five of the most statistically promising markets for further assessment. Now you can undertake more intensive market research as well as complete the second half of your SWOT analysis (opportunities and threats). Add the evaluation of the opportunities and threats offered by the markets into your planning. Opportunities and threats focus on the external factors present in the company's environment that may impact the success or failure of the firm. A big new customer for your company would be an opportunity, and a threat might be the introduction of a newer, better, cheaper product by the competition. Using this analysis, you should be able to gauge the gap between your current capabilities and the capabilities you will need to successfully enter a market abroad. The key to a successful international strategy is prioritizing markets based on how they align with your product or service and your company's strengths and then controlling the variables in the environment (such as marketing and customer service) to maximize your success. You have located the markets with the greatest potential and now you need to examine them in detail. Ask yourself questions such as:

- How does the quality of your product or service compare with similar goods that already are available in your target foreign markets?
- Is your price competitive?
- Who are you major customers?
- What is the best promotional strategy to use?
- How should our company modify existing marketing materials or even the product or service?

Many resources to help you answer these questions are available online.

Start at Export.gov's Market Research page. Here you will find a library containing over 100,000 industry- and country-specific market reports authored by U.S. government specialists working in overseas posts. The Country Commercial Guides are open to all but the industry overviews, market updates, best markets, and industry or regional reports require free registration as they are only available to U.S. companies. Many more resources are listed in the Appendix at the end of this book.

Another good general site to use is Export Help for Businesses. A Web site created and maintained by the University of Washington Business School students, with articles and tips organized under how to export, industry data, country information, and other Web sites, this site will lead you through the process of examining a market. Find this resource at http://www.exportinfo.org.

DEVELOP YOUR EXPORT MARKETING PLAN

Before you develop your export marketing plan, however, be sure to check your business plan to see that it reflects your domestic operation and is current and comprehensive. If you have an out-of-date plan, now is the time to review and renew it. For more information and resources on writing and updating the business plan, see Chapter 5.

Now develop the export marketing plan, an essential management tool, to help your company reach its overseas market potential. This step takes time and investment, but by prioritizing opportunities against your resource constraints and time frame, you increase your chances for success. The first time an export marketing plan is developed, it should be simple— just a few pages. The initial planning effort will generate more information and insights for this living document that can be incorporated into more sophisticated planning documents. Objectives in the plan must be compared with actual results as measures of success for different strategies tried.

What should you include in your plan? Companies choosing to export directly should complete a very detailed plan; however, if your company chooses indirect export methods, develop a simpler plan. An export plan is a modified business plan that focuses on international markets. Generally, it identifies your target market(s), export goals, necessary resources, and anticipated results. A suggested organization of elements to include follows:

1. *Table of Contents*

2. *Introduction*: why this company should export?

3. *Background Analysis*: product or service and HTS number, resources, industry structure, competition, supply and demand, location and facilities, personnel, international market goals, and business history.

4. *Marketing Overview*: target foreign market(s), economic and political environment, main industrial users with brief description, industry trends and market outlook, characteristics of important market segments, tariff and non-tariff barriers, rules and regulations, methods of promotion and cost of promotional assistance expected of exporters, locating foreign distribution company, and when and how much foreign travel.

5. *Schedule of Activities or Action Steps*: key activities, indirect marketing efforts, distribution, pricing and trends plus discounts used in the trade, evaluation criteria and process, competitive analysis, and logistics of transportation and payment.

6. *Financial Plan*: revenues or sources of funding, cost of sales, promotion costs, operating budget, travel costs, and product launch.

An addendum may include Background Data on Target Country(s) and Market: basic market statistics, historical and projected, background facts, competitive environment.

ACCIDENTAL EXPORTING

If a company receives unsolicited orders from abroad, you may begin to export without conducting market research or competitive analysis, of course. And, while this selling is valuable to the company, you may discover better, more promising markets by conducting a systematic search. In addition, if your company determines to export indirectly (see Chapter 4) by using an intermediary, export management company (EMC) or export trading company (ETC), you should select markets to enter before selecting the intermediary.

REFERENCES

(Starred titles discussed in the chapter)

Print Resources

Addison, Doug. *Small Websites, Great Results: The Blueprint for Creating Websites That Really Work.* Paraglyph, Inc., 2004. 352p. ISBN 1-932111-90-5. $29.99.

If you want a simple, well-designed, highly focused Web site, Addison's approach will work for your small business. Design ideas and marketing techniques are showcased in profiles of 20 small businesses. You will discover new approaches to creating sites; find out what really makes small sites work; learn about strategies for getting, keeping, and satisfying customers; and pick up tips on how to work with professional designers to get the results they want and need. Learn how to create an update or editorial calendar and how to organize the files on your Web site so that your business site is always different, current, and easy to change. Discover what to leave off your site to keep it simple and uncluttered. Addison will convince you that quality is much better than quantity.

A Basic Guide to Exporting: Official Government Resource for Small and Medium-sized Businesses. 10th ed. U.S. Department of Commerce, 2007. 190p. ISBN 0-16079-20-4-5. $19.95. Also available online: http://www.unzco.com/basic-guide/index.html

Conventional wisdom once held that U.S. businesses should be content selling within their domestic market as international markets were too difficult and too expensive to penetrate. However, in the past decade, barriers to trade have been lowered and advances in communications technology have been and are tremendous. Today exporting is seen as a prime growth area, and this title describes the costs and risks associated with exporting, how to develop a strategy for success, and where to get the knowledge to enter exporting. Assistance from the federal and state government is also discussed.

Capela, John J. *Import/Export for Dummies.* Wiley Publishing, Inc., 2008. 338p. ISBN 978-0-470-26094-4. $19.99.

Capela is an international business consultant, and this practical guide covers how to evaluate import/export opportunities, expand your global operations, identify target markets, find customers, follow the rules and regulations of different countries, and develop a marketing strategy. The introductory discussion of what environmental forces make international business different is essential reading before you start your international adventure. Another important section discusses the selection of products and suppliers. Learn about the various approaches to exporting and importing and some of the qualities you need to possess to be successful.

Cohen, William A *The Marketing Plan*. 4th ed. John Wiley and Sons, Inc., 2004. 368p. ISBN 0-471-23059-6. $41.95.

This updated edition presents step-by-step procedures to help you produce a clear plan that defines your marketing goals and how you plan to achieve them. Tools and techniques help you scan your industry and local environment, establish goals and objectives, and develop marketing strategies and tactics to sell your product or service successfully. Also included are time-saving forms to help you accomplish a variety of marketing planning tasks. Three new sample marketing plans from readers who have used previous editions to develop them are included in this edition. This practical guide will help you understand how and why a good marketing plan is so essential to every business venture.

Cyr, Donald, and Gray, Douglas. *Marketing Your Product*. 4th ed. Self-Counsel Press, Inc., 2004. 200p. ISBN 1-55180-394-1. $18.95.

Covering all the essentials of marketing, this expanded edition of a marketing classic demonstrates how your business can carve a niche for its products or services. Learn about market researching, market positioning, marketing strategy planning, product launching, and competitor awareness. Cyr and Gray answer help readers answer questions such as what you should know about global marketing and why people choose one product over another. One highlight in this edition is a chapter on the value of the Internet as a marketing tool in the global marketplace. Good worksheets help entrepreneurs and new small business owners develop individualized marketing plans.

Doman, Don, et al. *Market Research Made Easy*. 3rd ed. Self-Counsel Press, Inc., 2006. 146p. ISBN 1-55180-676-2. $14.95.

The authors describe market research as a process of asking questions or finding existing information about the market, the competition, and potential customers. Written for the first-time, do-it-yourself market researcher, this book guides readers step by step through marketing any business. Worksheets and explanations in nontechnical language help you decide if you want to consult a professional, determine how much you want to spend, and gather and analyze data to create a marketing strategy. Learn how to write a questionnaire. Analyze the global market and understand your industry. Various real-life case studies scattered throughout bring the importance of market research and doing it well home. The authors ascertain that the most difficult part of market research is that it can burst your bubble—demolish a cherished idea—but it will save you money and point you in the right direction. Learn how to expand your market share internationally. The Canadian resources included are especially useful.

Dorsey, Jennifer. *Start Your Own Import/Export Business*. 2nd ed. Entrepreneur Press, 2007. 252p. ISBN 1-59918-108-8. $15.95.

This book contains insights and practical advice for entering global markets. It covers aspects of the start-up process, including collecting money from overseas transactions, using the Internet to simplify your transactions, accessing trade law information to keep your business in compliance, finding contacts in the United States and abroad, using the Internet to simplify your transactions, and choosing a customs broker. Chapters on market research, working online, employees, pricing, and insurance will help run a business efficiently and effectively. A brief appendix on international trade resources may also prove useful. Interviews with successful importer/exporters and an updated resource list will help show the way to success.

Encyclopedia of Associations. Thomson-Gale. Annual. $2310.

This comprehensive list of national organizations provides a brief entry for each group including name, address, telephone number, URL, cost of membership, and a short description of publications and members. Organizations are grouped in general subject areas. Indexes provide access to the organizations by name, key word, and geographic area. An international directory is also available. This work has become a standard in its field.

Europa World Year Book. Annual. Routledge, Taylor & Francis. 2 v.

This well-respected annual provides a great deal of detailed information on the political, economic, and commercial institutions of the world. Each country is covered by an individual chapter composed of an introductory survey that includes recent history, economic affairs, government, and defense; followed by data on social welfare, finance, telecommunications, trade and industry, utilities, and education. Now also an online product, a free trial electronic subscription is available from the Europa World Web site at http://www .europaworld.com/

Exporters' Encyclopaedia. Annual. Dun & Bradstreet.

This comprehensive world reference guide summarizes requirements business people must meet to export products and services to countries around the world. This encyclopedia is divided into 220 country-specific sections; firms specializing in international business, laws, and legislation; international trade associations; government agencies; shipping practice; and reference data on weights and measures for overseas ports. Find key contacts, trade and safety regulations, and information on documentation needed. Marketing data include legal requirements for importer or agents, procurement standards, environmental protection or pollution control, marking, and labeling. The encyclopedia also provides passport regulations and business etiquette guidelines.

Hague, Paul, Hague, Nick, and Morgan, Carol-Ann. *Market Research in Practice: A Guide to the Basics (Market Research in Practice Series)*. Kogan Page, 2004. 226p. ISBN 0-7494-4180-1. $32.50.

Fully international in scope, this practical guide to the basics of market research takes a clear and concise, step-by-step approach, explaining the many tools and techniques used by market researchers. The authors offer comparative examples and case studies from Europe, the United States, and the rest of the world. With a decidedly British tone, the authors detail qualitative market research, questionnaire design, administered interviews, response bands, telephone interviewing, conjoint analysis, quota samples and more. The Sampling and Statistics chapter is particularly useful and succinct. As a refresher or as an introduction, this title is outstanding.

Hinkelman, Edward, et al. *Importers Manual.* Annual. World Trade Press. 960p.

Information on how to import virtually any commodity into the United States can be found in this practical reference. It is precisely organized for ease of use and is divided into the major sections of Commodity Index; U.S. Customs Entry and Clearance; International Banking; Legal Considerations of Importing; and Packing, Shipping, and Insurance. The heart of the work, the Commodity Index, contains entry procedures, documentation, restrictions, and prohibitions; marking and labeling requirements; and contact information for regulatory agencies for all products that can be imported into the United States.

Horowitz, Shel. *Grassroots Marketing: Getting Noticed in a Noisy World.* Rev. ed. Chelsea Green Publishing, 2004. 320p. ISBN 0-890132-68-3. $22.95.

Horowitz maintains that the average small business, individual, or organization needs to market very inexpensively. Learn how to identify your target market, get the message to your market, and convince the customer to do business with your company. If you need help with choosing a company name, writing press releases, using Yellow Page ads and direct mail advertising effectively, and navigating the Internet, learn the basics here. Case histories and examples illustrate the effectiveness or ineffectiveness of many marketing vehicles for different types of businesses. Nine chapters cover using the "Incredible Internet" in Part IV. Chapter 21, Getting Started in Cyberspace, is particularly useful for those unfamiliar with e-commerce. An appendix of useful resources is also included. Learn how to attract favorable attention for your small business in the global market through the Internet.

Jagoe, John R. *Export Sales and Marketing Manual 2008: The Bible of Exporting.* Annual. Export Institute of the United States. 520p. ISBN 0-943677-66-1. $295.

Having been updated annually for 21 consecutive years, this international trade publication has achieved longevity and global reach. This manual covers all the steps involved in selling products in world markets. Over 120 illustrations, 85 graphs, 40 flow charts, and 60 sample international trade documents, lead the user through the process. Jagoe helps users conduct market research through 1200 Web site addresses providing information on various markets and products or services, and he provides a lengthy glossary of export terms and detailed index for quick access to important information. This professional and practical resource will help you effectively enter and succeed in the global market.

Johnson, Winslow "Bud." *Powerhouse Marketing Plans.* AMACOM, 2004. 352p. ISBN 0-8144-7219-2. $29.95.

Learn how to maximize market research initiatives such as phone surveys, focus groups, online surveys, and test marketing. Walking readers through the planning process, Johnson's sample plans will help importers as well as exporters plan their business expansion or develop a new market. You can explore the details of new marketing ventures and the interrelationship among those details. Watch the process from name development to package creation and from researching the competitive environment to understanding consumer segments and their motivations and interests. Each chapter takes a real product or service and works through the process to produce a sample marketing plan summary at the end. The comprehensive sample marketing plan concluding the book is outstanding and a real example of what can be pulled together by using the advice Johnson presents. Discover the creative thinking and problem-solving processes behind good marketing plans.

Karlson, Carolyn Boulger. *Writing and Presenting a Business Plan*. Cengage South-Western, 2008. 295p. ISBN 0-324-58422-9. $37.95.

From idea generation through feasibility analysis, and from writing the plan to presenting it to various audience groups, Karlson covers all steps necessary to develop and start a business. She also provides guidance on meeting with investors and getting funding for the new venture, and it provides numerous samples of effective plans and presentations. Market analysis, SWOT analysis, timetables, and break-even analyses are all presented in clear, easy-to-read, and easy-to-understand formats. Karlson's guide is very useful for completing your export marketing plan.

Kotler, Philip. *Ten Deadly Marketing Sins: Signs and Solutions*. John Wiley & Sons, 2004. 132p. ISBN 0-471-66206-2. $19.95.

Well-known and respected marketing expert Kotler identifies and describes the 10 glaring deficiencies companies make in their marketing efforts, whether domestic or international. Each mistake is covered thoroughly in its own chapter. Kotler explains how to remain customer-driven, understand your customers, tract the competition, find new opportunities, and develop effective marketing plans. He also includes using technology to the fullest in your marketing plan; and while some might argue that technology is covered too generally, it's still worthwhile to get Kotler's views. Find out if you are making any of these marketing mistakes and how to avoid or reverse them.

Levine, Michael. *Guerrilla PR Wired: Waging a Successful Publicity Campaign Online, Offline, and Everywhere in Between*. McGraw-Hill, 2003. 288p. ISBN 0-07-138232-1. $15.95.

This collection of cutting-edge, low-cost publicity techniques includes sample press releases and attention-getting strategies targeted for the wired environment. Focused on the Web or Internet, the chapters on Internet public relations (PR) and The Web and How to Unweave It, are particularly informative to those new to using the Internet for marketing. Levine has many years of experience in PR and more entrepreneurs will benefit from this discussion and hints gathered from his experiences.

Machado, R. and Cassim, S. *Marketing for Entrepreneurs*. Juta Academic, 2004. 224p. ISBN 0-7021-5544-6. $24.95.

Covering all aspects of marketing, this title is especially strong in the product-service mix, branding, trademarks, packaging, warranties, and developing new products.

Also learn how to identify, collect, analyze, and use the information collected through market research. This practical handbook has an international slant and will help develop a good marketing plan for expanding your business abroad.

McKeever, Mike. *How to Write a Business Plan*. 7th ed. Nolo Press, 2005. 256p. ISBN 1-4133-0092-8. $34.99.

This logically organized, thoughtfully presented book uses examples and worksheets to help anyone prepare a successful business plan. The importance of planning in any business venture cannot be overemphasized. Included are business plans for a small service and a manufacturing business. The chapter on writing your marketing and personnel plans is particularly helpful for the marketing section of a business plan or to develop a new market. Before proceeding with the marketing plan, McKeever suggests you return to your written business description to see if it still is an accurate statement of how you view your business or if the thinking and writing experiences between chapters have changed your current ideas. A business plan and the accompanying marketing plan are dynamic documents that need constant revision to keep you and your business current. This new edition has good new online and offline resources to help the new entrepreneur plan their business.

McKinney, Anne. *Real Business Plans and Marketing Tools: Including Samples to Use in Starting, Growing, Marketing, and Selling Your Business*. PREP Publishing, 2003. 224p. ISBN 1-885288-36-0. $24.95.

In this book designed to help entrepreneurs prepare paperwork relating to starting, marketing, and growing a business, McKinney presents real business plans for 17 different types of businesses including a hair salon, brew pub, auto body shop, home-based wholesale company, and janitorial supply company. The section on marketing tools will help new small business owners understand the fine points of marketing. You will also find samples of financial statements and other documents used to obtain bank loans and equity financing. This title will help all business owners in strategic planning.

Morrison, Terri, and Conaway, Wayne A. *Kiss, Bow, or Shake Hands: The Bestselling Guide to Doing Business in More than 60 Countries*. Adams Media Corp., 2006. 592p. ISBN 1593373686.

This encyclopedic resource presents information for each country on the country history, type of government, languages, religions, business practices, titles and forms of address for 60 countries. A cultural orientation for each country with negotiation strategies and value systems is included. Well-organized and concise, this newly revised guide will make learning to do business in a foreign country will be easier.

Mullins, John. *The New Business Road Test: What Entrepreneurs and Executives Should Do Before Writing a Business Plan*. Financial Times/Prentice Hall, 2004. 288p. ISBN 0-273-66356-9. $24.95.

Before writing a business plan or investing any money, use Mullins's seven domains model for assessing your new business ideas. Learn how to run a customer-driven feasibility study to assess that new business opportunity. Case studies use real businesses like Honda, Enterprise Car Rental, and Starbucks to illustrate industry trends and opportunities. What are critical success factors and niche markets? Avoid the "me too" trap and more. Use his practical advice and guidance to help your new business succeed.

Murphy, Christopher. *Competitive Intelligence: Gathering, Analysing, and Putting It to Work*. Gower Publishing Company, 2005. 304p. ISBN 0-566-08537-2. $120.00.

Businesses need intelligence to find suppliers, mobilize capital, win customers, and beat the competition. Murphy advocates a conscious, systematic approach to getting intelligence and using it to recognize and seize opportunities. Learn how companies try to stay ahead of their rivals, about different methods of research and sources of information, and about analytical techniques that transform facts and opinions into a platform of knowledge to support informed business decision-making. Learn how to read between the lines of company reports and press releases, how to understand corporate cultures, and how to research industries and companies in other countries. While focused on the British business world, the lessons presented have universal application, and examples are taken from across the globe. The final chapter, Intelligence Countersteps, will help you protect your company from the practices of unscrupulous researchers and investigators.

Parasuraman, A. and Colby, Charles L. *Techno-Ready Marketing: How and Why Your Customers Adopt Technology*. The Free Press, 2001. 240p. ISBN 7-806-84864-945. $27.00.

Presented here is a compelling framework for measuring the propensity of customers to welcome and use technology-intensive products and services. Learn how to determine each customer's technology readiness, how to motivate customers to use new technology, why people either embrace or resist technology, and how to divide your consumers into five distinct groups. CEOs, small business owners or managers, and marketing professionals will learn how to succeed in the technology-driven future.

Phillips, Michael and Rasberry, Salli. *Marketing Without Advertising*. 4th ed. Nolo Press, 2003. 240p. ISBN 0-87337-930-6. $24.00.

This book takes readers on an in-depth, practical journey through marketing strategies. One valuable section illustrates how to design and implement a marketing plan. Other topics include updating the physical appearance of your business, educating and helping prospective customers find your business, and using the Internet to market your business internationally. Sections on the importance of good relations with your employees and how they influence the perception of your business are interesting and informative. Questionnaires, checklists, and worksheets help readers understand important points and make decisions about expanding their marketing efforts by using the Internet.

Salmon, Robert and de Linares, Yolaine. *Competitive Intelligence: Scanning the Global Environment*. Economica Ltd., 1999. 200p. ISBN 1-902282-04-3. $24.95.

Broadening the concept of economic business intelligence, Salmon believes that companies must "scan their environment" for everything happening around them. Human relations and intangible factors are assuming increasing importance, and business success depends on agility, creativity, and proactivity.

Product life cycles are getting shorter, consumer tastes are more unpredictable, technological innovation advances at a dizzying pace, and information circulates in real time. Businesses must learn to refocus economic thinking on people and identify future trends on the basis of what we observe around us. Learn how to decipher the signals and identify opportunities and risks for your business.

Small Business Sourcebook. 2v. Thomson-Gale. Annual. $405.00.

You will find a wealth of information for the small business owner or manager in this guide, but here we will concentrate on trade associations. In the Small Business Profiles, the second part of the entry is entitled Associations and Other Organizations, and listed here are trade and professional associations that gather and disseminate information and statistics of interest to its members. This resource lists each association's name, address, phone, toll-free and fax numbers, company e-mail, URL, contact name, purpose and objective, description of the membership, and a listing of its publications with frequency. Also in the Small Business Profiles, users will find a long and complete list of resources grouped under categories such as licensing, trade publications, trade shows, franchises, and sources of supply about any type of business from bagel shop to restaurants including import/export. Each resource in a profile has a complete citation as well as a short description. Often URLs or e-mail addresses are provided. The two-volume set helps entrepreneurs start up, develop, and grow their businesses.

SRDS Media Solutions. *The Lifestyle Market Analyst.* Annual. $460.

Compiled from 12 million households, this annual market analysis tool provides demographic, lifestyle, and consumer segment profiles to help users locate where consumers live and how they spend their money and free time. This volume takes interests, hobbies, and activities like bicycling, fishing, gambling, and reading and combines them with demographic and geographic data. Use it to help you find regional buying powers, your target audience(s), and analyze 40 demographic segments. Check their Web site for more information, http://www.srds.com, including their International Media Guides. Find information on Mexican and Canadian print, TV, and radio opportunities.

**Vibert, Conor. *Competitive Intelligence: A Framework for Web-based Analysis and Decision Making.* South-Western, 2003. 264p. ISBN 0-324-20325-X. $39.95.

Vibert explains how to conduct competitive research using the Internet. Part I contains chapters on Strategically Searching the Web and Differentiating Good Online Information from Bad. Part II has chapters on Analysis: Why It is Important and Web-Based Research Mission: Incorporating the Internet into Analysis. Part III's best chapter is Using Web CI to Understand the Online Music Business, A Case Example. The contributors all focus on free, publicly available information sources rather than expensive commercial databases. Learn about Internet research on competitors and how it can be used to help your business compete on an international basis.

Weiss, Kenneth D. *Building an Import/Export Business.* 4th ed. John Wiley & Sons, Inc., 2008. 320p. ISBN 0-470-18577-5. $19.95.

Weiss, an entrepreneur and international trade consultant, offers tips and instructions for every aspect of an import/export business. Learn how to get started in the post-9/11 import/export landscape. He explains how to take advantage of GATT, WTO, CAFTA, NAFTA, and other trade agreements. Weiss covers all new and updated regulations, laws, and customs and shipping procedures to help ensure that businesses are in compliance with the Transportation Security Administration (TSA), U.S. Customs and Border Protection (CBP), and U.S. Immigration and Customs Enforcement (ICE). Besides helping importers and exporters plan their business expansion, Weiss describes how to research a raw idea and then successfully launch a stable, profitable business operation. Learn from the real-life examples presented here.

World Directory of Trade and Business Journals 2007. 3rd ed. Euromonitor International PLC (Gale), 2007. 670p. ISBN 1-84264-416-5.

If you can find this huge directory in a library, it will provide you with a powerful business research tool. All major industries are represented and are indexed by sector and country for an easy-to-use, well-organized approach. An index of the journals listed by country adds another access point. Countries from Algeria and Belarus, through Guyana and Mali, to Yemen are covered with industries ranging from confectionery, domestic electrical appliances, media, pet food and pet care products, to vegetables. Entries include language, frequency, content summary, country coverage, format, and publisher with contact information including e-mail, fax, and URL.

Zodl, Joseph A. *Export-Import: Everything You and Your Company Need to Know to Compete in World Markets.* 4th ed. IIEI Press, 2005. 174p. ISBN 0-9773098-0-0. $39.95.

In easy-to-understand language and writing style, Zodl leads you into the world of international business, dispels the myths, simplifies tasks and processes, and illustrates important points with real-world examples. Zodl defines the vocabulary and terminology needed to understand the world of international business and points out sources to turn to for expert advice. This title provides the information the exporter needs to take a U.S.-manufactured product, sell it to a foreign buyer, make the shipment correctly, and get paid in U.S. dollars. It shows a middleman how to buy a product made by someone else and resell it at a profit to an overseas customer. Zodl also has a Web site users may be interested in checking out at http://www.zodl.net/firstpage.htm.

Online Resources

About.com: Small Business Information: http://sbinformation.about.com (accessed Spring 2009).

This large site has many different parts, but the Small Business Information and Business Plan Writing sections are especially well done. Learn about the SWOT Analysis for Small Business in a short article that will help users understand the important of a SWOT analysis. Find articles about the importance of writing a plan and how to complete a useful plan. There is a business plan FAQ and more. International trade advice is also provided, as well as many downloadable business forms. Some industry information can be accessed here as well. Continually updated and well organized, this site will help with online business activities as well as help you write your business plan and continue to plan your business activities.

American Association of Exporters and Importers (AAEI): http://www.aaei.org/ (accessed Spring 2009).

Begun in 1921, this organization "has been the national voice of American business in support of fair and open trade among nations" with its expertise in custom matters and global trade issues. Members include manufacturers, distributors, and retailers as well as organizations serving carriers, banks, freight forwarders, and brokers. The Trade FAQs will answer many questions those new to exporting or importing may have. The association works with many U.S. government agencies. Access to news and press releases along with additional information is provided at the Web site.

American Marketing Association: http://www.marketingpower.com (accessed Spring 2009).

This Web site has many articles that will help you start and continue learning how to market your small business. The section on marketing plans asks users questions to help them start thinking about the plan, their target consumers, the product, and the like. The structure of a marketing plan is discussed and more. Other areas of the site provide articles on best practices in marketing, trends in marketing, networking opportunities, and practitioner resources. Joining the association gives you access to additional member-only resources. A directory of marketing suppliers as well as excellent marketing tools and templates are also available for free.

BBC News (Country Profiles): http://news.bbc.co.uk/2/hi/country_profiles/ default.stm (accessed Spring 2009).

The BBC's full country profiles include a complete guide to history, politics, and economic background for many countries divided into six major regions of the world. Nineteen international organizations are also profiled, many including sections on facts, leaders, and issues. The country profiles also are divided into the overview, facts, leaders, and media. Related Internet links as well as related BBC links are also useful. The timeline of important events for each country provides practical, relevant information.

BEOnline: Business and Economics Online: http://www.loc.gov/rr/business/ beonline/ (accessed Spring 2009).

Compiled by the Library of Congress Business Reference Services for researchers, this site has, under Subject Lists, a lengthy list of business topics such as associations, business plans (forms), companies by industry, data sets, e-commerce, economic indicators, international trade, and legal resources. If you click on Associations, you will find a short list of associations. Clicking on the association name takes you to its Web site. Under the International Trade Listing, you will find Foreign Trade Statistics, the Trade Compliance Center, and more.

BizMove.com: http://bizmove.com (accessed Spring 2009).

The International Section of this site is outstanding. Users will find information on developing an export strategy, learning how to sell overseas, writing an international business plan, as well as documentation and pricing for international businesses. Forms and questionnaires for business planning, industry analysis, goal setting, and more are provided. Thorough and written in jargon-free language, small companies aspiring to international expansion will find this site useful.

BizTradeShows: http://www.biztradeshows.com (accessed Spring 2009).

This site contains the largest directory of trade fairs and business events and brings users exhaustive coverage of exhibitions, trade shows and expositions, conferences, and seminars for various industries worldwide. Users can browse through the most comprehensive information on individual trade events worldwide, along with their event profile, organizer, exhibitor and visitor profile, venues, and dates to plan your participation in advance as nearly a full year of shows is included. Shows are arranged by industry, month, major city, or country, and you can also find trade show display ideas.

Bplans.com: http://www.bplans.com (accessed Spring 2009).

This well-established, frequently updated site, sponsored by Palo Alton Software, Inc., is the best for help in writing your business plan. The section entitled Write a Business Plan contains articles, calculators on cash flow, starting costs, break even and more, a business plan template, and executive summary and mission statement help, plus access to expert advice. Currently 60 free plans are viewable online for free. On this fully searchable site, you can quickly find topics that you need. Other sections include finance and capital, marketing and advertising, buying a business, market research, and a monthly newsletter. Sample marketing plans include SWOT analysis and further explain how to use it in marketing your business. Closely examine a sample marketing plan to help you write a good marketing strategy. Bplans.com is a useful, practical site that also offers fee-based experts and assistance.

Business.gov: http://www.business.gov (accessed Spring 2009).

Business.gov is another government site developed to help businesses find the information they need and want. The Advertising and Marketing section is especially useful. Links to information on major industries, population and demographic resources, plus Rural America Facts provide users with a multitude of useful resources. International trade connections are outstanding for global or Internet businesses too. You will find links to International Economic Trends, Import and Export Statistics, and Foreign Trade Statistics.

Business Owners Idea Café: http://www.businessownersideacafe.com (accessed Spring 2009).

Developed by successful entrepreneurs and authors of published guides on starting a business, this large site presents short articles on all aspects of small business or entrepreneurial life. The main divisions include CyberSchmooz, Starting your Biz, Running Your Biz, Take Out Info, Classifieds, The "You" in your Biz, De-Stress and Have Fun, About Idea Café, and Join Idea Café. The Managing and Operations section contains tools to help you maintain and grow your new international business. The Links to Business Resources section provides Internet services, market research, and marketing and sales information. The large Running Your Biz: eCommerce section has excellent coverage on all things e-commerce plus links to outside information on e-commerce. Here you can find experts to answer your questions or discuss your current business crisis. You will find sample business plans, financing help, and a variety of business forms.

Buyusa.gov: http://www.buyusa.gov/home/export.html (accessed Spring 2009).

This simple-to-use government Web site offers to help businesses get into international sales through market research, trade events, introductions to buyers and distributors, and counseling for any and every step of the export process. One part of the Web site helps importers to the United States, and another helps exporters from the United States. Both parts cover products and services. When you click on a country, you get the Country Commercial Guide (CCG), a calendar of events, employment opportunities, market information, and services for U.S. exporters/suppliers. Also part of this site is *Commercial News USA*, the "official export promotion magazine of the U.S. Department of Commerce." This online publication also contains a wealth of information including franchising, trade shows, a company index, and more. Part of the Web site, AsiaNow, promotes trade with 14 Asia-Pacific markets and provides single point access to regional trade events, extensive services, and research covering Asian markets. Access Eastern Mediterranean provides U.S. companies with information on the region's markets and its 180 million consumers. The Americas and Showcase Europe provide information and services to those areas of the globe.

Canada Business Services for Entrepreneurs: http://www.canadabusiness.ca/ (accessed Spring 2009).

Though this site is aimed at Canadian businesses, you will find help and information here for exporting, importing, e-commerce, selling to the Canadian government and more. The entire Exporting section is a wealth of information for small and medium-sized businesses, from writing the export plan to Business Trip Planning for Exporters. The links under E-Business will help you in many phases of starting or expanding your markets in Canada.

Centers for International Trade Development: http://www.citd.org/StartupKit/ index.cfm (accessed Spring 2009).

This very useful site has a guide for new exporters, an export readiness assessment tool, and an excellent Export FAQ for companies just getting into international trade. Their Trade Information Database includes U.S. and world trade and economic data, trade contacts and leads, trade reference tools, foreign market research, trade/investment regulations, trade documentation, finance & insurance sections and more. A trade resources directory provides information on numerous trade associations and organizations. A trade show calendar is also available, along with booklets on best markets for various U.S. industries. Start gathering import/export information here.

Commercial News USA: http://www.thinkglobal.us/ (accessed Spring 2009).**

Commercial News USA is the official export promotion magazine of the Department of Commerce, and it showcases U.S.-made products and services. You will find lists of companies already exporting grouped in about 15 different industries. Trade show opportunities are highlighted and described, often letting businesses know who attends and who should attend. This publication is also an excellent source for trade leads and to advertise your products or services to find customers or partners; subscribe online or by mail. Issues may be read online for download in PDFs. Franchising information is available, as well as success stories to inspire new exporters.

Country Studies: http://lcweb2.loc.gov/frd/cs/ (accessed Spring 2009).

These in-depth country studies and handbooks were prepared by a team of scholars under the direction of the Federal Research Division of the Library of Congress, as sponsored by the U.S. Army. At present, 102 countries and regions are covered, primarily focusing on lesser-known areas of the world or regions in which U.S. forces might be deployed. One word of warning, however: because funding for the country studies was cancelled in 1999, the studies range in date of preparation from 1988 to 1998. However, the Country Profiles also accessible from this site are being updated. The front page of the Profiles lists when they were updated, mostly in 2006 and 2007. Highlights of the individual studies include photographs, historical and economic backgrounds, tables, glossaries, and bibliographies. The site is searchable by topic.

Department of the Treasury Internal Revenue Service: http://www.irs.gov (accessed Spring 2009).

The IRS's Market Segment Specialization Program focuses on particular market segments that may be an industry like auto body and repair, a profession like ministers, or an issue like aviation tax. Their guides discuss common and unique industry issues, business practices, and industry terminology. They are produced and updated on an as needed basis so some are quite old. Despite their age, however, you may find that, like the overview of the Bars and Restaurants industry from April 2003, the information presented is very useful for your business.

Economist.com: http://www.economist.com (accessed Spring 2009).

Providing excellent coverage of world news, the Economist.com also contains information on world markets, the latest exchange rates, and country and city guides geared to the business traveler. It is the companion site to the print journal *The Economist*. Although much of the site is free and fully searchable, the Economist.com does charge to view archived articles. Other portions of the site are considered to be premium content viewable by subscription only.

Entrepreneur.com: http://www.entrepreneur.com (accessed Spring 2009).

Entrepreneur Magazine provides a wealth of information and assistance to the new entrepreneur. A thorough understanding of the need for the right type of marketing plan to fit your business and your style of planning and working is very important; and this site guides you through the process of discovering the right type for you. Learn how to determine your marketing goals and objectives and how a plan will help you achieve them. Under Marketing and Sales, you will also find tips on building buzz, branding, word-of-mouth advertising, and marketing materials. Learn about the "9 Tools for Building Customer Loyalty," for example. Discover how to create an ad budget and create great ads and direct mail pieces. The E-business section explains legal issues, setting up an e-commerce site, e-mail marketing, Internet security, and more. International marketing research is well covered in the Marketing section. Use this outstanding site often during the planning and opening of your global business.

Entrepreneurs' Help Page: http://www.tannedfeet.com/ (accessed Spring 2009).

Find here help with business plans, financial statements, legal structure and legal forms, marketing and PR, human resources (HR), and strategy. Designed, created, and published by a group of young professionals in Chicago, Entrepreneurs Help Page does not claim to substitute for professional advice and judgment but provides information to entrepreneurs to get them started in the right direction. Experts offer advice on finding the right customers, selecting and working with an advertising agency, and marketing budgets. The idea for a marketing database to trace bits of information about your customers such as purchase history, demographics, service history, and so forth, has been shown to work for companies such as Amazon.com. Articles are usually not lengthy but ask questions to help the new business person start thinking about what is needed and what questions will be asked of him/her. Down-to-earth advice from peers is often the most valuable.

Entrepreneurship: http://entrepreneurship.org/ (accessed Spring 2009).

The Ewing Marion Kauffman Foundation is the entrepreneur's trusted guide to high growth. This large site is filled with relevant, practical, and timely information on how to manage and expand your business. Included are original articles written for the site by entrepreneurs drawing on their own experiences and an aggregation of the "best of the best" existing articles and tools to guide you on the path to high growth. Topics are arranged around eight key subject areas: Accounting and Finance, Human Resources, Marketing and Sales, Products and Services, Business Operations, The Entrepreneur, Public Policy, and Entrepreneurship Law. The Sales and Marketing section includes a section on Global Markets. Search on Global and find articles like Eleven Pitfalls to Avoid in Going Global and Entrepreneurs, Manage Your Global Growth.

Euromonitor International: http://www.euromonitor.com/ (accessed Spring 2009).

Euromonitor International offers quality international market intelligence on industries, countries and consumers. They have some 30 years of experience publishing market reports, business reference books, online information systems, and bespoke consulting projects. Their Web site has a huge article archive with short articles on topics like trends in retail, food prices, brand growth, in various parts of the world. Many articles are on a specific company, country, or product. Complete company profiles and industry reports can be purchased

Eurostat: http://epp.eurostat.ec.europa.eu/portal/page/portal/eurostat/home/ (accessed Spring 2009).

This large portal is sponsored by the European Commission. Listed along the left side of the home page are the general themes: General and Regional Statistics; Economy and Finance; Population and Social Conditions; Industry, Trade, and Services; Agriculture and Fisheries; External Trade; Transport; Environment and Energy; and Science and Technology. Elsewhere you will find tables on employment, demographic changes, environment, economic reform, and much more. Business and consumer surveys and consumer prices are also available. Much of the information is available free in PDF file downloads. This is a good place to start for anyone looking to trade with Europe.

The Exporter. Trade Data Reports, Inc.: http://www.exporter.com (accessed Spring 2009).

The focus of this publication is to provide information on exporting services and resources for businesspeople involved in international trade who need to understand and meet foreign import and U.S. export requirements. The Web site provides this and more, including a very current news feed and supplemental commentary and white papers focusing on international trade issues. Additional information can be accessed through free membership subscription.

**Export.gov: http://www.export.gov (accessed Spring 2009).

Created as a government-to-business initiative, Export.gov is the government's portal to exporting and trade services. It is designed to simplify the exporting process by being a single point of access to export-related services and thus reducing the need to view multiple government sources. Over 19 U.S. departments and agencies contribute the information it provides including the U.S. International Trade Administration, the U.S. Commercial Service, the Department of Commerce, the Export-Import Bank, the Agency for International Development, and the U.S. Trade and Development Agency. Companies new to exporting will find step-by-step help through the export process. To facilitate international trade, companies can also find references on foreign tariff and tax information, search foreign and domestic trade events, subscribe to receive trade leads and industry specific market intelligence as well as gain access to federal export assistance and financing. The National Trade Data Bank (NTDB) provides access to Country Commercial Guides, market research reports, best market reports and other programs. Find global business opportunity leads as well as market and country research. FedBizOpps (formerly known as Commerce Business Daily) is linked here too. Also linked is the TradeStats Express page for national and state export data. Export.gov is fully searchable and allows you to search globally the contents of all of its contributing entities. Use this site to start market research, international statistics searches, and for getting advice and counseling.

**Export Help for Businesses: http://www.exportinfo.org (accessed Spring 2009).

This well-organized, practical site was created and is maintained by the students at the University of Washington Business School. It includes practical information for small and medium-sized businesses. It describes and links to country sites like Japan's JETRO (Japan External Trade Organization) and EC21, Korea's huge company database. Government and international organizations links are also highlighted.

ExportHelp, your online export helpdesk: http://www.exporthelp.co.za/index.html (accessed Spring 2009).

This large export assistance site from South Africa has an abundance of information and advice for new exporters. Find information on documentation, marketing, an initial SWOT analysis, country selection, and more. A lengthy article on trade fairs and getting the most out of them is also a highlight. The section on e-commerce is also practical.

EXPORT911.com: http://www.export911.com/ (accessed Spring 2009).

This business and educational Web site focuses on international business. It provides in-depth information on export/import marketing, management, letters of credit, export cargo insurance, shipping, logistics, manufacturing, purchasing, bar codes, and more. Major sections include Gateways to Global Markets, Purchasing Department, Production Department, and Product Coding (bar codes). Business Tool titles include Conversion Tables, Abbreviations, Acronyms, and Symbols, and General References. Case studies and samples are also provided. This large site provides a plethora of educational and informational articles and data.

The Export Yellow Pages: http://www.exportyellowpages.com (accessed Spring 2009).

The Export Yellow Pages are administered by the Export Trading Company Affairs of the International Trade Administration in partnership with the U.S. Department of Commerce. Containing information on U.S. business products and suppliers, this site is designed to promote and connect SMEs, improve market visibility, help establish international contacts, simplify sales sourcing, and solve language barriers. This site is often used by foreign buyers as a reference tool to find U.S. goods and services. U.S. firms can register their businesses without charge at http://www.myexports.com. In addition, export intermediaries such as freight forwarders, sales agents, and other service companies that help export businesses can register at no charge in the U.S. Trade Assistance Directory. Find trade leads and other resources here in a wide variety of industries. Products and services are offered by over 27,000 U.S. companies. The U.S. Trade Assistance Directory is available online or in print.

Federation of International Trade Associations (FITA): http://www.fita.org (accessed Spring 2009).

This huge, very useful site covers all areas of importing and exporting. Users will find help with market research, transportation and logistics, documentation, trade finance and currencies, trade law, directories, trade show calendar, and worldwide trade leads. Find links to Export 1001, a user-friendly introduction to the fundamental aspects of exporting, links to practical sites from other countries, importers' directories, a trade information database and much more. FITA has a China Business Guide and Trade Software, used to manage international trade enterprises. This large site is well organized, annotated, and easy to use.

Foreign Government Resources on the Web: http://www.lib.umich.edu/govdocs/foreign.html (accessed Spring 2009).

Maintained by the University of Michigan's Documents Center, this Web site provides an extensive collection of foreign government Web sites. Also accessible from the site are country background information, the text of constitutions and treaties, embassy information and statistics on demographics, economics, health, and military. Many of the links are briefly annotated by the documents center's staff. The center also updates the site frequently: the What's New section is updated weekly and provides annotated links to new resources of interest. Use this site to keep current on foreign government information.

The Global Connector: http://www.globalconnector.org (accessed Spring 2009).

Part of Indiana University's Center for International Business Education and Research (CIBER), this gateway leads to thousands of international trade sites. The Global Connector allows searching by either country or by industry. Country data include links to data on government, domestic economy, news and media, entry requirements, transportation, and international trade. Industry specific information can be searched by the type or source of information including trade shows, trade publications, trends/analysis, and regulatory matters.

GlobalEDGE: http://globaledge.msu.edu (accessed Spring 2009).

Managed by Michigan State University's Center for International Business Education and Research (MSU_CIBER), this site links to a broad selection of international trade data including economic trends, statistical data sources, government resources, trade portals, journals, and mailing lists. Its Global Resources section provides access to more than 2,000 online resources. MSU _CIBER has also contributed its own resources including an interactive forum for business professionals and portions of the information contained in the Knowledge Room, GlobalEDGE's section on the latest issues/trends effecting international
business.

Global Trade and Technology Network (GTN): http://www.usgtn.net (accessed Spring 2009).

The GTN, established in 1994 as part of the U.S. Agency for International Development trade facilitation program, focuses on facilitating trade between the United States and foreign countries and helps develop international markets to bolster steady economic growth in the United States and abroad. Now a part of the U.S. Commercial Service, the premier global export business solutions provider of the U.S. Government, this global network of approximately 1800 trade specialists working in 109 domestic offices and in 80 markets worldwide, the Commercial Service helps U.S. companies make international sales with world-class market research, trade events that promote their products or services to qualified buyers, introductions to qualified buyers and distributors, and counseling through every step of the export process. Register here to obtain Import and/or Export assistance.

Home Business Magazine (HBM): **http://www.homebusinessmag.com (accessed Spring 2009).**

The Marketing and Sales categories accessible through the frame on the left side of the screen provide a wealth of articles on marketing any type of small business. Short courses on marketing success, information on how you could be hurting your sales, and other articles as well as subcategories on direct marketing, Web marketing, publicity, and selling provide more inexpensive but effective marketing ideas. Advice and ideas on business start-up, management, e-commerce, and money are also included. The How to Write a Business Plan section is also very detailed and helpful. Learn about selling on eBay in the eBay Start Up Guide. The *HBM* archives include a large number of articles grouped by category. Really good information on using the Internet for e-commerce and marketing plus good hints on improving your Web site are provided.

International Monetary Fund (IMF): http://www.imf.org/external/index.htm (accessed Spring 2009).

The IMF database contains approximately 32,000 time series covering more than 200 countries and areas and includes all series appearing on the International Financial Statistics (IFS) Country Pages, exchange rate series for all Fund member countries, plus Aruba and the Netherlands Antilles, and most other world, area, and country series from the IFS World Tables. Find here the *Export and Import Price Index Manual.* Under the Country Info tab, users will find detailed, current information about the economic situation in the country. The site is fully searchable and easy to use. The complete text of the *World Economic Outlook* is also available online; learn how the economic slowdown in the United States in 2007 affected other areas of the world and continues to affect the global economy.

International Trade Administration (ITA): http://trade.gov/index.asp (accessed Spring 2009).

Part of the Department of Commerce, ITA's site tries to strengthen the U.S.'s competitiveness, promote trade and investment, and encourage fair trade and compliance with trade laws and agreements. Find statistics through its TradeStats Express and some PDFs of free publications, though many are only available for purchase. The *Basic Guide to Exporting* is probably the most thorough and useful. Part of the site is entitled How Do I Go Global? and is very useful (http://www.ita.doc.gov/td/sif/how_do_i_go_global.htm) The ITA's Customized Market Analysis (CMA) offers a quick, accurate assessment of how your services will sell in a given market. This custom-tailored market research provides firms with specific information on marketing and foreign representation for their services in selected countries. Interviews or surveys are conducted to determine overall marketability of the services, key competitors, price of comparable services, trade barriers, possible business partners and applicable trade events. Besides national trade and industry statistics, find state and local trade data and links to key foreign country data sources.

International Trade Considerations: http://www.wiuec.org/workshops/inttrade/index.html (accessed Spring 2009).

Developed by the Western Illinois Entrepreneurship Center, this well-organized site will help business owners and managers develop an import/export Plan, identify partners, complete market research, and learn about legal, licensing, and cultural issues, as well as costs of doing business internationally. Use this site to organize your research and identify the questions you need to have answered.

KnowThis.com: Marketing Virtual Library http://www.knowthis.com (accessed Spring 2009).

This large site is a smorgasbord of data and guidance on marketing, including how to conduct market research, promotion versus advertising, using current technologies, and a large section on Internet marketing, divided into methods and strategies and research. Find guidance on creating marketing plans as well as sample plans. The large section on finding secondary research will prove very valuable to new market researchers. New topics include selling virtual clothes for avatars and reviews of software to enhance small e-commerce sites. Tutorials on managing customers, personal selling, targeting markets, and more are available.

Market Research, Industry Research, Business Research: http://www.virtualpet.com/ industry (accessed Spring 2009).

This major portal for researching companies and industries presents a step-by-step process to begin researching an industry. Here you can find sources to help you learn about legal issues, regulatory issues, competition, markets, and even history of the industry for your new business. Additional links to Industry Portals are also available. Three other linked sites offer help on How to Learn about a Company by Examining its Products, How to Review, Evaluate, Critique a Web Site, and How to Conduct a Patent Search.

MoreBusiness.com: http://www.morebusiness.com (accessed Spring 2009).

Sections on this site include Startup, Running SmallBiz, Templates, and Tools. The Templates section provides sample business contracts and agreements, business and marketing plans, press releases, and business checklists. Sample marketing plans for various types of businesses are also provided. A large collection of articles and advice under Business Technology will help you understand the Internet, online shopping, Web site technology, hacking, and even laptop issues. The section Build Your Own Website is very useful. Many of the articles are lengthy and thorough. Use this site to help improve your marketing and management skills.

Piers Global Intelligence Solutions: http://www.piers.com (accessed Spring 2009).

This large commercial site is a leader in providing current, accurate, and comprehensive data on international trade. Here users can find new suppliers, new markets, and business opportunities as well as benchmark performance against the competition. Check this site out to see if it can help your company start exporting, especially to Latin America and Asia.

Quick MBA: http://www.quickmba.com/entre/bplan/ (accessed Spring 2009).

For those new to business plans and SWOT analysis, this site is thorough and practical. Learn the basics of both these concepts and many more here. Management and marketing articles are useful and helpful to new owners and managers as well as to experienced ones. A political, economic, social, technical (PEST) analysis is presented, why to use it, and how it relates to SWOT. Often articles include recommended readings.

SBDCNET: http://sbdcnet.utsa.edu (accessed Spring 2009).

The Small Business Development Center National Information Clearinghouse provides timely, Web-based information to entrepreneurs. Small Business Development Centers (SBDC) are located in all 50 states. SBDCs offer free, confidential business counseling. This Web site provides information on business start-up, e-commerce, industry research, marketing, trends, and more.

Entrepreneurs will find plenty of links and information here to help plan and run a new business.

Service Corps of Retired Executives: http://www.score.org (accessed Spring 2009).

SCORE (Counselors to America's Small Business) is an organization of volunteer members that provides business advice to small businesses throughout the nation. Visiting their Web site, you can receive free counseling via e-mail; ask to have a counselor look at the first draft of your plan. The Business Toolbox provides important links and a template gallery with many templates to help the new business owner with several parts of a good business plan. As with the SBA site, solid business planning help is available here.

Small Business Administration: http://www.sba.gov (accessed Spring 2009).

This official government site offers a wealth of resources and programs for starting and growing a small business. Under Startup Basics, check out the areas you need help with while doing your business planning. Other major sections cover business planning, financing, international trade, managing, marketing, employees, taxes, legal aspects, and business opportunities. Find here online forms, sample business plans, loan information, and many publications. The *Export Library* contains titles like Breaking into the Trade Game, Export Working Capital Program, Export Financing for Small Businesses, and SBA & Ex-Im Bank Co-Guarantee Program. Some contents are available in Spanish. Also part of the SBA program are the Small Business Development Centers (SBDC) at http://www.sba.gov/sbdc. SBDCs are located in every state and deliver counseling and training for small businesses in the areas of management, marketing, financing, and feasibility studies.

**STAT-USA/Internet: http://www.stat-usa.gov/ (accessed Spring 2009).

This service of the U.S. Department of Commerce is a single point of access to authoritative business, trade, and economic information from across the federal government. An important part of this resource is http://www.stat-usa.gov/tradtest.nsf—Obtain current and historical trade-related releases, international market research, trade opportunities, country analysis, and our trade library from the National Trade Data Bank (NTDB). The NTDB provides access to Country Commercial Guides, market research reports, best market reports and other programs. USA Trade *Online* provides current and historical import and export statistics for over 18,000 commodities traded worldwide as well as the most current merchandise trade statistics available in a spreadsheet format. The International Trade Library is a comprehensive collection of over 40,000 documents related to international trade. All are full text searchable, as well as keyword searchable by country or product.

Tradeport Global Trade Center: http://www.tradeport.org (accessed Spring 2009).

TradePort is a repository of free information and resources for businesses that seek to conduct international trade. Created in 1996, TradePort is backed by an alliance of regional trade associations that assist California export and import businesses, but companies in all states will find plenty of information to assist their export or import efforts. The Export Tutorial as well as the Import Tutorial are full of valuable resources and information. The Market Research section, which has a large Trade Leads section, and the Trade Library, which provides a bibliography of resources, a glossary, and links to trade statistics are current, very practical resources. This useful site is a great place to start researching your export/import adventure.

Trade Show News Network: http://www.tsnn.com (accessed Spring 2009).

Though the Internet definitely has had an impact on the trade show market, sometimes setting up a booth at a trade show is a great way to make contacts, find people, and even sell products or services. This comprehensive site provides information on more than 15,000 trade shows, which you can find by industry, month of the year, city, state, or country. The Small Business Guide also provides short articles on franchising, incorporating, Internet ads, temporary help, bartering, and home-based businesses. Also find advice on virtual trade shows, trade show planning, convention centers, online service providers, and more.

United Nation's Statistics Division: http://unstats.un.org/unsd/default.htm (accessed Spring 2009).

This large site gathers and presents UN statistical databases to global users through a single entry point. Find a wide variety of statistical resources on this well-organized and fully searchable site. The databases include economic statistics, demographic and social statistics, environment and energy statistics, geographic information, and seminars on statistics. The UN Statistical Commission also considers and approves international statistical standards, norms, and programs to address emerging issues. In addition, the United Nations supports countries' efforts to strengthen their national statistical systems. Publications of the UN Statistics Division are also described and available for purchase.

U.S. Bureau of Industry and Security: http://www.bis.doc.gov (accessed Spring 2009).

This agency of the Department of Commerce is responsible for advancing U.S. national security, foreign policy, and economic objectives by ensuring an effective export control and treaty compliance system and promoting continued U.S. strategic technology leadership. It issues export licenses, prosecutes violators of export control policies, and implements the Export Administration Act's antiboycott provisions. Export license requirements are triggered by the actual item (commodity, software, or technology) being exported, where it is going, who is going to use it, and what they will be using it for. The Web page's FAQs on Export Licensing will answer many questions.

**U.S. Census Bureau: http://www.census.gov (accessed Spring 2009).

This Web page is the best place to start searching for the multitude of data produced by census programs, publications, and statistics. The home page groups the data under Census 2000, People, Business, Geography, Newsroom, At the Bureau, and Special Topics. Under Business, you can click on the Foreign Trade, Economic Census, NAICS, E-Stats, and Survey of Business Owners subjects. Under Foreign Trade, learn directly from the Census Bureau how to properly classify your products for export and how to file your Shipper's Export Declaration online. The Bureau also processes, tabulates, and releases the data collected by the Bureau of Customs and Border Protection on exports and imports of goods. The catalog, a search feature, and links to related sites are also accessible on the left side of the home page. Another important part of the Census Bureau's Web page is the International Data Base (IDB) at http://www.census.gov/ipc/www/idb/ The IDB presents estimates and projections of basic demographic measures for countries and regions of the world. Country summaries, country rankings, and population pyramids all provide useful data. U.S. export and import statistics by commodity, country, customs district, and method of transportation provide value and quantity on a monthly, year-to-date, and annual history basis. U.S. state export data and port statistics for imports and exports are also available. Use this site frequently to help start and grow your business.

U.S. Department of State: http://www.state.gov/r/pa/ei/bgn/ (accessed Spring 2009).

Background Notes are publications are updated by the Office of Electronic Information when information is received from the department's regional bureaus and include facts about the people, economy, history, geography, government, political conditions, and foreign relations. Hundreds of countries of all sizes are covered. In addition, there is U.S. embassies and consulate information as well as a diplomatic List. Listings on the left side bar of the home page link to a wealth of topical information including a series of publications that contain factual information on all countries with which the United States has relations. Country Commercial Guides can also be accessed through this site.

U.S. International Trade Commission (USITC): http://www.usitc.gov (accessed Spring 2009).

This nonpartisan, quasi-judicial federal agency provides trade expertise, determines the impact of imports on U.S. industries, and directs actions against certain unfair trade practices. Publications available through this Web site include the Harmonized Tariff Schedule, general fact-finding reports, economic effects reports, and the International Economic Review. The USITC *Interactive Tariff and Trade DataWeb* provides international trade statistics and U.S. tariff data to the public full-time and free of charge, including import and export statistics, U.S. tariffs, U.S. future tariffs, and U.S. tariff preference information.

U.S. Trade and Development Agency (USTDA): http://www.ustda.gov (accessed Spring 2009).

The USTDA's mission is to promote economic growth in developing and middle income countries and to assist simultaneously U.S. businesses to export their products and services to create U.S. jobs. It is an independent U.S. Government foreign assistance agency funded by the U.S. Congress. Find business opportunities here as well as grant funding for overseas projects that support the development of modern infrastructure and open trading systems. The library contains completed USTDA-funded studies in various regions or countries as well as feasibility studies.

VIBES: Virtual International Business and Economic Sources: http://library.uncc .edu/display/?dept=reference&format=open&page=68 (accessed Spring 2009).

The more than 1,600 links to free sources of information at this site were selected by Jeanie Welch of the University of North Carolina Charlotte. The table of contents breaks the sites into three groups: comprehensive, regional, and national. The comprehensive section organizes its links by category, including banking and finance, business practices and company information, emerging markets, international trade law, and more. Research and tables and graphs are highlights of this site. The regional section allows searching devoted to a single region or continent such as Europe or the Middle East. The national section links to sites devoted to a particular country.

WebSite MarketingPlan: http://www.websitemarketingplan.com (accessed Spring 2009).

This large site contains a wealth of information for small businesses. A large assortment of articles and sample marketing plans are available as well as sample business plans, a newsletter, Internet marketing articles, marketing strategy articles, and more. Under the Internet Marketing tab, find articles grouped under Doing Business Online, Web Marketing Strategy, Improving Online Profit, and more. Learn about the four seasons of public relations. Lengthy articles on advertising, using PR for communicating to customers and finding new ones, and customer retention are outstanding. There are many commercial links but plenty of free help for the new entrepreneur too. This site is especially helpful for those interested in e-commerce. Easy to navigate, this site will help you develop a marketing plan that you can use.

World Bank: http://www.worldbank.org (accessed Spring 2009).

Established in 1944, the World Bank is composed of five separate organizations all with distinct but related missions: the International Bank for Reconstruction and Development (IBRD) and the International Development Association (IDA), the International Finance Corporation (IFC), Multilateral Investment Guaranty Agency (MIGA), and the International Centre for Settlement of Investment Disputes (ICSID). Resources provided from its Business Center include World Bank project and program summaries, documents, and reports. The side bar provides links to data and statistics on countries and regions, evaluations, news, and more. Arranged hierarchically, each of these categories allows you to drill down to even more specific information. In addition to providing access to its own collection of resources, the World Bank provides access to each member organization's site. Doing Business (http://www.doingbusiness.org) is a database that provides objective measures of business regulations and enforcement for 175 countries.

World Trade Organization (WTO): http://www.wto.org (accessed Spring 2009).

Established in 1995, the WTO is composed of more than 140 countries that cooperate on global economic policymaking and provides the ground rules for international commerce. The organization's world-renown annual report *International Trade Statistics* is available on its Web site via the Resources link. Also available are documents published by the WTO, information on trade topics, and links to publications of many member countries, news, and international trade resources.

Yahoo! Directory, Business and Economy/Trade: http://dir.yahoo.com/Business _and_Economy/Trade/ (accessed Spring 2009).

Especially important categories are organizations, e-commerce, software, and use tax issues. This large site includes a wealth of information with good international coverage on a wide variety of topics. Under International Trade Organizations, users will find listings for 148 useful organizations involved in global trade. Under its small business site (http://smallbusiness.yahoo.com/) the e-commerce section covers online shopping centers, privacy seal programs, and digital money. For industries it covers manufacturing as well as the retail industry. Check this site for current, accurate business information.

Yahoo! Directory, National Governments: http://dir.yahoo.com/government (accessed Spring 2009).

This site is a quick way to find links to governments around the world. Countries from Brunei, Burkina Faso, and Moldova to Oman and Vanuatu are listed. Some countries have few links under their category at this time, but many, like Australia, are a gateway to departments, documents, local governments, research labs, statistics, taxes, and more. Links are often briefly annotated.

4

Approaches to Exporting and Importing

Chapter Highlights:

How to Find Foreign Customers

Exporting Approaches

Foreign Market Entry

Indirect Exporting: Benefits and Disadvantages

Direct Exporting: Benefits and Disadvantages

Importing

Transportation

Many options exist for selling your products or services internationally. Expansive market selection is an approach that involves selecting foreign markets that are similar to your home market and then expanding on a market-by-market basis. Some markets are high risk and high cost while others are low risk and low cost. To begin, your company will need to identify foreign buyers, qualify potential buyers, locate overseas distributors, and advertise globally. For most newcomers to going global, the task of identifying potential customers in foreign countries is daunting.

HOW TO FIND FOREIGN CUSTOMERS

Several avenues for locating potential foreign buyers are available generally. The U.S. Department of Commerce, individual state offices for economic development, local and foreign chambers of commerce and industry and trade groups, and business associations are just some of the organizations willing to help companies find legitimate buyers. The following is a partial list of specific sources to start you off:

1. *Advertise in Trade Journals.* As in accidental exporting, foreign buyers may find you. A listing in the Department of Commerce's *Commercial News USA* (*CNUSA*) at http://www.thinkglobal.us/ may yield inquiries from overseas. This monthly catalog or magazine is designed to promote U.S. products and services abroad. Ads are inexpensive but costs vary with the size of the listing; and because of the Internet, it is available and visible around the world. Listings in *CNUSA* identify the major features of an export product or service along with the name, address, and telephone and fax numbers of the U.S. manufacturer or distributor. A photo or illustration may also be included. Many companies have used this outlet very successfully.

2. *Pursue Trade Leads.* Instead of waiting for potential foreign customers to contact you, search out foreign companies looking for your product or service. Again, the *CNUSA* is a good source of trade leads and places to find them. Also be sure to try the *Export Yellow Pages* at http://www.exportyellowpages.com.

Home page. The Export Yellow Pages.

Source: http://www.exportyellowpages.com

3. *Exhibit at Trade Shows or Fairs.* Several levels of international events and organized trips are held both in the United States and abroad.
   U.S. government and state agencies organize these events, as do trade

associations and chambers of commerce. These events often attract potential buyers from around the world and are an excellent opportunity to showcase your company and products as well as to make valuable contacts. One place to locate these events is the Trade Show News Network at http://www.tsnn.com. Well-organized and easy to use, it lists events by country, industry, month of the year, city, and state. Careful planning and follow through are needed if overseas travel is involved because of the expense. Select events carefully, and prepare materials and translators. Also be sure to follow up on any potential leads promptly.

4. *Participate in Trade Missions.* Public and private trade missions are organized and promoted cooperatively by federal and state international trade agencies and trade associations. They make the arrangements, so the process of meeting prospective partners or buyers is simplified. Your company is matched with potential agents and distributors interested in your product or service. To be properly prepared for the types of inquiries you might encounter, plan to attend a pre-mission training session or other trade mission training sessions offered by the U.S. government. The U.S. Trade and Development Agency (USTDA) brings foreign project sponsors to the United States to observe the design, manufacture, demonstration, and operation of U.S. products and services that can potentially help them achieve their development goals. The USTDA uses pre-qualified contractors to assist in the preparation and management of these customized visits. The orientations are usually cofunded by U.S. industry. Contact USTDA by telephone at (703) 875-4357 or visit the USTDA Web site on the Internet at http://www.tda.gov for more information. Additionally, the Small Business Administration's (SBA) Trade Mission Online program can be accessed at http://www.sba.gov/aboutsba/sbaprograms/internationaltrade/tmonline/index.html. The Trade Mission Online program's searchable database of U.S. small businesses trying to export their products or seeking U.S. partners or suppliers for trade-related activities is designed to enable international small business sales, franchising, joint ventures, and/or licensing. The SBA also uses this program to recruit and provide time-sensitive trade promotion information to registered companies. The U.S. Department of Commerce offers several types of trade missions: commercial missions, market access missions, policy missions, combined missions, and certified trade missions. Find information on all these missions at http://export.gov.

5. *Bid on or subcontract to bidders of Multilateral Development Bank (MDB) projects.* Multilateral Development Banks include the World Bank, the African, Asian, and Inter-American Development Banks and the European Bank for Reconstruction and Development. The purpose of the MDBs is to provide a funding source for less-developed countries that otherwise might not be able to borrow for needed projects. MDB projects can be an excellent way to start exporting and often represent extensive opportunities for U.S. businesses to compete for project work. Check out the World Bank site, http://worldbank.org, for more information and projects from the MDBs.

6. *Sell globally over the Internet.* Your Web site, if designed properly, will attract foreign interest and potential buyers for your products or services.

Prompt follow-up is essential. STAT-USA helps small companies with limited sales staff sell their products internationally. It is a source for sales leads and export information. See Chapter 8 for more help on e-commerce.

Once you have determined the level of difficulty of finding good foreign buyers or customers for your products or services, it may make the decision on an approach to exporting easier.

EXPORTING APPROACHES

Closely related to finding foreign customers are the four basic approaches to exporting that may be used alone or in any combination. The differences between the approaches relate primarily to the company's level of involvement in the export process.

1. Passive exporting occurs when companies just fill orders for domestic buyers who then export the product or service. Those buyers have determined the foreign demand, taken the risks, and handled the exporting details.

2. Companies can seek out domestic buyers who represent foreign customers often known as global trading companies. These buyers often represent a wide variety of goods and services, and they assume the risk and handle the details and documentation. Sales agents, commission merchants, manufacturers' representatives, commodity brokers, sales brokers, procurement agents, and buying agents all perform various aspects of facilitating trade.

3. Indirect exporting through an intermediary firm capable of finding foreign markets and buyers is a third option. export management companies (EMCs), export trading companies (ETCs), international trade consultants, and other intermediaries will provide exporters with access to well-established expertise and trade contacts. The EMC does it all—hiring dealers, distributors and representatives; handling advertising, marketing and promotions; overseeing marking and packaging; arranging shipping; and sometimes arranging financing. They are usually paid by commission, salary, or retainer plus commission. If the EMC takes the title to your goods, it becomes, for you, just another domestic sale. His overseas experience permits evaluation of the market, access to his overseas customers, and minimal financial risks for you. ETCs, sometimes called export jobbers, identify what foreign buyers want to purchase and hunt down domestic sources willing to export and sometimes work on a commission basis. They often take title to the product and pay you directly. ETCs are demand driven and transaction oriented. Officially, an ETC is a legally defined entity under the Export Trading Company Act, with specific responsibilities and obligations. The ETC Act permits these companies to apply for certificates of review that provide immunity from prosecution for activities that may otherwise be in violation of antitrust regulations from the U.S. Department of Commerce. Learn more about the ETC Act and the International Trade Administration's Export Trading Company Affairs program at http://www.ita.doc.gov/TD/OETCA/staff.html.

Export agents, merchants, and remarketers purchase goods directly from a domestic or foreign manufacturer and then pack, ship and resell the goods on his own, which means they assume all the risks and all the profits. Often the exporter will realize the benefits of exporting such as learning more about foreign competitors, new technologies, and new market opportunities with less risk by starting in indirect exporting.

Finding export intermediaries is not difficult. Two places to check are the National Association of Export Companies (http://www.nexco.org) and the Federation of International Trade Associations (http://fita.org). For more information on ETCs and the U.S. Government Export Trade Certificate of Review program, check out http://export.gov. Often these kinds of exporting companies (ETCs) have specific influence in certain markets and select product representations to suit that affinity. They then have the ability to combine shipments of different products to a common destination in a single container to minimize freight costs. The economy of scale they offer is important in global marketing for a smaller business just beginning to develop overseas markets. The EMT/ETC frequently provides warehousing, receipt of goods from many sources, as well as packing and shipment services. Trade channels are created for each product or market combination to transport, insure, finance, collect payment, and provide aftermarket support.

4. Direct exporting is the most ambitious, risky, and difficult as the exporter handles all aspects of the process from market research, planning for the foreign distribution, through collections. However, maximum profits and long-term growth can be part of the rewards. This decision requires a large commitment of time and effort and should not be taken lightly.

Many new exporters use approaches 1 and 2, as they do not require deep involvement in the export process. Companies may begin small and grow into direct exporting as experience is gained and sales volume justifies more investment. Advisers from state or federal government agencies may help make this decision.

FOREIGN MARKET ENTRY

Many options for market entry strategies or approaches already exist. This list includes direct and indirect exporting as discussed above, joint ventures, strategic alliances, and acquisitions of foreign companies through direct investment or licensing technology abroad. Benefits and risks are associated with each method, which are contingent on many factors, including the type of product or service you produce, the need for product or service support, and the foreign economic, political, business, and cultural environment you are seeking to penetrate. Which strategy you choose depends on your company's level of resources and commitment, and the degree of risk you are willing to incur. Accidental exporting or waiting for foreign distributors to contact your company is another but more passive approach.

For the purpose of this book, we will now look more comprehensively at the two most common methods of exporting for small and medium-sized enterprises (SMEs), which are indirect selling and direct selling.

INDIRECT EXPORTING: BENEFITS AND DISADVANTAGES

SMEs must examine their relationships with EMC and ETC carefully and structure them properly. Benefits include:

- With very little commitment of staff and resources, product or service exposure in international markets can quickly build sales and profits.
- The years of experience and well-established networks of contacts of the EMC/ETC will improve chances of success.
- Negotiating contracts that stipulate the SME pays nothing until the first order is received will save start-up costs and associated risks.
- Faster entry into the overseas market is usually possible.
- Expertise in dealing with the special details involved in exporting, as well as its strategies.

Disadvantages of using EMCs/ETCs include:

- The SME loses control over the manner in which the product or service is marketed and positioned in the market. The company's image and brand are at stake. The contract must incorporate concerns and requirements as well as include close monitoring of the intermediary's activities and progress by the SME.
- Profits can be lost if the SME must deeply discount its price. However, the economies of scale realized through increased production may offset this loss.
- If the EMC/ETC passes on the higher price to foreign customers, the competitive position of the product may be adversely affected. It is very important to negotiate prices at the outset of the contract.
- It is possible that there will be competition from the other products marketed by the EMC/ETC. This could result in neglect of the client's product in favor of other products that are easier to sell or more profitable.
- Some foreign buyers may be reluctant to deal with a third-party intermediary.

DIRECT EXPORTING: BENEFITS AND DISADVANTAGES

As stated earlier, initial costs and risks are greater using direct exporting, and direct exporting also means the company is more committed to successfully entering foreign markets. Sufficient and appropriate staff must be able to support the company's export efforts, and company representatives may need to travel abroad at times. Benefits include:

- Higher profits are possible.
- Control over marketing, positioning and pricing is retained.

Disadvantages include:

- Unfamiliar languages, laws, and accounting practices will require more time and effort to learn and analyze.
- Analyzing credit information may be difficult, time-consuming, and costly.
- Unfamiliar export licensing and shipping practices must be identified.
- Internal organization changes may be needed to support the more complex functions.

You will more easily achieve success in direct exporting with the assistance of many companies and organizations specializing in exporting.

IMPORTING

Generally, businesses start with a product, look to see who may purchase it, and then adapt to meet the buyer's needs or specifications. In starting to import, if they do not have a product or service, companies might try working the other way: find the buyer(s), discover their specifications, and locate the product that will fill the buyer's needs. Importing is as complex a business as exporting.

Trade shows are another important avenue for locating new needs of consumers or new products to meet those needs. To determine why your company is thinking of importing, answer these three questions to start:

- Is the product(s) you need or want to see available domestically?
- Have you found a lucrative and untapped domestic market for an imported product(s)?
- Does importing a product increase your competitiveness as a business?

If your company is acting as the importer for a foreign manufacturer, the prime objective is to reach your targeted market. You need a clear definition of the trade channel through which the product will travel to reach that market. A "trade channel" is the method through which products or services are distributed from the maker to the end users. If you determine that importing can benefit your business, like an exporter, you will want to develop a thorough international business plan. See the next chapter for help with your plan.

When you build your plan, identify the domestic target market, evaluate government regulations, and determine the nature of the product(s) to identify the proper Harmonized Tariff Schedule (HTS) product classification.

For comprehensive HTS tariff determination for your imports, check out the U.S. International Trade Commission's Tariff Information Center at http://www.usitc.gov/tata/hts/. Both importer and supplier must agree on the full code number to be listed on all documents. Remember to check the reputation of your foreign supplier. You can find some information on foreign sellers or suppliers through the U.S. Commercial Services program in the International Company Profile accessible through http://export.gov or *Commercial News USA*. Ask a foreign supplier for references and follow them up. A first-time importer may want to consult a licensed Customs Broker, a company that handles the clearance of imported goods for you. Customs brokers are licensed by U.S. Customs and Border Protection (CBP), so check their Web site (http://www.cbp.gov) for more information. Importing procedures may be complicated, so hiring a customs broker will facilitate the process and minimize future problems in your first import experience.

TRANSPORTATION

Now the new exporter or importer must investigate the best way to ship the product overseas, and one of the easiest ways to determine the best shipment method is to consult an international freight forwarder. Find one who is experienced in shipping to the region or country you are targeting, and they will be familiar with the foreign country's import regulations, the U.S. import or export regulations, the freight and associated costs, the best way to package and pack your goods, and what documentation you need. The freight forwarder can assist you in weighing the pros and cons of different modes of transportation, i.e., land, ocean, or air. You, as exporter, may also ask the freight forwarder to make arrangements with the customs broker to ensure that the goods comply with customs export documentation regulations and have the goods delivered to the carrier in time for loading. After shipment, they may also forward all documents to the customer or to the paying bank.

Develop a basic familiarity with the basic kinds of shipping documentation needed, which are the following:

1. Commercial Invoice: is often prepared in two languages, proves ownership and secures payment and corresponds exactly to the description of goods in the letter of credit or documents accompanying the payment.
2. Shipper's Export Declaration: enables the Census Bureau to monitor exports for statistical purposes. It must be presented to the carrier before a shipment can be made. This form is available for download from the Census Bureau (http://www.census.gov) and can be filed electronically.
3. Certificate of Origin: allows for preferential duty rates and is needed in countries subject to special free trade treaties. Export.gov has more information on this topic.

4. Export Packing List: is used by the shipper to determine weight and volume of the total shipment as it itemizes the goods by individual package and exactly how they are packaged.

5. Inspection Certificate: is sometimes required to prove the goods ordered are actually contained in the shipment and are in good condition.

6. Insurance Certificate: is required if exporter is responsible for insurance and should be negotiable and endorsed before shipping documents are submitted to a bank for payment.

7. Air Waybill: sets forth the international carrier's responsibility to transport the goods to their destination and conveys the title to the goods being shipped. Most air waybills contain a customs declaration form. Marine bills of lading provide evidence of title to the goods as well as the responsibility to transport the goods to their named destination.

Whether exporting or importing, finding and keeping customers is still the key issue. Make great customer service the most important mission of your company and the goal of every employee. Communicate frequently with your international contacts and visit the overseas markets and manufacturers.

REFERENCES

(Starred titles discussed in the chapter)

Print Resources

A Basic Guide to Exporting: Official Government Resource for Small and Medium-sized Businesses. 10th ed. U.S. Department of Commerce, 2007. 190pp. ISBN 0-16079-20-4-5. $19.95. Also available online: http://www.unzco.com/basic-guide/index.html

Conventional wisdom once held that U.S. businesses should be content selling within their domestic market as international markets were too difficult and too expensive to penetrate. However, in the past decade, barriers to trade have been lowered and advances in communications technology have been and are tremendous. Now exporting is seen as a prime growth area, and this title describes the costs and risks associated with exporting, how to develop a strategy for success, and where to get the knowledge to enter exporting. Assistance from the federal and state governments is also discussed.

Capela, John J. *Import/Export for Dummies.* Wiley Publishing Inc., 2008. 360p. ISBN 978-0-470-26094-4. $19.99.

This clear, practical primer provides SMEs and entrepreneurs with the needed information to begin exporting their products around the world and importing goods to sell in the United States. Covering the ins and outs of developing or expanding operations to capture a share of this developing market, Capela, a professor at St. Joseph's College in Brooklyn, details the top 10 countries with which the U.S. trades. Well-organized and inexpensive, this title is a good purchase for new exporter and importers.

Collins, Robert, and Block, Carson. *Doing Business in China for Dummies.* Wiley Publishing Inc., 2007. 364p. ISBN 0-470-20920-8. $14.95.

Though this work concentrates on China, you will find help on strategies to enter the foreign market of your choice. But if you are interested in China, learn how to navigate Chinese business culture and etiquette with this authoritative guide. Collins and Block start with the basics and continue through helping you negotiate the Chinese bureaucracy. Travel tips are also included. Find help here to understand the Chinese markets, develop a strong business plan, find employees, work through currency controls and the Chinese banking system, and more. Get tips on advertising and deciding where to set up shop. Also find useful top-10 lists and tear-out cheat sheets.

Dorsey, Jennifer. *Start Your Own Import/Export Business.* 2nd ed. Entrepreneur Press, 2007. 252p. ISBN 1-59918-108-8. $15.95.

This book contains insights and practical advice for entering global markets. It covers aspects of the start-up process, including collecting money from overseas transactions, using the Internet to simplify your transactions, accessing trade law information to keep your business in compliance, how to find contacts in the United States and abroad, using the Internet to simplify your transactions, and choosing a customs broker. Chapters on market research, working online, employees, pricing, and insurance will help run a business efficiently and effectively. A brief appendix on international trade resources may also prove useful. Interviews with successful importer/exporters and an updated resource list will help show the way to success.

Exporters' Encyclopaedia. Annual. Dun & Bradstreet.

A comprehensive world reference guide, this encyclopedia is divided into 220 country-specific sections; firms specializing in international business, laws, and legislation; international trade associations; government agencies; shipping practice; and reference data on weights and measures for overseas ports. Find key contacts, trade and safety regulations, and information on documentation needed. Marketing data include legal requirements for importer or agents, procurement standards, environmental protection or pollution control, marking, and labeling. The encyclopedia also provides passport regulations and business etiquette guidelines.

Hinkelman, Edward, et al. *Importers Manual.* Annual. World Trade Press. 960p.

Information on how to import virtually any commodity into the United States can be found in this practical reference. It is precisely organized for ease of use and is divided into the major sections of Commodity Index; U.S. Customs Entry and Clearance; International Banking; Legal Considerations of Importing; and Packing, Shipping, and Insurance. The heart of the work, the Commodity Index, contains entry procedures, documentation, restrictions, and prohibitions; marking and labeling requirements; and contact information for regulatory agencies for all products that can be imported into the United States.

International Marketing Data and Statistics. Annual. Euromonitor Publications Ltd.

This data handbook provides marketing and business information spanning 24 years and covers 161 non-European countries. International organizations such as the IMF and United Nations and 1,000 information sources in total are contacted for this information. Data are presented in easy-to-use and -understand tables. You can find current statistics on socioeconomic trends, consumer market sizes, expenditure patterns, number of telephone lines, and more here.

International Trade Centre. *Export Quality Management: An Answer Book for Small and Medium-Sized Exporters.* International Trade Centre (UN Publications), 2005. 252p. ISBN 978-92-9137-214-0. $50.00.

Using a question and answer format, exporters or importers can learn how to navigate the world of international standards, mandatory technical regulations, metrology, ISO 9000 series standards, accreditation, conformity assessment procedures and more. Organized in section, each section is comprehensive and well written. This work covers various aspects of quality requirements, quality assurance, conformity assessment and certification, and trade-related environmental issues. This guide is especially helpful in trading with developing countries and transitional economies.

Jagoe, John R. *Export Sales & Marketing Manual 2008: The Bible of Exporting.* Annual. Export Institute of the United States. 520p. ISBN 0-943677-66-1. $295.

Having been updated annually for 21 consecutive years, this international trade publication has achieved longevity and global reach. This manual covers all the steps involved in selling products in world markets. Over 120 illustrations, 85 graphs, 40 flow charts, and 60 sample international trade documents lead the user through the process. Jagoe helps users conduct market research through 1200 Web site addresses providing information on various markets and products or services. A lengthy glossary of export terms and detailed index for quick access to important information is also provided.

Salacuse, Jeswald W. *The Global Negotiator: Making, Managing, and Mending Deals Around the World in the Twenty-First Century.* Palgrave Macmillan, 2003. 312p. ISBN 0-312-29339-9. $39.95.

This unique, outstanding guidebook breaks down the intricacies of international negotiations into understandable segments and provides the tools to ensure success in the creation, management, and remediation of international deals. Salacuse even explains how to deal with negotiations that go wrong, illustrating how deals may falter and methods to save them. Managers, lawyers, executives, and government officials will use this comprehensive guide to understand the transformations global business has experienced in the last decade.

Sherlock, Jim, and Reuvid, Jonathan. *The Handbook of International Trade: A Guide to the Principles and Practice of Export.* GMB Publishing, Ltd., 2007. 440p. ISBN 978-1-84673-035-1.

This handbook for practitioners and students provides a thorough understanding of the underlying issues involved in developing and managing cross-border trade. Contributors provide a comprehensive guide to the methods, procedures, conventions, documentation, and laws of the export trade. A thorough understanding of the structure of the global economy and the dynamics governing world trade is a great basis for developing a strong and success export or import business.

Travis, Tom. *Doing Business Anywhere: The Essential Guide to Going Global*. John Wiley & Sons, Inc., 2007. 202p. ISBN 0-470-14961-2. $24.95.

Travis presents his six tenets of global trade and illustrates them in the context of real stories of global trade. He emphasizes the importance of international trade to the economic prosperity of all the world's nations. If you want to start a new venture or expand your present one, Travis helps you organize, plan, operate, and execute with a global mind-set. Learn how to navigate conflicting and confusing laws, deal with different cultures, and operate in different countries. He also explains how to leverage the benefits of free trade agreements to set up and operate a competitive and profitable business, and he highlights how to protect your brand through patents, copyrights, and trademarks. Security concerns and measures are also discussed. Travis will convince readers that embracing his six tenets is key to "doing business anywhere."

Weiss, Kenneth D. *Building an Import/Export Business*. 4th ed. John Wiley & Sons, Inc., 2008. 320p. ISBN 0-470-18577-5. $19.95.

Weiss, an entrepreneur and international trade consultant, offers tips and instructions for every aspect of an import/export business. Learn how to get started in the post-9/11 import/export landscape. He explains how to take advantage of GATT, WTO, CAFTA, NAFTA, and other trade agreements. Weiss covers all new and updated regulations, laws, and customs and shipping procedures to help ensure that businesses are in compliance with the Transportation Security Administration (TSA), U.S. Customs and Border Protection (CBP), and U.S. Immigration and Customs Enforcement (ICE). Besides helping importers and exporters plan their business expansion, Weiss describes how to research a raw idea and then successfully launch a stable, profitable business operation. Learn how to find suppliers and the importance of foreign travel. Let the real-life examples presented here help you build your export/import business.

Zodl, Joseph A. *Export Import: Everything You and Your Company Need to Know to Compete in World Markets*. 4th ed. IIEI Press, 2005. 174p. ISBN 0-9773098-0-0. $39.95.

In easy-to-understand language and writing style, Zodl leads the reader into the world of international business, dispels the myths, simplifies tasks and processes, and illustrates important points with real-world examples. Zodl defines the vocabulary and terminology needed to understand the world of international business and points out sources to turn to for expert advice. This title provides the information the exporter needs to take a U.S.-manufactured product, sell it to a foreign buyer, make the shipment correctly, and get paid in U.S. dollars. It shows a middleman how to buy a product made by someone else and resell it at a profit to an overseas customer. Zodl also has a Web site users may be interested in checking out at http://www.zodl.net/firstpage.htm.

Online Resources

American Association of Exporters and Importers (AAEI): http://www.aaei .org/ accessed Spring 2009).

Begun in 1921, this organization "has been the national voice of American business in support of fair and open trade among nations" with its expertise in custom matters and global trade issues. Members include manufacturers, distributors, and retailers as well as organizations serving carriers, banks, freight forwarders, and brokers. The association works with many U.S. government agencies. Access to news and press releases along with additional information is provided at the Web site. The Trade FAQs may prove useful, as may the Education and Training opportunities described on the site.

BEOnline: Business and Economics Online: http://www.loc.gov/rr/business/beonline/ (accessed Spring 2009).

Compiled by the Library of Congress Business Reference Services for researchers, this site has, under Subject Lists, a lengthy list of business topics such as associations, business plans (forms), companies by industry, data sets, e-commerce, franchises, economic indicators, legal resources and more. If you click on Associations, you are taken to an associations database that includes contacts, descriptions, addresses, and events data for the organizations listed. Over 10,000 business organizations in the United States are listed. Find here a link to the Herb Growing and Marketing Network or the Association of Bridal Consultants. Under the Title listing, you will find Airlines of the Web, America's Business Funding Directory, American Chambers of Commerce Abroad, American City Business Journals, and more.

BizMove.com: http://www.bizmove.com (accessed Spring 2009).

The International section of this site is outstanding. Users will find information on developing an Export Strategy, learning how to sell overseas, writing an international business plan, as well as documentation and pricing for international businesses. Forms and questionnaires for business planning, industry analysis, goal setting, and more are provided. Thorough and written in jargon-free language, small companies aspiring to international expansion will find this site useful.

BizTradeShows: http://www.biztradeshows.com (accessed Spring 2009).

This site contains the largest directory of trade fairs and business events and brings users exhaustive coverage of exhibitions, trade shows and expositions, conferences, and seminars for various industries worldwide. Users can browse through the most comprehensive information on individual trade events worldwide, along with their event profile, organizer, exhibitor and visitor profile, venues, and dates to plan your participation in advance as nearly a full year of shows is included. Shows are arranged by industry, month, major city, or country, and you can also find trade show display ideas.

Business.gov: http://www.business.gov (accessed Spring 2009).

Business.gov is another government site developed to help businesses find the information they need and want. The Import/Export section of this site is especially noteworthy. Links to information on major industries, population and demographic resources, plus Rural America Facts provide users with a multitude of useful resources. International trade connections are important for global or Internet businesses too. You will find useful links under Importing/Exporting Specific Products. Under E-Commerce, the section on Selling Internationally will be enlightening.

Buyusa.gov: http://www.buyusa.gov/home/export.html (accessed Spring 2009).

This simple-to-use government Web site offers to help businesses get into international sales through market research, trade events, introductions to buyers and distributors, and counseling for any and every step of the export process. One part of the Web site helps importers to the United States, another helps exporters from the United States, and both parts cover products and services. When you click on a country, you get the Country Commercial Guide (CCG), a calendar of events, employment opportunities, market information, and services for U.S. exporters or suppliers. Also part of this site is *Commercial News USA*, the "official export promotion magazine of the U.S. Department of Commerce." This online publication also contains a wealth of information including franchising, trade shows, a company index, and more. See separate entry below for more about *CNUSA*. Part of the Web site, AsiaNow, promotes trade with 14 Asia-Pacific markets and provides single point access to regional trade events, extensive services, and research covering Asian markets. Access Eastern Mediterranean provides U.S. companies with information on the region's markets and its 180 million consumers. The Americas and Showcase Europe provides information and services to those areas of the globe.

Centers for International Trade Development: http://www.citd.org/StartupKit/index.cfm (accessed Spring 2009).

This very useful site has a guide for new exporters, an export readiness assessment tool, and an excellent Export FAQ for companies just getting into international trade. Their Trade Information Database includes U.S. and world trade and economic data, trade contacts and leads, trade reference tools, foreign market research, trade/investment regulations, trade documentation, finance and insurance sections and more. A trade resources directory provides information on numerous trade associations and organizations. A trade show calendar is also available, as are booklets on best markets for various U.S. industries. Start gathering import or export information here.

***Commercial News USA*: http://www.export.gov/cnusa (accessed Spring 2009).**

Commercial News USA is the official export promotion magazine of the Department of Commerce and showcases U.S.-made products and services. Users will find lists of companies already exporting grouped in about 15 different industries. Trade show opportunities are highlighted and described, often letting businesses know who attends and who should attend. This publication is also an excellent source for trade leads and to advertise your products or services to find customers or partners; subscribe online or by mail. Issues may be read online for download in PDFs. Franchising information is available, as well as success stories to inspire new exporters.

Entrepreneur.com: http://www.entrepreneur.com (accessed Spring 2009).

Entrepreneur Magazine provides a wealth of information and assistance to the new entrepreneur. A thorough understanding of the need for the right type of marketing plan to fit your business and your style of planning and working is very important; and this site guides you through the process of discovering the right type for you. Learn how to determine your marketing goals and objectives and how a plan will help you achieve them. International marketing research is well covered in the Marketing section. Under How-to Guides, How to Start an Import/Export Business is articulate, and articles on the Target Market will inspire new exporters or importers. The International Expansion area articles may prove useful. Use this outstanding site often during the planning, opening, and running of your global business.

Export America. **U.S. Department of Commerce: http://www.trade.gov/exportamerica/ (accessed Spring 2009).**

The official magazine of the International Trade Administration (ITA) of the U.S. Department of Commerce, this publication offers practical export advice and is very valuable to small and mid-sized exporters. It includes country- and industry-specific opportunities, trade events, online marketing tips, and export statistics. Articles cover such topics as export documentation, market research, U.S. customs, and success stories, which are available here. Selected articles from current journal issues can be viewed at this Web site. Although not globally searchable, full text of past journal issues from November 1999 through the most current completed year are also available.

**Export.gov http://www.export.gov (accessed Spring 2009).

Created as a government-to-business initiative, Export.gov is the government's portal to exporting and trade services. It is designed to simplify the exporting process by being a single point of access to export-related services and thus reducing the need to view multiple government sources. Over 19 U.S. departments and agencies contribute the information it provides, including the U.S. International Trade Administration, the U.S. Commercial Service, the Department of Commerce, the Export-Import Bank, the Agency for International Development, and the U.S. Trade and Development Agency. Companies new to exporting will find step-by-step help through the export process. To facilitate international trade, companies can also find references on foreign tariff and tax information, search foreign and domestic trade events, and subscribe to receive trade leads and industry specific market intelligence as well as gain access to federal export assistance and financing. The MDB Lead Line is a tool found here that alerts businesses to new development projects funded by the multilateral development banks. Other important areas are the Export Trade Certificate of Review program and the Export Yellow Pages. The Overseas Trade Fair Certification program certifies a limited number of private trade show organizers to recruit and manage U.S. pavilions at approximately 90 overseas trade shows globally. The Export Yellow Pages list export service providers looking for new export business. Trade Leads, a service of the U.S. Commercial Service, provides U.S. companies with current sales leads from international firms and foreign governments seeking to buy or represent U.S. products and/or services. Export.gov is fully searchable.

Export-Import Bank of the United States (Ex-Im Bank): http://www.exim.gov (accessed Spring 2009).

Begun 65 years ago, the bank's mission is to match officially supported foreign competition and fill financing gaps to support U.S. exports and contribute to the promotion and maintenance of U.S. jobs. Ex-Im Bank offers working capital guarantees to U.S. companies, export credit insurance, and direct loans or guarantees of commercial loans to foreign buyers of U.S. goods and services. Find economic impact notices, credit reviews and compliance, forms and publications, handbooks, statistics, seminars, and related links here. Also find seminars on topics such as finding international buyers and extent credit, and trade finance solutions for exporters.

**Export Trading Company Affairs (ETCA): http://www.ita.doc.gov/TD/OETCA/staff.html (accessed Spring 2009).

The ETCA was created by Congress as part of the Export Trading Company Act of 1982. It promotes the formation and use of export trade intermediaries and the development of joint export ventures by U.S. companies. It administers the Export Trade Certificate of Review program, which helps businesses lower their export costs and protects U.S. firms from antitrust accusations relating to joint export activities, and the myEXPORTS program which is a multimedia advertising tool for U.S. firms advertising their export interests.

**The Export Yellow Pages: http://www.exportyellowpages.com (accessed Spring 2009).

The Export Yellow Pages are administered by the Export Trading Company Affairs of the International Trade Administration in partnership with the U.S. Department of Commerce. Containing information on U.S. business products and suppliers, this site is designed to promote and connect SMEs, improve market visibility, help establish international contacts, simplify sales sourcing, and solve language barriers. This site is often used by foreign buyers as a reference tool to find U.S. goods and services. U.S. firms can register their businesses without charge at http://www.myexports.com. In addition, export intermediaries such as freight forwarders, sales agents, and other service companies that help export businesses can register at no charge in the U.S. Trade Assistance Directory. Find trade leads and other resources here in a wide variety of industries. Products and services are offered by over 27,000 U.S. companies. The U.S. Trade Assistance Directory is available online or in print.

**Federation of International Trade Associations (FITA): http://fita.org (accessed Spring 2009).

This huge, very useful site covers all areas of importing and exporting. Users will find help with market research, transportation and logistics, documentation, trade finance and currencies, trade law, directories, trade show calendar, and worldwide trade leads. Find links to Export 1001, a user-friendly introduction to the fundamental aspects of exporting, links to practical sites from other countries, importers' directories, a trade information database and much more.

FITA has a China Business Guide and Trade Software, used to manage international trade enterprises. Also look here for a lengthy list of export intermediaries. This large site is well organized, annotated, and easy to use.

The Global Connector: http://www.globalconnector.org (accessed Spring 2009).

Part of Indiana University's Center for International Business Education and Research (CIBER), this gateway leads to thousands of international trade sites. The Global Connector allows searching by either country or by industry. Country data include links to data on government, domestic economy, news and media, entry requirements, transportation, and international trade. Industry-specific information can be searched by the type or source of information including trade shows, trade publications, trends/analysis, and regulatory matters.

GlobalEDGE: http://globaledge.msu.edu (accessed Spring 2009).

Managed by Michigan State University's Center for International Business Education and Research (MSU_CIBER), this site links to a broad selection of international trade data including economic trends, statistical data sources, government resources, trade portals, journals, and mailing lists. Its Global Resources section provides access to more than 2,000 online resources. The section called Trade Leads is outstanding. MSU_CIBER has also contributed its own resources including an interactive forum for business professionals and portions of the information contained in the Knowledge Room, GlobalEDGE's section on the latest issues/trends effecting international business.

Global Trade and Technology Network (GTN): http://www.usgtn.net (accessed Spring 2009).

The GTN, established in 1994 as part of the U.S. Agency for International Development trade facilitation program, focuses on facilitating trade between the United States and foreign countries and helps develop international markets to bolster steady economic growth in the United States and abroad. Now a part of the U.S. Commercial Service, the premier global export business solutions provider of the U.S. government, this global network of approximately 1800 trade specialists working in 109 domestic offices and in 80 markets worldwide, the Commercial Service helps U.S. companies make international sales with world-class market research, trade events that promote their products or services to qualified buyers, introductions to qualified buyers and distributors, and counseling through every step of the export process. Register here to obtain Import and/or Export assistance.

International Trade Administration (ITA): http://trade.gov/index.asp (accessed Spring 2009).

Part of the Department of Commerce, ITA established this site to strengthen the U.S.'s competitiveness, promote trade and investment, and encourage fair trade and compliance with trade laws and agreements. Find statistics through its TradeStats Express and some PDFs of free publications, though many are only available for purchase. The *Basic Guide to Exporting* is probably the most thorough and useful publication. Find trade events and missions and get export counseling through this site. The FAQ section has many links to more information for exporters and importers. Besides national trade and industry statistics, find state and local trade data and links to key foreign country data sources.

Market Entry Assistance: http://faculty.philau.edu/russowl/market.html (accessed Spring 2009).

Professor Lloyd C. Russow at Philadelphia University has organized a large number of Web resources useful for new exporters and importers. You will find country information, product classification systems, and international organizations, as well as market entry resources. The section titled Are You Ready to Go International is very useful as is the Documentation section. Refer to this useful site often.

**National Association of Export Companies (NEXCO): http://nexco.org (accessed Spring 2009).

This international trade association provides pertinent and timely information to importers, exporters, freight forwarders, bankers, and other professionals engaged in global trade. It is a forum for networking, business solutions, and advocacy through its Global Business Roundtable program and sponsors online conferences and an annual trade mission. Monthly seminars are given in New York City on export compliance, international trade research on the Internet, trade statistics, customs law, and more. WEBINARs are also becoming very popular and accessible to anyone with an Internet connection. The Directory section is very useful to locate export partners and help.

National Foreign Trade Council (NFTC): http://www.nftc.org (accessed Spring 2009).

Founded in 1914, the 300-plus member companies that comprise this organization advocate a rules-based world economy. Dedicated to advocacy in trade policy, export finance, international taxes, and human resources issues, the council works to advance open markets, fight protectionism, and advocate for the Export-Import Bank, IMF, and more. The council's site provides links to current news and information related to NFTC activities and Positions. The Web site also provides full-text white papers produced by the organization.

New York Public Library, International Trade Research Guide: http://www.nypl.org/research/sibl/trade/trade.html (accessed Spring 2009).

This wonderful guide produced by the Science, Industry and Business Library (SIBL) will provide invaluable information in learning how to conduct business between the United States and another country. Guides, business directories, periodicals, and trade statistic sources can be located through this large and practical site. It is well organized and easy to navigate; find information grouped under market research, trade leads, shipping and logistics, and cross-cultural business communication.

SBDCNET: http://sbdcnet.utsa.edu (accessed Spring 2009).

The Small Business Development Center National Information Clearinghouse provides timely, Web-based information to entrepreneurs. Small Business Development Centers (SBDC) are located in all 50 states. SBDCs offer free, confidential business counseling. This Web site provides information on business start-up, international trade, e-commerce, industry research, marketing, trends, and more. The International Trade section has many links to more information and more help in moving into exporting or importing. Templates for business plans and marketing tools are also available. A free newsletter will help you keep up on trends in small business. Entrepreneurs will find plenty of links and information here to help plan, expand and run a new business.

**Small Business Administration: http://www.sba.gov (accessed Spring 2009).

This official government site offers a wealth of resources and programs for starting and growing a small business. Under Startup Basics, check out the areas you need help with while doing your business planning. Other major sections cover business planning, financing, international trade, managing, marketing, employees, taxes, legal aspects, and business opportunities. Find here online forms, sample business plans, loan information, and many publications. The *Export Library* contains titles like Breaking into the Trade Game, Export Working Capital Program, Export Financing for Small Businesses, and SBA & Ex-Im Bank Co-Guarantee Program. Some contents are available in Spanish. Trade Mission Online is also found on the SBA site and is useful to businesses that want to export their products for use by foreign firms and U.S. businesses seeking U.S. partners or suppliers for trade-related activities. Also part of the SBA program are the Small Business Development Centers (SBDC) at http://www.sba.gov/sbdc. SBDCs are located in every state and deliver counseling and training for small businesses in the areas of management, marketing, financing, and feasibility studies. (see the SBDCNET entry in this list for more.)

**STAT-USA/Internet: http://www.stat-usa.gov/ (accessed Spring 2009).

This service of the U.S. Department of Commerce is a single point of access to authoritative business, trade, and economic information from across the federal government. Thousands of international market reports and U.S. economic indicators from many federal agencies are available in an easy-to-use online database. An important part of this resource is GLOBUS & NTDB—obtain current and historical trade-related releases, international market research, trade opportunities, country analysis, and our trade library from the National Trade Data Bank (NTDB). The NTDB provides access to Country Commercial Guides, market research reports, best market reports and other programs. Find Global Business Opportunity Leads as well as Market and Country Research. FedBizOpps (formerly known as Commerce Business Daily) is linked here too. USA Trade *Online* provides current and historical import and export statistics for over 18,000 commodities traded worldwide as well as the most current merchandise trade statistics available in a spreadsheet format. The International Trade Library is a comprehensive collection of over 40,000 documents related to international trade. All are full text searchable, as well as keyword searchable by country or product.

365-Trade: http://www.365-trade.com/ (accessed Spring 2009).

This world directory of importers, exporters, manufacturers, suppliers, and trade leads for buyers and sellers groups trade leads into large categories including Arts and Furniture, General and Leisure, Services Industry, Textile and Wear, and Transport. One click takes you into a list of Offers to Buy or Offers to Sell. Company catalogs are also available on the site, grouped in the same categories. Jobs are listed as well as requests for agents to purchase or ship and so forth.

TradeKey: http://www.tradekey.com (accessed Spring 2009).

This commercial site, a global business-to-business marketplace, states that it connects over five million importers and exporter in 220 countries with over five million visitors monthly, 1.7 million registered users, and 23 million page views, it seems likely. Registration is free with premium services offered for paid subscribers. Find manufacturers and wholesalers here, suppliers and buyers. The front page lists a column of Latest Buy Offers and one of Latest Sell Offers indicating the date and country of origin. Look for trade leads here.

TradeNet: http://www.tradenet.com (accessed Spring 2009).

This international business directory is easily searchable. You can place listings on the Web site, and help is available for using the site and putting your listings up. Trade leads are grouped by industry categories such as Automotive, Health Care, Personal Services and Care, as well as by categories like Pets, Religious Organizations, and Travel. Recent Listings are highlighted in a sidebar. News and other links are available from this large frequently updated site.

Tradeport Global Trade Center: http://www.tradeport.org (accessed Spring 2009).

TradePort is a repository of free information and resources for businesses that seek to conduct international trade. Created in 1996, TradePort is backed by an alliance of regional trade associations that assist California export and import businesses, but companies in all states will find plenty of information to assist their export or import efforts. The Export Tutorial as well as the Import Tutorial are full of valuable resources and information. The Market Research section, which has a large Trade Leads section, and the Trade Library, which provides a bibliography of resources, a glossary, and links to trade statistics are current, very practical resources. This useful site is a great place to start researching your export/import adventure.

**Trade Show News Network: http://www.tsnn.com (accessed Spring 2009).

Though the Internet definitely has had an impact on the trade show market, sometimes setting up a booth at a trade show is a great way to make contacts, find people, and even sell products or services. This comprehensive site provides information on more than 15,000 trade shows that you can find by industry, month of the year, city, state, or country. The Small Business Guide also provides short articles on franchising, incorporating, Internet ads, temporary help, bartering, and home-based businesses. Also find advice on virtual trade shows, trade show planning, convention centers, online service providers, and more.

U.S. Bureau of Industry and Security: http://www.bis.doc.gov (accessed Spring 2009).

This agency of the Department of Commerce is responsible for advancing U.S. national security, foreign policy, and economic objectives by ensuring an effective export control and treaty compliance system and promoting continued

U.S. strategic technology leadership. It issues export licenses, prosecutes viola-tors of export control policies, and implements the Export Administration Act's antiboycott provisions. Export license requirements are triggered by the actual item (commodity, software or technology) being exported, where it is going, who is going to use it, and what they will be using it for. The Web page's FAQs on Export Licensing will answer many questions.

**U.S. Census Bureau: http://www.census.gov (accessed Spring 2009).

This Web page is the best place to start searching for the multitude of data pro-duced by Census programs, publications, and statistics. The home page groups the data under Census 2000, People, Business, Geography, Newsroom, At the Bureau, and Special Topics. Under Business, you can click on the Foreign Trade, Economic Census, NAICS, E-Stats, and Survey of Business Owners. Under For-eign Trade, learn directly from the Census Bureau how to properly classify your products for export and how to file your Shipper's Export Declaration online. The Bureau also processes, tabulates, and releases the data collected by the Bureau of Customs and Border Protection on exports and imports of goods. The catalog, a search feature, and links to related sites are also accessible on the left side of the home page. Another important part of the Census Bureau's Web page is the International Data Base (IDB) at http://www.census.gov/ipc/www/idb/. The IDB presents estimates and projections of basic demographic measures for countries and regions of the world. Country summaries, country rankings, and population pyramids all provide useful data. U.S. export and import statistics by commodity, country, customs district, and method of trans-portation provide value and quantity on a monthly, year-to-date, and annual history basis. U.S. state export data and port statistics for imports and exports are also available. Use this site frequently to help start and grow your business.

**U.S. Customs and Border Protection (CBP): http://www.cbp.gov/ (accessed Spring 2009).

Under the Department of Homeland Security, the CBP unifies and integrates the work of several separate government entities including functions of the U.S. Customs Service, the Immigration and Naturalization Service, and the Agri-cultural Department's Animal and Plant Health Protection Service. It provides protection, advice, and control of merchandise shipped into the country as well as enforcement and compliance with many diverse regulations concerning homeland security, the flow of trade, inspections at ports of entry, and seizures of illegal drugs and contraband. The Importing and Exporting sections of the CBP Web site contain a wealth of information on current trade issues, export licenses and fees, news on specific products, the Harmonized Tariff Schedule, pertinent statutes and regulations, and other publications, forms and videos.

U.S. Department of Agriculture: http://www.usda.gov/wps/portal/usdahome (accessed Spring 2009).

Through the AgExport Connections office, agricultural exporters can keep abreast of foreign market development opportunities with marketing research reports, trade leads, product publicity, and listings of prospective foreign importers. Agricultural counselors, attaches, and trade officers transmit market information, trade, and economic statistics electronically to offices in Washington, DC. U.S. companies can take advantage of the following export services: (1) Trade Leads, which are inquiries, submitted by foreign buyers for specific products, and are transmitted electronically to the AgExport Connections office from 95 countries. Trade Leads may be accessed through the following means: (a) *Internet*—Trade Leads are available on a daily basis, organized by country, product, or date. In addition to Trade Leads, the Home Page contains information on a wide range of USDA programs and services, as well as trade statistics and foreign market report. Trade Leads are also available on other private and public bulletin boards or some newspapers, trade journals, or newsletters. Contact your state agriculture department, trade office or Chamber of Commerce to determine if this service is available locally. (2) Foreign Buyer Lists are drawn from a database that includes more than 25,000 foreign buyers of food, fish and seafood, farm and forest products in nearly 80 countries. The lists provide important details on each firm such as contact person, address, telephone, fax, and type of product(s) imported. Lists are available by product for a specific country—all known buyers of a specific product identified in a specific country in MS Excel format. You can access the form to order lists from http://www.fas.usda.gov /agexport/forbuy.html.

U.S. International Trade Commission's Tariff Information Center: http:// www.usitc.gov/tata/hts (accessed Spring 2009).

This large site provides Harmonized Tariff Schedule, HTS Tools, and HTS Help! Besides the official Harmonized Tariff Schedule, this nonpartisan, quasi-judicial federal agency provides trade expertise, determines the impact of imports on U.S. industries, and directs actions against certain unfair trade practices. Publications available through this Web site include the General Fact-finding Reports, Economic Effects Report, and the International Economic Review. The USITC *Interactive Tariff and Trade DataWeb* provides international trade statistics and U.S. tariff data to the public full time and free of charge, including import and export statistics, U.S. tariffs, U.S. future tariffs, and U.S. tariff preference information.

**U.S. Trade and Development Agency (USTDA): http://www.ustda.gov (accessed Spring 2009).

The USTDA's mission is to promote economic growth in developing and middle income countries and to assist simultaneously U.S. businesses to export their products and services to create U.S. jobs. It is an independent U.S. government foreign assistance agency funded by the U.S. Congress. Find business opportunities here as well as grant funding for overseas projects that support the development of modern infrastructure and open trading systems. The Library contains completed USTDA-funded studies in various regions or countries as well as feasibility studies. The USTDA brings foreign project sponsors to the United States to observe the design, manufacture, demonstration, and operation of U.S. products and services that can potentially help them achieve their development goals. USTDA uses pre-qualified contractors to assist in the preparation and management of these customized visits. The orientations are usually cofunded by U.S. industry. Also available here is the Federal Business

Opportunities list of domestic and overseas opportunities (http://www.ustda
.gov/businessopps).

**VIBES: Virtual International Business and Economic Sources: http://library.uncc
.edu/display/?dept=reference&format=open&page=68 (accessed Spring 2009).**

The more than 1,600 links to free sources of information at this site were
selected by Jeanie Welch of the University of North Carolina Charlotte. The
table of contents breaks the sites into three groups: Comprehensive, Regional,
and National. The Comprehensive section organizes its links by category,
including Banking and Finance, Business Practices and Company Information,
Emerging Markets, and International Trade Law. Research and tables and
graphs are highlights of this site. The Regional section allows searching devoted
to a single region or continent such as Europe or the Middle East. The National
section links to sites devoted to a particular country.

**WorkZ: http://www.workz.com/content/view_content.html?section_id=480
(accessed Spring 2009).**

Hot topics on this large site include e-mail marketing, Web design, podcasting,
blogs, e-commerce, and more. You will also find Forms and Templates and
Web Techniques very useful. The Run Your Business section includes a wealth
of articles of good business practices for all areas of your business. The Ecommerce section covers many facets of selling and marketing online and offline,
and the Trade Show section includes many hints on how to make good use of
your time attending and making use of the contacts after the show.

World Bank: http://www.worldbank.org (accessed Spring 2009).

Established in 1944, the World Bank is composed of five separate organizations
all with distinct but related missions: the International Bank for Reconstruction
and Development (IBRD) and the International Development Association
(IDA), the International Finance Corporation (IFC), Multilateral Investment
Guaranty Agency (MIGA), and the International Centre for Settlement of
Investment Disputes (ICSID). Resources provided from its Business Center
include World Bank project and program summaries, documents, and reports.
The side bar provides links to data and statistics on countries and regions, evaluations, news, and more. Arranged hierarchically, each of these categories
allows you to drill down to even more specific information. In addition to providing access to its own collection of resources, the World Bank provides access
to each member organization's site. Doing Business (http://www.doing
business.org) is a database that provides objective measures of business regulations and enforcement for 175 countries.

**World Wide Chamber of Commerce Guide: http://www.chamberfind.com (accessed
Spring 2009).**

The local chamber of commerce has long been the best source for community
data, local businesses, attractions, festivals, relocation data, tourist information,
and more. This site can be searched by U.S. chambers by state, world chambers
by regions, or keywords. Local businesses that are chamber members can also be
located here. Chamber sites vary but most can be very useful before visiting an

area. Many of the foreign site provide at least some information in English by clicking on a U.S. or British flag.

Yahoo! Directory, National Governments: http://dir.yahoo.com/government (accessed Spring 2009).

This site is a quick way to find links to governments around the world. Countries from Brunei, Burkina Faso, and Moldova to Oman and Vanuatu are listed. Some countries have few links under their category presently but many, like Australia, are a gateway to departments, documents, local governments, research labs, statistics, taxes, and more. Links are often briefly annotated.

5

Basics of Setting Up an International Business

Chapter Highlights:

Parts of an International Business Plan
> The Executive Summary
> Long-Term Goals
> Purpose
> Industry Profile or Competitive Analysis
> Approach to Exporting
> Identify Products and/or Services
> Target Markets and Customers
> Distribution
> Advertising/Promotion/Pricing
> Financial Projections

Sample Plans: Where to Find and How to Use
Organization of the Essential Elements of a Business Plan
Review, Update, Change Your Business Plan
The Executive Summary

By now you know you want to import or export and what type of products or services you will sell. Your company has a business plan, but now it is important to incorporate the international activities into your plan. Focus on the aspects of the international plan that are different from the business plan you have for domestic markets. An international business plan helps you anticipate the future and make well-informed decisions. Planning is a continuous process in the management of any business. It involves the plan, the action, the evaluation, and the control of the events according to your plan. For each new region you explore and/or any new product you plan to introduce into foreign markets, you need a plan. The entire plan should be revised as needed but at least once per year. How to begin? Take an objective and unemotional look at your business. Use the tools at the Centers for International Trade Development Web site: www.citd.org/startupkit/index.cfm. Here you will find a huge practical guide entitled Exporting Basics by Maurice Kogon. Its divisions are Export Prerequisites, Costs of Exporting, Risks of Exporting, and the like and include several excellent start-up aids. A sample Export Market Plan is included as well as the Export Market Plan Template, which has six parts including the strengths, weaknesses, opportunities, and threats (SWOT) analysis; Current Export Status; Product Focus for Export; and Current Export Resources, Functions and Requirements. You will also find a sample Export Market Strategy: Next 2 Years.

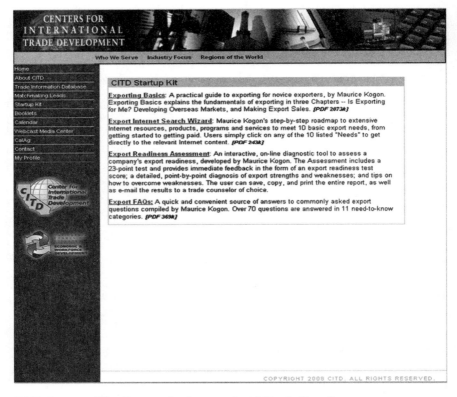

CITD Start-up Kit. Centers for International Trade Development.

Source: California Community Colleges,
Economic and Workforce Development Program

PARTS OF AN INTERNATIONAL BUSINESS PLAN

This section details the parts of an international business plan—you may or may not wish to include all of them. The format is flexible and will be covered later. Remember that life is what is happening while you are making plans, but the business plan helps you anticipate the future and make better-informed decisions. Planning is a continuous process in the management of a business, so be sure to revise and update as needed but at least once per year.

1. **The Executive Summary.** This important section begins your Business Plan, but I will cover it thoroughly at the end of the chapter. Write this summation of your plan after you have finished all the other sections.

2. **Long-Term Goals.** State the mission of your business and define the long-term goals. Why does or should your business exist and sell internationally? What are your personal and business goals for the next 10 years? How does entering international trade help you reach your goals? What are your one-, three-, and five-year goals for the business? Answers to these questions are fundamental to the understanding of your purpose in entering overseas trade. Conversely, state what your mission is not. Profit is not a goal or a mission but an outcome of the successful achievement of your mission. Emphasize the thing or things that set your business apart from others.

3. **Purpose.** What is the purpose of your business and for beginning to export? Outline and study your purpose for entering international business. Who will use your business plan and for what purposes? Now identify specific goals such as sales volume expected, gross profit, your compensation, the amount of time you will commit, your personal and business goals, and any other objectives that may apply.

4. **Industry Profile or Competitive Analysis.** Investigate and describe the history and background of your industry. When and how was it developed? How quickly has it been growing? How competitive is it in international markets? What does its future look like? What are the trends? Next find and list sources of industry information. What industry trade associations exist? Find any existing government studies or compiled export (import) statistics? Define the role of small to medium-sized businesses like yours. Do SMEs fit the roles well? Why have you been successful domestically? What has been your pattern of growth in the domestic market? What external factors have contributed to the growth? Has the growth been seasonal? Describe and rank your competitors. What are your competitive advantages over other domestic or international firms? In effect, you are doing a SWOT analysis: what are the company's strengths, weaknesses, opportunities, and threats. But also ascertain if there are foreign coproduction or assembly requirements an issue. Is there a requirement to maintain and service the products locally? Will and how will the government of the target market influence the marketing of your product? Find out the import regulations and restrictions.

5. **Approach to Exporting.** Describe the method of exporting chosen by your company. For direct exporting, identify who in the company is responsible

for market research and selection, establishment of distribution networks, performance of functions involved in exporting, and aftermarket servicing. Identify and analyze international skills available to you and your company. For indirect exporting, you will need to hire or appoint an Export Management Company (EMC) or Export Trading Company (ETC) to represent you, locate buying offices of large foreign firms or governments, or sell to large U.S. firms for export through their own overseas networks. Identify essential key employees for your export team. Also determine outside resources required, such as an accountant, lawyer, banker, freight forwarder, export consultant, and any other key advisors. Find an advisor at the U.S. Department of Commerce. Determine when you need to write policies. Limit the effects of your inevitable mistakes by starting slowly.

6. **Identify Products and/or Services.** List the products and/or services that your company will offer internationally. Products that sell well domestically should be considered first if they meet a known need. Describe your product, the function it serves, why customers value it, and the problems it solves. In foreign markets like at home, needs are satisfied with regard to function, price, and esthetic value. What makes them unique? Is the quality good? What products are now available in the target export market to meet the needs of your potential customers? Why should foreign buyers purchase from you? Will it change the way things are presently done? Describe your product's strengths and weaknesses in relation to your competitors' products. Will it save time, improve accuracy, do a better job, or do the job more cheaply. Technologically, will its introduction be compatible with the technological capabilities or degree of readiness for product acceptance or will changes be necessary? Additionally, determine what levels of inventory will be necessary.

7. **Target Markets and Customers.** In Chapter 3, you determined which markets offer the best prospects for export or import sales. Identified were three to five countries who were the largest purchasers of like products for the past three or so years. How are those customers similar and/or different from your current customer base? Do they have the same or different buying patterns? Are those customers loyal to suppliers and products presently in use? Will these loyalties present problems in penetrating the market? Can you also identify which markets were the best when considering freight rates? Which have the best projected growth rates? Which countries offer the most potential in general? How quickly can your company begin assembly or manufacturing activities? Will the market continue expanding? Try to determine projected sales levels. What is your company's current market share domestically? What is the anticipated overseas volume? What are projects for the first year and then following years? Can you project sales in your targeted markets? Identify companies, agents, or distributors in your chosen market. Of this group, have any made inquiries or asked for information? You may also want to identify a major international competitor in each market you target so you can compare your international business to them. Compare, for example, marketing, products, service, sales methods, pricing, and image.

8. **Distribution.** What are the main channels of distribution for your product or service currently, and will similar channels work in your new target export market? Is this the most effective distribution channel? What are the common industry distribution channel practices in the target market? Compare your proposed method in terms of cost, available middlemen, and so forth. Consider if your distributors or agents would make a good joint-venture partner? Could they gear up to assemble or partially manufacture your products? How quickly? Should you include this option in your long-term strategic plan? For your plan, also think about the quality of the infrastructure including available transportation (roads, planes, trucks, or trains), services (banks, electricians, movers), warehousing, telecommunications, and the legal system in your target market. Think about all the logistics of getting your product to the target market including transportation, insurance, documentation required, and terms of sale.

9. **Advertising/Promotion/Pricing.** What are your current promotional activities? What promotional vehicles have you identified in the target export market, e.g., trade publications, trade fairs, competent representatives and distributors? Are there packaging or labeling requirements in the target market that are different from the domestic market? Remember that packaging is the last five minutes of marketing. Any language barriers or modifications of the product or service needed? Does the price structure for the target market differ? What are the effects of the costs of transportation, insurance, duties, taxes, middle men markups, packaging changes, on the pricing structure? Create a price list in the target market's currency. What about the terms and prices of existing competitors' products? Will they affect your pricing? How will you communicate with customers, if needed? How often will you visit the territory to see customers and/or consumers and provide sales support to your distributors or representatives? Can you give the same order and delivery preferences to your international customers as you provide to domestic customers?

10. **Financial Projections.** Forecasting sales is a good starting point. The sales forecast shows the expected time that the sale is made. Actual cash flow will be impacted by delivery dates and payment terms. In international sales, costs of goods are determined by terms of sale and pricing strategies. Consult with a freight forwarder to determine costs. Determine overhead costs for export activities, such as legal fees, accounting fees, promotional materials, communication equipment or monthly fees, translation services, advertising, and promotional expenses like trade shows, travel. Figure out what payment terms you will quote and whether you need items like a letter of credit, export credit insurance, or open account.

SAMPLE PLANS: WHERE TO FIND AND HOW TO USE

Now is a good time to look at some resources specifically designed to help you make and write your international business plan. One of the best places to start on the Internet is Bplans.com at http://www.bplans.com.

Here you will find over 50 free sample business plans as well as helpful tools and know-how for creating a business plan. Sample plans, even if for the same business you plan to open, should not be simply copied. A sample plan suggests categories of things for you to consider. A business plan defines and reveals the relationship between the business and you, the owner or manager. A sample plan tells you what is needed in a well-written document. Take a careful look at the financial section in the sample plan as it can help you in developing your financial plans.

Home page. Bplans.com.

Source: http://www.bplans.com

Another good site for business plan guidance is sponsored by *Inc*. Magazine: http://www.inc.com/guides. This site provides two plans for business planning: one is an in-depth look at each section of a plan, and the other is a quick guide to building and improving your plan. You may also find the Small Business Administration sample business plan at http://www.sba.gov/

smallbusinessplanner/plan/writeabusinessplan/index.html useful. Its business plan section was written by Linda Pinson, who is a well-known author on business planning. You will also find her business plan book listed in the References at the end of this chapter. An exceptionally good, current book on business plans is *Business Plans That Work* by Jeffry A. Timmons, Andrew Zacharakis, and Stephen Spinelli. Using this work will enable you to create a plan that crystallizes and legitimizes your ideas for customers, investors, and yourself. In the For Dummies series, Steven Peterson, Peter Jaret, and Barbara Findlay Schenck have written an outstanding resource entitled *Business Plans Kit for Dummies* (with a CD-ROM). In an easy-to-use, easy-to-follow humorous manner, the authors lead you through the steps of writing a business plan for all types of businesses, including nonprofits as well as businesses in later steps of development or in need of restructuring. The CD-ROM contains lots of forms, government documents, sample by-laws, and more.

ORGANIZATION OF THE ESSENTIAL ELEMENTS OF A BUSINESS PLAN

The format for elements of a business plan includes:

1. *The Cover Page* contains the name of business, brief description or mission statement, "Business Plan" as title, date written, your name (and contact information if you want to list different ones from your business), address, and phone number for the business. If you have a business logo, include it here.

2. *Table of Contents* includes the name of each section and the page number where sections begin and subheadings if needed for clarity. The purpose of this page is to get your readers to the section that they are most interested in reading.

3. *Executive Summary* identifies the key ideas you want to emphasize (write this after your plan is finished). Summarize all sections briefly and keep the summary to only a page or two in length. As many readers will only read this section, it is very important that it be done well. This section is expanded upon later in this chapter.

4. *Business Overview* describes the services and/or products you will be selling, the country or countries you will be targeting, and some short-term and long-term goals. Focus here on customer benefits.

5. *Business Environment* identifies all the major aspects that affect your company's situation that are beyond your control, such as how your industry operates including industry regulation, the intensity of your competition and who they are, foreign governments, and the movement and trends of the marketplace globally.

6. *Marketing Plan* describes how to get the products or services to your targeted consumer or market. Also describe your pricing philosophy and

competitive advantage, if any. Describe how you will promote your business
and its wares (advertising) and how it will differ from your domestic
operations.

7. *Financial Plan* tells your story in numbers. You will include a projected
   balance sheet and a profit and loss statement that shows when you anticipate
   profits to start and how long you can afford to absorb losses. Here is where
   you show your international startup or expansion costs and operating cash
   needs.

8. *Outside Advice* lists those individuals you plan to hire or have hired such as
   insurance agents, lawyers, export counselor, accountants, foreign distributors,
   and/or bankers, domestic and foreign.

9. *Supporting Documents* includes any contracts, agreements, or leases that you
   feel are important to the operation of your business.

After reading through the list of sections in a business plan, start a list of
things you need to research in connection with your business and preparing
your business plan. Set a deadline for completion. Ask someone to read it
and comment on your work so you will have a reason to write and complete
your plan in a timely fashion.

If you would like to compare your plan to other business plans, try Anne
McKinney's book, *Real Business Plans and Marketing Tools: Including Samples
to Use in Starting, Growing, Marketing, and Selling Your Business*. She presents
useful plans for a Brew Pub, Home-based Wholesale Company, Gift Shop, Fit-
ness Center, and Janitorial Supply Company, 17 different business plans in all,
to help you compare and develop your own plan:

McKinney, Anne. *Real Business Plans and Marketing Tools: Including Samples to Use in Starting, Growing, Marketing, and Selling Your Business*.
PREP Publishing, 2003. 224p. ISBN 1-885288-36-0. $24.95.

Designed to help entrepreneurs prepare paperwork relating to starting,
marketing, and growing a business, McKinney presents real business plans
for 17 different types of retail businesses including a hair salon, auto body
shop, and restaurant. You will also find samples of financial statements
and other documents used to obtain bank loans and venture capital. A valuable section of the book is the part describing and showing how to use marketing tools. This title will help business owners with strategic planning to
expand into international trade.

REVIEW, UPDATE, CHANGE YOUR BUSINESS PLAN

Be committed to continually reviewing and updating your plan. Note in
your calendar to "Review international business plan" in six months, or less
if you know things will change sooner. Business events that should trigger an
update of your business plan include:

1. Something in your business changes, such as you hire an employee; you add a new product or service; you export or import to a new country or market; or you take on a partner.

2. Your target market or customer base changes, and you change your product line or price or inventory that reflects this change and meets a new need or request.

3. Technology continues to change and some of its changes will affect the way you do business such as new software packages, Internet resources, desktop environments, or new hardware.

Experts who critique business plans frequently state that the business owners are not realistic in their business plans. Try not to be overly enthusiastic and inflate your potential or expectations. Be precise, concise and clear but demonstrate a thorough knowledge of the market and the competition, and your industry as a whole. Emphasize what is different or unique about your venture and find a niche. For help with keeping your plan current, find Mike McKeever's book, *How to Write a Business Plan*:

McKeever, Mike. *How to Write a Business Plan.* 7th ed. Nolo Press, 2005. 256p. ISBN 1-4133-0092-8. $34.99.

This well-written book uses examples and worksheets to help business owners or managers prepare a practical business plan. McKeever includes business plans for a small service and a manufacturing business. His explanation of the breakeven analysis and sales forecasting are very thorough and easy to understand. His step-by-step guidance on how to write a successful business plan is perfectly suited for new owners or managers just starting or expanding a business. The chapter "Selling Your Business Plan" will especially those interested in obtaining financing for their new venture. This new edition has good current online and offline resources to help the new business owner or manager plan their business.

THE EXECUTIVE SUMMARY

This snapshot of your company's history, objectives, financial status, industry overview, and marketing plan is sometimes the only section people will read carefully. It must be a complete, yet brief, overview of your entire plan. It must be specific, exciting, and succinct. Grab your readers' attention. Cover the type of international business you want, what you hope to achieve, how you hope to achieve it, and your capabilities.

First, outline your business's philosophy, goals, and commitments. Identify the type of business you have, such as a new venture or expansion into international business or an international franchise. Define your legal structure with name, location, hours of operation, and years in operation, if any. Name the principle owner(s). State the objective of the international business plan. What do you need to help you accomplish your business goals?

What business opportunity have you identified? If you need expansion or new capital or a bank loan, state the amount and generally how the money will be used, and the potential return on investment. The proposed payback period should be stated. Also, mention the industry overview, target market identified, and competitive advantage.

Again remember that although this document appears at the beginning of your international business plan, prepare it last because it summarizes the deep learning that has taken place through the entire planning process. You know your niche in the market, understand and continually research your industry and competition, and are ready to launch and grow this international business. If you are having trouble writing the Executive Summary, take a look at Linda Pinson's book, *Anatomy of a Business Plan*, for help in writing this snapshot of your business so that it will capture the attention and interest of your readers:

Pinson, Linda. *Anatomy of a Business Plan*. 7th ed. Dearborn Trade, 2008. 288p. ISBN 0-944-205-37-2. $22.95.

This useful guide now includes four sample business plans, plus blank forms to help you write a thoughtful, comprehensive and professional business plan. Pinson understands that the Executive Summary needs to grab attention, and she presents ways for you to do just that. She includes a resource section to help businesses research financial and marketing information so essential for an outstanding plan. Four real-life business plans and blank forms and worksheets provide readers with additional user-friendly guidelines for the creation of the plans. New chapters on financing resources and business planning for nonprofits as well as a sample restaurant business plan will help many business owners or managers create a better plan. She also provides guidelines for updating and packaging your plan.

Below are resources to help you learn how to write an international business plan and where to get help in preparing your plan. Sample several different resources and find one that helps you work through the process.

REFERENCES

(Starred titles discussed in the chapter)

Print Resources

Doman, Don, et al. *Market Research Made Easy*. 3rd ed. Self-Counsel Press, Inc., 2006. 146p. ISBN 1-55180-676-2. $14.95.

The authors describe market research as a process of asking questions or finding existing information about the market, the competition, and potential customers. Written for the first-time, do-it-yourself market researcher, this book guides readers step by step through marketing any business. Worksheets and explanations in nontechnical language help you decide if you want to consult a professional, determine how much you want to spend, and gather and analyze data to create a marketing strategy. Learn how to write a questionnaire. Analyze the global market and understand your industry. Various real-life case studies scattered throughout bring the importance of market research and doing it well home. The authors ascertain that the most difficult part of market research is that it can burst your bubble—demolish a cherished idea—but it will save you money and point you in the right direction. Learn how to expand your market share internationally. The Canadian resources included are especially useful.

Dorsey, Jennifer. *Start Your Own Import/Export Business*. 2nd ed. Entrepreneur Press, 2007. 252p. ISBN 1-59918-108-8. $15.95.

This book contains insights and practical advice for entering global markets. It covers all aspects of the start-up process, including collecting money from overseas transactions, using the Internet to simplify your transactions, accessing trade law information to keep your business in compliance, finding contacts in the United States and abroad, using the Internet to simplify your transactions, and choosing a customs broker. Interviews with successful importer/exporters and an updated resource list will help show the way to success.

Exporters' Encyclopaedia. Annual. Dun & Bradstreet.

A comprehensive world reference guide, this encyclopedia is divided into 220 country-specific sections; firms specializing in international business, laws, and legislation; international trade associations; government agencies; shipping practice; and reference data on weights and measures for overseas ports. Find key contacts, trade and safety regulations, and information on documentation needed. Marketing Data includes legal requirements for importer agents, procurement standards, environmental protection or pollution control, marking, and labeling. The encyclopedia also provides passport regulations and business etiquette guidelines.

Gendron, Michael P. *Creating the New E-Commerce Company*. South-Western, 2005. 304p. ISBN 0-324-22485-0. $34.95.

Gendron discusses how emerging technologies should be viewed in a total corporate context as an intrinsic part of the organization's structure and mission. Learn how new technologies will revamp the way we do business every day and learn to use them to maximize your company's potential. Management in all sizes of businesses need to think about how organizations and industries can adapt to the electronic future. E-thinking in day-to-day business tactics and strategic plans is essential. Discover how this conversion to e-commerce thinking can boost the bottom line.

Jagoe, John R. *Export Sales & Marketing Manual 2008: The Bible of Exporting*. Annual. Export Institute of the United States. 520p. ISBN 0-943677-66-1. $295.

Having been updated annually for 21 consecutive years, this international trade publication has achieved longevity and global reach. This manual covers all the steps involved in selling products in world markets. Over 120 illustrations, 85 graphs, 40 flow charts, and 60 ample international trade documents lead the user through the process. Jagoe helps users conduct market research through 1200 Web site addresses providing information on various markets and products or services. A lengthy glossary of export terms and detailed index for quick access to important information is also provided.

Karlson, Carolyn Boulger. *Writing and Presenting a Business Plan*. Cengage South-Western, 2008. 295p. ISBN 0-324-58422-9. $37.95.

From idea generation through feasibility analysis, and from writing the plan to presenting it to various audience groups, Karlson covers all steps necessary to develop and start a business. She also provides guidance on meeting with investors and getting funding for the new venture, and provides numerous samples of effective plans and presentations. Market analysis, SWOT analysis, timetables, and break even analyses are all presented in clear, easy-to-read and -understand formats.

Magos, Alice. *Business Plans That Work*. 3rd edition. Toolkit Media Group, 2008. 244p. ISBN 0-8080-0858-7. $19.95.

The essential elements of a professional business plan have been updated in accordance with new laws and regulations in this revised edition, which translates complicated marketing and financial concepts into down-to-earth, practical guidance. The major highlight of this title is the five updated sample business plans that include a wealth of detailed information about the operation of a successful small business. Find plans for simple one-person companies, as well as for corporations with numerous employees. Learn how to create a professional plan, describe the mission and objectives, analyze the competition, target market, create sales and marketing plans, generate financial statements, and use the business plan as a management tool long after it is completed.

**McKeever, Mike. *How to Write a Business Plan*. 7th ed. Nolo Press, 2005. 256p. ISBN 1-4133-0092-8. $34.99.

McKeever's logically organized, thoughtfully presented work uses examples and worksheets to help owners or managers prepare a successful business plan. He includes business plans for a small service and a manufacturing business. The chapter on writing your marketing and personnel plans is particularly helpful for the marketing section of a business plan. Before proceeding with the marketing plan, McKeever suggests you return to your written business description to see if it still is an accurate statement of how you view your business or if the thinking and writing experiences between chapters have changed your current ideas. A business plan is a dynamic document that needs constant revision to keep you and your business current. His explanation of the breakeven analysis and sales forecasting are very thorough and easy to understand. The tear out forms in the back for filling in numbers are invaluable, and for some, the task of filling in the profit and loss forecast will bring the term "bottom line" into sharp focus. The chapter called Selling Your Business Plan will especially help those interested in obtaining financing for their new venture. This new edition has good new online and offline resources to help the new owner or manager plan their business.

**McKinney, Anne. *Real Business Plans and Marketing Tools: Including Samples to Use in Starting, Growing, Marketing, and Selling Your Business*. PREP Publishing, 2003. 224p. ISBN 1-885288-36-0. $24.95.

In this book designed to help entrepreneurs prepare paperwork relating to starting, marketing, and growing a business, McKinney presents real business plans for 17 different types of businesses including a hair salon, auto body shop, home-based wholesale company, and janitorial supply company. You will also find samples of financial statements and other documents used to obtain bank loans and equity financing. This title will help new business owners in strategic planning.

Moss, Rita. *Strauss's Handbook of Business Information*. 2nd ed. Libraries Unlimited, 2004. 453p. ISBN 1-56308-520-8. $85.00.

Business information has experienced a revolution in the past few years, i.e., user-friendly and sometimes free access to online databases filled with company, industry, association, and government information. The basic organization of the first edition has been followed here, dividing the Handbook into two main sections: Formats and Fields of Business Information. Additionally, with the globalization of business and economies, international resources are featured in each chapter. The Format section includes guides, directories, periodicals, loose-leaf services, and electronics. Fields covered include marketing, accounting and taxation, banking, stocks and bonds, futures, insurance and real estate. Appendices cover acronyms, federal government agencies, state agencies, and selected Web sites. A title and a subject index complete the volume.

Mullins, John. *The New Business Road Test: What Entrepreneurs and Executives Should Do Before Writing a Business Plan*. Financial Times/Prentice Hall, 2004. 288p. ISBN 0-273-66356-9. $24.95.

Before writing a business plan or investing any money, use Mullins's seven domains model for assessing your new business ideas. Learn how to run a customer-driven feasibility study to assess that new business opportunity. Case studies use real businesses like Honda, Enterprise Car Rental, and Starbucks to illustrate industry trends and opportunities. What are critical success factors and niche markets? Avoid the "me too" trap and more. Use his practical advice and guidance to help your new business succeed.

**Peterson, Steven D., PhD., Jaret, Peter E., and Schenck, Barbara Findlay. *Business Plans Kit for Dummies*. Wiley Publishing Inc., 2005. 2nd Edition. 360p. ISBN 978-0764597-947. $23.09.

Updated and expanded, this revised edition helps you put your business plan to work. Every chapter has checklists and forms. The examples in the case studies illustrate how real-life businesses succeed. The analysis of business plans for businesses that didn't make it is an unusual and useful feature. An excellent sample business plan is included and lists ten final questions to ask your business plan before you show it to anyone or decide it is complete. Every entrepreneur will want to test his plan. Plus the CD-ROM with its wealth of forms and useful documents will help entrepreneurs in many areas of business. Learn how to forecast and budget, identify your company's mission and competitors, and obtain needed funding.

**Pinson, Linda. *Anatomy of a Business Plan*. 7th ed. Dearborn Trade, 2004. 288p. ISBN 0-944-205-37-2. $22.95.

This user-friendly guide includes four sample business plans, plus blank forms to help you write a thoughtful, thorough, and professional business plan. Business plans and blank forms and worksheets provide readers with user-friendly guidelines for the creation of their plan. This updated seventh edition features new chapters on financing resources and business planning for nonprofits as well as a sample restaurant business plan. Pinson includes a resource section to help businesses research financial and marketing information so essential for an outstanding plan. You will also find guidelines for updating and packaging your plan.

RMA Annual Statement Studies. Risk Management Association, Annual.

These studies collect and compile current and historical financial data for almost 350 industries by company asset and sales size. An annual volume is expensive, so check your library or their Web site for information on buying one industry (www.rmahq.org). Find the Web site description below in online resources. Banks use this information for analyzing business loan applications. Libraries have traditionally purchased this data for their business collections but subscription costs keep rising.

Rogoff, Edward G. *Bankable Business Plans*. 2nd ed. Rowhouse Publishing, 2007. 258p. ISBN 0-9791522-0-7. $16.49.

This well-written, no-nonsense approach to putting in writing what lenders and investors want to see illustrates how style counts along with content. Rogoff shows the user how to create professional financial projects and address the needs of investors and lenders. Part I explains why you need to plan; Part II is broken into "Ten Essential Action Steps" in order to develop the plan; and Part III covers creating a time line and presenting yourself and the plan in the best light. Outlines and samples of simple and complex plans are included. A list of resources and complete index round out this practical guide.

Salmon, Robert and de Linares, Yolaine. *Competitive Intelligence: Scanning the Global Environment*. Economica Ltd., 1999. 200p. ISBN 1-902282-04-3. $24.95.

Broadening the concept of economic business intelligence, Salmon believes that companies must "scan their environment" for everything happening around them. Human relations and intangible factors are assuming increasing importance, and business success depends on agility, creativity, and proactivity. Product life cycles are getting shorter, consumers tastes are more unpredictable, technological innovation advances at a dizzying pace, and information circulates in real time. Businesses must learn to refocus economic thinking on people and identify future trends on the basis of what we observe around us. Learn how to decipher the signals and identify opportunities and risks for your business.

Small Business Sourcebook. 2v. Thomson Gale, Annual. $405.00.

This directory provides a wealth of information for the small business owner or manager. The Small Business Profiles cover 340 different small businesses. Businesses profiled include catering, cooking schools, fish farms, antique shops, bookstores, and car washes. Entries contain as many as 17 subheadings, such as start-up information, educational programs, reference works, sources of supply, statistical sources, trade periodicals, trade shows and conventions, consultants, and franchises and business opportunities. The chapter on import and export services will prove very useful as will the section on trade shows and exhibiting, which lists publications to help you get more out of exhibiting. The Small Business Topics section covers general ideas such as budgets or budgeting, retailing, service industry, franchising, insurance, and seasonal business. Like the small business profiles, these entries have the same 17 subheadings and lead users to many resources relating to the topics. The State Listings and Federal Government Assistance sections list programs and offices that provide information and support to businesses. Check your library for this practical, well-organized source.

Stutely, Richard. *The Definitive Business Plan*. Financial Times/Prentice-Hall, 2002. 312p. ISBN 0-273-65921-9. $27.00.

This excellent work has a more international focus and viewpoint and is written by a UK businessman. Some of the terminology is slightly different but the basics are the same. Stutely presents many short case studies to illustrate the use or importance of sections or strategies in business planning, which often target misconceptions. Stutely also includes many quotes and proverbs that will help the important ideas and concepts of business planning stick in your mind. This outstanding work will help write a great business plan.

**Timmons, Jeffry A. et al. *Business Plans That Work*. McGraw-Hill, 2004. 128p. ISBN 0-07-141287-5. $16.95.

Based on work with hundreds of entrepreneurs and entrepreneurial ventures, this book illustrates a proven, innovative and strategic approach to writing a business plan. Business planning allows practitioners to anticipate the resources required and the pitfalls that may arise in their new business. Learn how to write, adapt, focus, and revise your business plan. An entire chapter is devoted to each section of a business plan, and each includes exceptional samples for those sections. Chapters on the industry and the competition as well as the start-up team are particularly practical. The Financial Plan chapter will guide new owners and managers through the process of generating realistic financials. Flow charts and tables illustrate every step in the development of an outstanding and complete business plan.

Travis, Tom. *Doing Business Anywhere: The Essential Guide to Going Global*. John Wiley & Sons, Inc., 2007. 202p. ISBN 0-470-14961-2. $24.95.

Travis presents his six tenets of global trade and illustrates them in the context of real stories of global trade. He emphasizes the importance of international trade to the economic prosperity of all the world's nations. If you want to start a new venture or expand your present one, Travis helps you organize, plan, operate, and execute with a global mind-set. Learn how to navigate conflicting and confusing laws, deal with different cultures, and operate in different countries. He also explains how to leverage the benefits of free trade agreements to set up and operate a competitive and profitable business, and he highlights how to protect your brand through patents, copyrights, and trademarks. Security concerns and measures are also discussed. Travis will convince readers that embracing his six tenets is key to "doing business anywhere."

Troy, Leo. *Almanac of Business and Industrial Financial Ratios*. Aspen Publishers, Inc., 2004. 801p. ISBN 0-7355-4319-4. $139.

This updated business reference standard covers 50 operating and financial factors in 192 industries and derives its data from IRS figures on U.S. and international companies. Data for each industry are subdivided into 13 categories based on company size. Troy presents all variety of factors relating to operations, operating costs, financial performance, and an array of financial factors in percentages including debt ratio, return on assets, return on equity, and profit margins. Tables are divided into 13 asset sizes to help with making comparisons.

U.S. Department of Commerce. Census Bureau. *Statistical Abstract of the United States.* Government Printing Office, annual. Web version at: http://www .census.gov/compendia/statab/ (also available on CD ROM).

This collection of statistics on U.S. social, political, and economic conditions provides statistics on things like the number of cell phones in the United States, average cost of a home in different areas of the United States, educational level in various parts of the country, fastest growing jobs, where population growth is happening, and more in over 1,400 tables and charts. First published in 1878, the data are collected from over 220 different government and private agencies. Each chapter begins with a description of the data being presented and definitions of terms and concepts. The International Statistics section presents statistics for the world as a whole and for many countries on a comparative basis with the United States. Data are shown for population, births and deaths, social and industrial indicators, the economy, agriculture, and communication. Use the subject index to quickly locate the statistical tables you need. Most tables present information for the past 5 to 10 years. Footnotes under the tables provide source information.

Walsh, Ciaran. *Key Management Ratios: Master the Management Metrics that Drive and Control Your Business.* 3rd ed. Financial Times/Prentice Hall, 2003. 400p. ISBN 0-273-66345-3. $24.95.

Business ratios are the standards and targets that help owners or managers work toward achieving their goals in running a successful business. Fully international, using companies in the United Kingdom, United States, European Union, and Japan, Walsh proceeds to teach readers everything needed to know about key business ratios, linking them to day-to-day operations. He also covers financial statements, balance sheets, cash flow, liquidity, and cost, volume and price relationships. You will take some knowledge away from studying this thorough and well-organized book.

Weiss, Kenneth D. *Building an Import/Export Business.* 4th ed. John Wiley & Sons, Inc., 2008. 320p. ISBN 0-470-18577-5. $19.95.

Weiss, an entrepreneur and international trade consultant, offers tips and instructions for every aspect of an import/export business. Learn how to get started in the post-9/11 import/export landscape. He explains how to take advantage of GATT, WTO, CAFTA, NAFTA, and other trade agreements. Weiss covers all new and updated regulations, laws, and customs and shipping procedures to help ensure that businesses are in compliance with the Transportation Security Administration (TSA), U.S. Customs and Border Protection (CBP), and U.S. Immigration and Customs Enforcement (ICE). Besides helping importers and exporters plan their business expansion, Weiss describes how to research a raw idea and then successfully launch a stable, profitable business operation. Learn how to find suppliers and the importance of foreign travel. Let the real-life examples presented here help you build your export or import business.

Zodl, Joseph A. *Export Import: Everything You and Your Company Need to Know to Compete in World Markets*. 4th ed. IIEI Press, 2005. 174p. ISBN 0-9773098-0-0. $39.95.

In easy-to-understand language and writing style, Zodl leads the reader into the world of international business, dispels the myths, simplifies tasks and processes, and illustrates important points with real-world examples. Zodl defines the vocabulary and terminology needed to understand the world of international business and points out sources for expert advice. This title provides the information the exporter needs to take a U.S.-manufactured product, sell it to a foreign buyer, make the shipment correctly, and get paid in U.S. dollars. It shows a middleman how to buy a product made by someone else and resell it at a profit to an overseas customer. Zodl also has a Web site users may be interested in checking out at http://www.zodl.net/firstpage.htm.

Online Resources

About.com: Small Business Information: http://sbinformation.about.com (accessed Spring 2009).

This large site has many different parts, but the Small Business Information and Business Plan Writing sections are especially well done. On the left side of this main page, you will find Business Ideas on a Budget, Choosing a Business to Start, Business Plan Outline, Step-by-Step, Business Legal Organizational Structures, and "How to" Library. Further down topics like Financing, Case Studies and Interviews, and Resources also provide more links to information. Learn about SWOT Analysis for Small Business in a short article that will help you understand the important of a SWOT analysis. Find articles about the importance of writing a plan and how to complete a useful plan. There is a business plan FAQ and more. International trade advice is also provided as well as many downloadable business forms. Some industry information can be accessed here as well. Continually updated and well-organized, this site will help with online business activities as well as help you write your business plan and continue to plan your business activities.

American Association of Exporters and Importers (AAEI): http://www.aaei.org (accessed Spring 2009).

Begun in 1921, this organization "has been the national voice of American business in support of fair and open trade among nations" with its expertise in custom matters and global trade issues. Members include manufacturers, distributors, and retailers as well as organizations serving carriers, banks, freight forwarders, and brokers. The association works with many U.S. government agencies. Access to news and press releases along with additional information is provided at the Web site.

BEOnline: Business and Economics Online: http://www.loc.gov/rr/business/beonline/ (accessed Spring 2009).

Compiled by the Library of Congress Business Reference Services for researchers, this site has, under Subject Lists, a lengthy list of business topics such as associations, business plans (forms), companies by industry, data sets, e-commerce, economic indicators, international trade, and legal resources. If you click on Associations, you will find a short list of Associations. Clicking on the Association takes you to its Web site. Under the International Trade listing, you will find Foreign Trade Statistics and the Trade Compliance Center.

BizMove.com: http://www.bizmove.com (accessed Spring 2009).

The wealth of information covers a variety of topics including General Management, Small Business Marketing, Internet Business, and International Trade. Worksheets and sample plans will help guide you. Growing a Business on the Internet covers topics such as search engine positioning, Web site promotion, and e-mail marketing methods. International Trade centers on Exporting covers many diverse topics including how to export a service and how to sell overseas.

**Bplans.com: http://www.bplans.com (accessed Spring 2009).

This well-established, frequently updated site, sponsored by Palo Alton Software, Inc., is the best for help in writing your business plan. The section entitled Write a Business Plan, contains articles, calculators on cash flow, starting costs, break even and more, a business plan template, and executive summary and mission statement help plus access to expert advice. Currently 60 free plans are viewable online for free. On this fully searchable site, users can quickly find topics that they need, such as getting your plan funded and business plan legalities. Another nice feature is that they offer a Business Planning Audio for auditory learners. Other sections include Finance and Capital, Marketing and Advertising, Buying a Business, Market Research, and a monthly newsletter. Bplans.com is a useful, practical site that also offers fee-based experts and assistance.

Bureau of Labor Statistics (BLS): http://stats.bls.gov/ (accessed Spring 2009).

When you get to the BLS site, select International for BLS's International Price Program (IPP) including the Import Price Indexes and Export Price Indexes. Also find here publications like the *Dictionary of Occupational Titles* and the *Occupational Outlook Handbook* online. The *Handbook* provides training and education needed, earnings, and expected job prospects for a wide range of jobs. Here is help to write job ads, job descriptions, foreign labor statistics, and more. Also find out about current government regulations and legislation in regard to employees.

Business.gov: http://www.business.gov (accessed Spring 2009).

This is another government site developed to help businesses find the information they need and want. The Market Research section of this site is especially noteworthy. Links to information on major industries, population and demographic resources, plus Rural America Facts provide users with a multitude of useful resources. International trade connections are useful for global or Internet businesses too. Major categories include Laws and Regulations, Buying and Selling, Financial Assistance, Taxes, etc. Also find workplace issue information on interviewing, working environments, training, hiring procedures, and employing minors. The Site Map works like a table of contents and gets you where you want to go quickly and easily.

Buyusa.gov: http://www.buyusa.gov/home/export.html (accessed Spring 2009).

This simple to use government Web site offers to help businesses get into international sales through market research, trade events, introductions to buyers and distributors, and counseling for any or every step of the export process. One part of the Web site helps importers to the United States, another helps exporters from the United States, and both parts cover products and services. When you click on a country, you get the Country Commercial Guide (CCG), a calendar of events, employment opportunities, market information, and services for U.S. exporters or suppliers. Also part of this site is the *Commercial News USA*, the "official export promotion magazine of the U.S. Department of Commerce." This online publication also contains a wealth of information including franchising, trade shows, a company index, and more. Part of the Web site, AsiaNow promotes trade with 14 Asia-Pacific markets and provides single point access to regional trade events, extensive services, and research covering Asian markets. Access Eastern Mediterranean provides U.S. companies with information on the region's markets and its 180 million consumers. The Americas and Showcase Europe provides information and services to those areas of the globe.

Entrepreneur.com: http://www.entrepreneur.com (accessed Spring 2009).

Entrepreneur Magazine provides a wealth of information and assistance to the new entrepreneur. A thorough understanding of the need for the right type of marketing plan to fit your business and your style of planning and working is very important; and this site guides you through the process of discovering the right type for you. Learn how to determine your marketing goals and objectives and how a plan will help you achieve them. International marketing research is well covered in the Marketing section. Under How-to Guides, How to Start an Import/Export Business is articulate, and articles on the target market will inspire new exporters or importers. The International Expansion area articles may prove useful. Use this outstanding site often during the planning, opening, and running of your global business.

Entrepreneurs' Help Page: http://www.tannedfeet.com/ (accessed Spring 2009).

Find here help with business plans, financial statements, legal structure and legal forms, marketing and public relations (PR), human resources (HR), and strategy. Designed, created, and published by a group of young professionals in Chicago, the Entrepreneurs Help page does not claim to substitute for professional advice and judgment but provides information to entrepreneurs to get them started in the right direction. Experts offer advice on finding the right customers, selecting and working with an advertising agency, and marketing budgets. The idea for a marketing database to trace bits of information about your customers such as purchase history, demographics, service history, and the like has been shown to work for companies such as Amazon.com. Articles are usually not lengthy but ask questions to help the new business person start thinking about what is needed and what questions will be asked of him/her. Down-to-earth advice from peers is often the most valuable.

Entrepreneurship: http://www.entrepreneurship.org/ (accessed Spring 2009).

The Ewing Marion Kauffman Foundation is the entrepreneur's trusted guide to high growth. This large site is filled with relevant, practical, and timely information on how to manage and expand your business. Included are original articles written for the site by entrepreneurs drawing on their own experiences and an aggregation of the "best of the best" existing articles and tools to guide you on the path to high growth. Topics are arranged around eight key subject areas: Accounting and Finance, Human Resources, Marketing and Sales, Products and Services, Business Operations, The Entrepreneur, Public Policy, and Entrepreneurship Law. Search "global markets" on the entire site to find over 300 articles.

Euromonitor International: http://www.euromonitor.com/ (accessed Spring 2009).

Euromonitor International offers quality international market intelligence on industries, countries and consumers. They have some 30 years of experience publishing market reports, business reference books, online information systems, and bespoke consulting projects. Their Web site has a huge article archive with short articles on topics like trends in retail, food prices, brand growth, in various parts of the world. Many articles are on a specific company, country, or product. Complete company profiles and industry reports can be purchased.

Export.gov: http://www.export.gov (accessed Spring 2009).

Created as a government-to-business initiative, Export.gov is the government's portal to exporting and trade services. It is designed to simplify the exporting process by being a single point of access to export-related services and thus reducing the need to view multiple government sources. Over 19 U.S. departments and agencies contribute to the information it provides including the U.S. International Trade Administration, the U.S. Commercial Service, the Department of Commerce, the Export-Import Bank, the Agency for International Development, and the U.S. Trade and Development Agency, among others. Companies new to exporting will find step-by-step help through the export process. To facilitate international trade, companies can also find references on foreign tariff and tax information, search foreign and domestic trade events, subscribe to receive trade leads and industry-specific market intelligence, as well as gain access to federal export assistance and financing. Export.gov is fully searchable and allows you to search globally the contents of all of its contributing entities.

ExportHelp: http://www.exporthelp.co.za/index.html (accessed Spring 2009).

This large export assistance site from South Africa has an abundance of information and advice for new exporters. Find information on documentation, marketing, an initial SWOT analysis, country selection, and more. A lengthy article on trade fairs and getting the most out of them is also a highlight. The section on e-commerce is also practical.

EXPORT911.com: http://www.export911.com/ (accessed Spring 2009).

This business and educational Web site focuses on international business. It provides in-depth information on export/import marketing, management, letters of credit, export cargo insurance, shipping, logistics, manufacturing, purchasing, bar codes, and more. Major sections include Gateways to Global Markets, Purchasing Department, Production Department, and Product Coding (bar codes). Business Tool titles include Conversion Tables, Abbreviations, Acronyms, and Symbols, and General References. Case studies and samples are also provided. This large site provides a plethora of educational and informational articles and data.

Federation of International Trade Associations (FITA): http://www.fita.org (accessed Spring 2009).

Founded in 1984, FITA has more than 450 affiliates who are independent international associations that fall into one of the following categories: world trade clubs, associations or chambers of commerce with regional or bilateral interests, associations focused on international logistics, associations supporting international trade, associations supporting exporters, and professional associations. More than 400,000 groups are linked here. Neither individuals nor companies can become members but can join the member organizations. FITA provides an outstanding linking site, which is searchable, has annotated links, and is available in languages other than English. The organization also publishes the e-mail newsletter *Really Useful Sites for International Trade Professionals.*

FedStats: http://www.fedstats.gov (accessed Spring 2009).

The official Web site of the Federal Interagency Council on Statistical Policy is a gateway to statistics from over 100 U.S. Federal agencies and is well organized and easy to use. You can find under the titles Links to Statistics, Topic Links A–Z, MapStats, and Statistics By Geography from U.S. Agencies. MapStats provides statistical profiles of states, counties, cities, congressional districts, and federal judicial districts. The Statistical Reference Shelf, a bit further down on the home page, is a large collection of online reference sources like the *Statistical Abstract of the United States.* You will find a variety of other sources such as the *State and Metropolitan Area Data Book* and *Digest of Education Statistics,* which will provide statistics on many topics of interest to entrepreneurs. On the other half of the page, Links to Statistical Agencies, under Agencies by Subject, click Economic on the drop-down arrow to lead you to a list of Periodic Economic Censuses. Below this area, you will find Data Access Tools that link users to agency online databases.

The Global Connector: http://www.globalconnector.org (accessed Spring 2009).

Part of Indiana University's Center for International Business Education and Research (CIBER), this gateway leads to thousands of international trade sites. The Global Connector allows searching by either country or by industry. Country data include links to data on government, domestic economy, news and media, entry requirements, transportation, and international trade. Industry specific information can be searched by the type or source of information including trade shows, trade publications, trends or analysis, and regulatory matters.

Home Business Magazine (*HBM*): http://www.homebusinessmag.com (accessed Spring 2009).

The Marketing and Sales categories accessible through the frame on the left side of the screen provide a wealth of articles on marketing any type of small business. Short courses on marketing success, information on how you could be hurting your sales, and other articles as well as subcategories on direct marketing, Web marketing, publicity, and selling provide more inexpensive but effective marketing ideas. Advice and ideas on business start-up, management, e-commerce, and money are also included. The How to Write a Business Plan section is also very detailed and helpful. Learn about selling on eBay in the eBay Start Up Guide. The *HBM* archives include a large number of articles grouped by category. Really good information on using the Internet for e-commerce and marketing plus good hints on improving your Web site are provided.

**Inc.com: http://www.inc.com (accessed Spring 2009).

The publishers of *Inc.* magazine present a large directory of articles by topic targeting many problems, concerns, and decisions confronting new business owners or managers. Their section on business plans is precise and practical. Particularly strong is the article on writing your business description; you are encouraged to write out the problem your business solves for its customers and then describe how your business solves your customers' problem. As stated earlier, the executive summary is a critical section in the business plan. Get advice here on what *not* to include in it. Simple but effective advice is the hallmark of this outstanding, easy-to-use site.

International Trade Administration (ITA): http://trade.gov/index.asp (accessed Spring 2009).

Part of the Department of Commerce (DOC), ITA's site tries to strengthen the U.S.'s competitiveness, promote trade and investment, and encourage fair trade and compliance with trade laws and agreements. Find statistics through its TradeStats Express and some PDFs of free publications, though many are only available for purchase. The *Basic Guide to Exporting* is probably the most thorough and useful publication as it provides practical help for exporters/importers. Find trade events and missions and get export counseling through this site. The FAQ section has many links to more information for exporters and importers. The ITA conducts analytical studies of individual industries and of foreign countries. The huge site has many industry and gross domestic products statistics. All of the agency and related Web sites comprising the large DOC organization are globally searchable from this DOC site, including the Economic and Statistics Administration. Besides national trade and industry statistics, find state and local trade data and links to key foreign country data sources. A Spanish version of the site is also available.

International Trade Considerations: http://www.wiuec.org/workshops/inttrade/index.html (accessed Spring 2009).

Developed by the Western Illinois Entrepreneurship Center, this well-organized site will help business owners or managers develop an Import/Export Plan, identify partners, complete market research, and learn about legal, licensing, and cultural issues, as well as costs of doing business internationally. Use this site to organize your research and identify the questions you need to have answered.

National Association of Export Companies (NEXCO): http://nexco.org (accessed Spring 2009).

Dedicated to empowering small to mid-sized companies to build their global commerce efficiently and effectively, this group was founded in 1965. It is a forum for networking, business solutions, and advocacy through its Global Business Roundtable program and sponsors online conferences and an annual trade mission. Its Web site links directly to a comprehensive searchable database maintained by the Federation of International Trade Associations (FITA).

New York Public Library, International Trade Research Guide: http://www.nypl .org/research/sibl/trade/trade.html (accessed Spring 2009).

This wonderful guide produced by the Science, Industry and Business Library (SIBL) will provide invaluable information in learning how to conduct business between the United States and another country. Guides, business directories, periodicals, and trade statistic sources can be located through this large and practical site. It is well organized and easy to navigate; find information grouped under market research, trade leads, shipping and logistics, and cross-cultural business communication.

Quick MBA: http://www.quickmba.com/entre/bplan/ (accessed Spring 2009).

For those new to business plans and SWOT analysis, this site is thorough and practical. Learn the basics of both these concepts and many more here. Management and marketing articles are useful and helpful to new owners and managers as well as experienced ones. A Political, Economic, Social, Technical (PEST) analysis is presented, why to use it, and how it relates to SWOT. Often articles include recommended readings.

RMA Universe: http://www.rmahq.org/RMA/ (accessed Spring 2009).

After 85 years in the business, Robert Morris and Associates no longer produces the RMA Annual Statement Studies. The name of the association is now Risk Management Association. *RMA Annual Statement Studies* are one of the standards in business ratios. This resource will help you show investors that you understand your business and are prepared to compete. Financial ratio benchmarks are included for over 700 industries, now using the NAICS codes. Trend data are available for five years. Using these data, you can make more informed decisions for your new business.

SBDCNET: http://sbdcnet.utsa.edu (accessed Spring 2009).

The Small Business Development Center National Information Clearinghouse provides timely, Web-based information to entrepreneurs. Small Business Development Centers (SBDC) are located in all 50 states. SBDCs offer free, confidential business counseling. This Web site provides information on business start-up, e-commerce, industry research, marketing, trends, and more. Entrepreneurs will find plenty of links and information here to help them plan and run their new business.

Service Corps of Retired Executives: http://www.score.org (accessed Spring 2009).

SCORE (Counselors to America's Small Business) is an organization of volunteer members that provides business advice to small businesses throughout the nation. Visiting their Web site, you can receive free counseling via e-mail; ask to have a counselor look at the first draft of your plan. The Business Toolbox provides important links and a template gallery with many templates to help the new business owner with several parts of a good business plan. Like the SBA site, solid business planning help is available here.

Small Business Administration: http://www.sba.gov (accessed Spring 2009).

This official government site offers a wealth of resources and programs for starting and growing a small business. Under Startup Basics, check out the areas you need help with while doing your business planning. Other major sections cover business planning, financing, international trade, managing, marketing, employees, taxes, legal aspects, and business opportunities. Find here online forms, sample business plans, loan information, and many publications. The *Export Library* contains titles such as Breaking into the Trade Game, Export Working Capital Program, Export Financing for Small Businesses, and SBA & Ex-Im Bank Co-Guarantee Program. Some contents are available in Spanish. Also part of the SBA program are the Small Business Development Centers (SBDC) at http://www.sba.gov/sbdc. SBDCs are located in every state and deliver counseling and training for small businesses in the areas of management, marketing, financing, and feasibility studies.

STAT-USA/Internet: http://www.stat-usa.gov/ (accessed Spring 2009).

This service of the U.S. Department of Commerce is a single point of access to authoritative business, trade, and economic information from across the federal government. An important part of this resource is http://www.stat-usa.gov/tradtest.nsf—Obtain current and historical trade-related releases, international market research, trade opportunities, country analysis, and our trade library from the National Trade Data Bank (NTDB). The NTDB (National Trade Data Bank) provides access to Country Commercial Guides, market research reports, best market reports and other programs. USA Trade *Online* provides current and historical import and export statistics for over 18,000 commodities traded worldwide as well as the most current merchandise trade statistics available in a spreadsheet format. The International Trade Library is a comprehensive collection of over 40,000 documents related to international trade. All are full-text searchable, as well as keyword searchable by country or product.

USA.gov: http://www.usa.gov (accessed Spring 2009).

Information by Topic will interest and amaze first-time visitors. Topics include Defense and International, Environment, Energy and Agriculture, Money and Taxes, Reference and General Government, and Science and Technology. Tabs at the top of the page include one for Businesses and Nonprofits, which has a section on International Trade. Clicking on Data and Statistics brings up an alphabetical list of links to resources chock full of statistics. Economic Indicators is the Web site of the Economics and Statistics Administration, part of the U.S. Department of Commerce (http://www.economicindicators.gov), and it provides timely access to the daily releases of key economic indicators from the Bureau of Economic Analysis (BEA) and the Census Bureau. In addition, under Businesses and Nonprofits is a section titled Foreign Businesses Doing Business in the U.S. Under Frequently Asked Foreign Business Questions is a section called Doing Business Abroad. Spanish translation of the site is also available. You can e-mail questions about the site and the statistics or telephone for help too. Your taxes pay for the collection, compiling, and publishing of these statistics, and they are available for your use.

U.S. Census Bureau: http://www.census.gov (accessed Spring 2009).

This Web page is the best place to start searching for the multitude of data produced by census programs, publications, and statistics. The home page groups the data under Census 2000, People, Business, Geography, Newsroom, At the Bureau, and Special Topics. Under Business, you can click on the Foreign Trade, Economic Census, NAICS, E-Stats, and Survey of Business Owners. Under Foreign Trade, learn directly from the Census Bureau how to properly classify your products for export and how to file your Shipper's Export Declaration online. The Bureau also processes, tabulates, and releases the data collected by the Bureau of Customs and Border Protection on exports and imports of goods in their International Data Base. Here you will find U.S. export and import statistics by commodity, country, customs district, and method of transportation providing value and quantity on a monthly, year-to-date, and annual history basis. U.S. state export data and port statistics for imports and exports are also available. The Catalog, a Search feature, and links to related sites are also accessible on the left side of the home page. Use this site frequently to help start and grow your business.

Valuation Resources.com: http://www.valuationresources.com (accessed Spring 2009).

This commercial site provides links to many industry information resources for over 250 industries. It pulls together industry resources from trade associations, industry publications and research firms. Topics also included are industry outlook, financial ratios, salary surveys, economic data, and public market data. Check here to see what information is available on your industry. Also find Trade Association directories and information here.

VIBES: Virtual International Business and Economic Sources: http://library .uncc.edu/display/?dept=reference&format=open&page=68 (accessed Spring 2009).

The more than 1,600 links to free sources of information at this site were selected by Jeanie Welch of the University of North Carolina Charlotte. The table of contents breaks the sites into three groups: Comprehensive, Regional, and National. The Comprehensive section organizes its links by category, including Banking and Finance, Business Practices and Company Information, Emerging Markets, and International Trade Law. Research and tables and graphs are highlights of this site. The Regional section allows searching devoted to a single region or continent such as Europe or the Middle East. The National section links to sites devoted to a particular country.

WebSite 101 (Expanding Your Business to the Web): http://website101.com (accessed Spring 2009).

This huge, helpful site has a large collection of articles entitled Business Planning Articles for Entrepreneurs. Two very useful articles are on common business plan mistakes. WebSite 101 takes surveys of its users and other groups, tallies results, and presents them on the Web site; they also collect surveys with results from other researchers and present them. This site is very dynamic and contains a wide variety of practical realistic data. Free, online tutorials are also available here. Besides their own tutorials, they link to other huge tutorial sites. Learn to write a business plan step-by-step, to use software like Frontpage or MSOffice, to buy health insurance, and how to buy and sell on eBay. Some of the sites offer one or two free tutorials and then want you to purchase books, more classes, or advanced instruction; as always, buyer beware.

Yahoo! Small Business Resources: http://smallbusiness.yahoo.com (accessed Spring 2009).

Under Getting Started on the far right hand side of this large site, the section on Business Plans is full of good links to articles on the basics, the risks, the need for updating, the financials, and the importance of a good Executive Summary. Special guidance is presented for home-based businesses and e-businesses, which are very popular today. The site is fully searchable and the listing of new articles covers a wide range of relevant information including, for example, hiring an e-mail marketing firm and choosing a Web host. And, in fact, Yahoo presents a whole section on e-commerce and the many decisions involved in setting up a store online. This useful large site is a good place to start learning about planning your new business.

6

Entering the World of International
Selling or Franchising

Chapter Highlights:
  Cross-Cultural Business Communication
  Preparing for Your First International Trip
  Greetings and Business Cards
  Barriers to Cross-Cultural Communications
      Language
      Interpreters and Translators
      Context of Cultures
      Gift Giving
      Humor
      Obtain Proper Documentation
  International Franchising
      Types of Franchises
      Uniform Franchise Offering Circular
      Understand before You Sign International Franchise Agreements
      Researching Franchise Opportunities

Companies must be aware of basic business practices that are essential to successful international selling. We all realize cultures vary, and there is no single code by which one conducts business worldwide. This chapter provides guidance on what you need to know to establish effective working relationships with businesspeople all over the globe and provides a brief introduction to the world of international franchises. Good business practices, however, transcend culture barriers and will help you conduct business overseas.

- Keep promises. One of the most frequent complaints from foreign importers and exporters about U.S. suppliers is failure to ship when promised. Your first order is particularly important as it shapes the customer's image of your firm as a dependable or undependable supplier or partner.
- Be polite, courteous, and friendly. Avoid undue familiarity or slang.
- Be flexible in your approach to international sales and do not make the mistake of forcing your U.S.-made product on an overseas market. Respond to the needs of the local market.
- Work on building and maintaining a good working relationship with the overseas customers, representative, or distributor. Keep foreign customers and contacts informed of all company changes, especially prices, personnel, addresses, e-mails, and phone numbers. Often monthly or quarterly visits to foreign customers will ensure your company and products maintain high visibility in the marketplace. If visits are impossible, at least use fax, e-mail, or telephone communications to keep the relationship active and up to date.
- Adapt to overseas customs when you build relationships globally and you will exceed your international business and social expectations. Understand that wrist watches are often worn for jewelry purposes as time has little meaning. In Hispanic countries, the Spanish word "mañana" literally means tomorrow or morning, but in everyday business languages it simply means "not today."

CROSS-CULTURAL BUSINESS COMMUNICATION

Globalization as described by Thomas L. Friedman in his book, *The Lexus and the Olive Tree* (Farrer, Straus, & Giraus, 2000), is a "dynamic, ongoing process that involves the integration of markets, nation-states, and technologies . . . enabling individuals and corporations to reach around the world farther, faster, deeper, and cheaper than ever before." Because globalization, therefore, is an ongoing, continuous process, the twenty-first century global marketplace offers many opportunities for international business expansion. These opportunities also come with a variety of intercultural communication challenges that businesspeople must comprehend in order to succeed. A variety of books, journals, and electronic databases are available that deal with the topics of international business communication and practices as well as current global business and economic conditions. These resources offer a foundation of information that will help prepare today's businessperson for the communication challenges of the multinational business community.

Every national government has an office of protocol because the observance of protocol standards is so important to developing lasting relationships between nations and similarly businesses from difference nations or cultures. Cultural differences and protocols must not be overlooked. The Appendix of this book will lead users to interesting and valuable information about foreign countries and regions with details about conducting business in cultures different from your own. The following sections will help you start thinking about many different issues involved and motivate you to seek more information to prepare yourself and your business to effectively enter the international marketplace.

PREPARING FOR YOUR FIRST INTERNATIONAL TRIP

Besides practical travel arrangements, business proposals, and financial data, take time to familiarize yourself with your destination's culture, local business practices, local customs, gift exchange practices, and dining protocols to make yourself look and sound like a professional international businessperson. Do your homework and you are more likely to succeed. Learn a few words in the language of the country or countries you will be visiting. You can learn some of the basics of a language much quicker than you think with today's courses for business executives.

GREETINGS AND BUSINESS CARDS

The handshake is quickly becoming a universal form of greeting around the world. In some cultures, however, the handshake may precede or follow a local custom, such as the bow in several Asian cultures. Gestures can be tricky as what is fine in one place may be extremely volatile and rude in another. Lack of awareness concerning the country's accepted form of greeting can also lead to awkward encounters. Proper use of names and titles is often a source of confusion in international business meetings. Learn what is proper in the countries you will be visiting. Formality is essential. Use titles correctly and honor formality. People from around the globe repeatedly mention that the casual American leap to first names is one of the most startling behaviors they encounter. The move from formal to informal is not automatic, and you must wait to be invited to use a person's first name. Eye contact is another tricky cultural norm, it can be considered disrespectful or challenging in Africa and Asia. Distribute business cards freely. However, you must remember that in some parts of the world, a business card is known as a name card and the emphasis is placed on the person. Always turn the card so the person receiving it does not have to turn it around to read it. Depending on how often and how long you visit one country or culture, you may want to have your business cards printed on the reverse side in the language and with the alphabet of that country. This simple act will facilitate introductions, will show respect for the people you meet, and will establish you as knowledgeable and courteous. If you do have your cards translated, use a professional translation organization and, if possible, have the translation confirmed by your in-country contacts (more on this below). Present the appropriate language side based on the primary language of the person receiving the card. Always look carefully at a card presented to you and at the person giving it to you. Receive cards with both hands, as if you were handling a precious object and present yours that way. Remember, it is a name card in many countries, and it is about a person, not about business. Writing on a business card may offend people in some countries, especially during a meeting.

BARRIERS TO CROSS-CULTURAL COMMUNICATIONS

Some cultural distinctions that U.S. companies often face include differences in business styles, attitudes toward development of business relationships, language, negotiating styles, attitudes concerning punctuality, context of cultures, gift-giving customs, significance of gestures, meanings of colors and numbers, and customs regarding titles.

1. **Language.** Keep in mind that English, though accepted as the international language of business, is still a second language for most of the world's population. You cannot assume that everyone who speaks English understands it the same way our own people in our hometown do. Beginning at birth, we each learn a set of symbols, meanings, and rules that constitutes our mother tongue. This original language is fully integrated into our beings, so much so that no matter how many languages you learn, you will automatically revert to your mother tongue to count, dream, and swear. Chinese ranks number one as a mother tongue. Language is more than a useful way to send and receive messages; it shapes our ideas, organizes our thinking and world view, and reveals what is important in a given culture. Because common understandings are not always shared, and to improve your chances of being understood correctly, speak a bit more slowly and try not to use colloquialisms, idioms, or acronyms. In addition, watch any body language signs that indicate you are being difficult to understand. Always remember to ask if there are questions or if you can clarify anything.

2. **Interpreters and Translators.** Closely related to language is the use of interpreters and/or translators. Some interpreters interpret consecutively and some simultaneously; you must be clear on what you need or want. Consecutive interpreting takes more time but is more cost effective. Long presentations will often require a second interpreter to allow for rest breaks. Even though clients may speak English, they often prefer to conduct business discussions in their own language. It is critical to have an interpreter when you are negotiating a business deal. An interpreter is crucial when it comes to drawing up a contract to ensure all parties have the same understanding of the agreement. Translators deal with the written word. One place to check, if you need an interpreter or translator, is the American Translators Association (ATA) at http://www.atanet.org/. Find more information about the ATA in the resources list.

3. **Context of Cultures.** A low-context culture is one in which information is usually explicitly conveyed through very specific exchanges and the written word is highly valued. Written agreements are considered binding. In low-context cultures, such as German, Swiss, or Scandinavian, it is essential to keep the focus of a business meeting strictly on the subject at hand. Conversely, information is conveyed implicitly in high-context cultures such as Japanese, Arab, or Mexican. The written word is de-emphasized and conversations appearing to say one thing on the surface may have quite another underlying meaning. Agreements based on personal relationships are much more binding than anything in writing. High-context cultures conduct business in what appears to be a much more social setting. Keep in mind that even in these casual surroundings, the development of trust is still essential to consummate business agreements. In low-context cultures, demonstrate an efficient use of time, and in high-context cultures, work on developing a personal relationship and trust.

4. **Gift Giving.** Giving and receiving gifts are integral parts of doing business. Customs vary greatly around the world. In some cultures, gifts are expected and failure to present them is an insult, whereas in other countries offering a gift is offensive. One key consideration is to not outspend your host! Gifts should be appropriate and not excessive. Tasteful items with the company logo on them work well in most places. Generally, gift giving is an important part of doing business in Japan where gifts are usually exchanged at the first meeting, but gifts are not the normal custom in Germany, Belgium, or the United States and may be considered inappropriate. Gifts can express hope that a new endeavor and relationship will go well, celebrate a success achieved, or express appreciation for hospitality and assistance provided, for example. Avoid a faux pas by researching undesirable symbolism. Like everything else, gift giving is shaped by tradition, culture, and personal attitudes. Issues with gifts include the color of the gift and/or wrapping paper or how the gift is wrapped, types and colors of flowers, and number of items given, as certain numbers in various countries have specific meanings. Two good gifts to consider are good quality pens and books. Learn how to graciously accept a gift too.

5. **Humor.** Humor often helps others feel at ease but it is another dangerous area when you are a foreign visitor. Do not tell jokes to foreigners when the humor may depend on having more knowledge of English than they might possess; i.e., double meanings can go very wrong. Once again, be sure to have some knowledge of culturally sensitive issues to avoid offending someone when your intention is the opposite.

6. **Obtain Proper Documentation.** You need proper documentation when traveling internationally. Check to be sure you have a valid passport. Check the U.S. State Department Web site http://travel.state.gov/travel/cis_pa_tw/cis/cis_1765.html to see if a Visa and/or immunizations are needed. An international driver's license is not essential but it can be an asset. To obtain the license, contact your local American Automobile Association (AAA) Motor Club for requirements (http://www.aaa.com/vacation/idpf.html). Finally, if

you plan to bring product samples or promotional materials, customs officials from other countries are concerned that you will leave foreign merchandise in their country without paying the proper duties. To avoid cash or bond payments, obtain a Carnet or special letter that guarantees payment of duties if the merchandise is left in the country. A Carnet is written to cover a set period of time and specific items. Find out more and apply for a Carnet at the U.S. Council for International Business's Web site at http://www.uscib.org/index.asp?documentID=718.

General Global Rules of Thumb

- You will never go wrong with a smile as it is always welcome.
- Avoid gestures of all kinds if at all possible as they are so easy to misconstrue.
- Do not make physical contact beyond a handshake. Generally, other cultures are more formal than the United States.
- Be ready for variations in personal space.
- Listen at least as much as you talk. Always be punctual.
- Assume the best about people and their actions. Do not be impatient and try to build trust and a long-term relationship.
- Slow down. Adjust your pace and speak lower and slower than you usually do.
- One of the easiest ways to differentiate yourself is to send a prompt, simple thank-you note for a gift, a dinner, or some extended kindness as people the world over remember the thanks they receive.
- Respect other cultures. People around the world admire our openness, our optimism, our creativity, and our independent spirit, but remember that the American way is not the only way.

The key to conducting business overseas and transcending cultural barriers is careful planning before you depart. Research and organization before you begin your overseas business venture will prove invaluable. Read some of the books and visit some of the Web resources listed at the end of the chapter for assistance.

INTERNATIONAL FRANCHISING

Perhaps you believe you do not have the experience or training necessary to start an international business from scratch or expand your current one overseas, but you still want to get into international selling. Consider buying a franchise. According to the Small Business Administration, franchise systems exist in over 200 industries with more than 1,200 franchise systems available for purchase by franchise in more than 160 countries. Estimates by the International Franchise Association are that total sales by franchised businesses will reach over $2 trillion in 2008 and a new franchise business opens every 8 minutes of every business day.

A franchise is not a separate type of small business entity. A franchise is a contractual licensing and distribution arrangement between two businesses, in which the franchiser, the owner of a business concept, gives the franchisee, another business person, the right to own and operate a business based on that concept. In fact, you are utilizing another's established business idea and plan. Franchisees borrow from another company's success and pay for their experience. However, though franchisees rarely go bankrupt and are found in nearly every industry in the United States and globally, in various sizes and requiring varying amounts of financial investment, be sure to do your market research. Refer to Chapter 3. Franchising is very popular and continues to expand, but market research for the place or country you are considering is essential.

The most important element in any international import is uniqueness. The Body Shop out of England pioneered the U.S. franchise market for bath products and toiletries while the Aussie Pet Mobile introduced mobile pet grooming franchises. Beard Papa seems to be entering the U.S. West coast as the first cream puff franchise and Oh Crepe is starting in California with sweet and savory crepes. Howard Schultz, CEO of Starbucks, needed to travel to Milan's espresso bars to understand European coffee service while today the Internet brings the world's fastest growing franchisors to our fingertips. According to Entrepreneur.com (www.entrepreneur.com), the Top Global Franchises in 2008 include Subway, KFC Corp., McDonald's, Curves, and UPS Store or Mail Boxes Etc.

The three major reasons franchisees do fail are lack of planning and research, under capitalization, and absentee ownership. Earlier in this chapter cultural differences, which too are very important when considering an international franchise, and how to discern them were discussed. Travel to the location is also essential before a contract is signed, and I list what to consider and why cultural differences need research too. Entrepreneur.com contains a really good article on Buying a Foreign-Based Franchise, by Jeff Elgin that will prove enlightening. See the description of Entrepreneur.com in the resources to see how useful it can be when expanding your business into the international arena.

Types of Franchises

Two main types of franchise operations exist generally for domestic and international franchises. The first one is the "Entire Business Format (EBF)," or turnkey package, where the franchiser grants the franchisee a license to use the logos, trademarks, business know-how, copyrights, trade secrets, standard operating procedures, purchasing power, and the like of the franchiser. The franchisee must pay a franchise fee plus start-up costs, ongoing royalty fees, and operating expenses (inventory, rent, and so forth). The franchiser provides site selection assistance, job training, an operating manual, and advice on marketing, management, personnel, and finance issues. Some

franchisers offer workshops, newsletters, an 800 telephone number for technical assistance, and other services. Popular franchises using this format include McDonald's, Blockbuster Video, Jenny Craig International, Midas International, and Berlitz International.

The second type of franchise is the "Product and Trade-Name Franchise," which involves the distribution of a product through a dealer. This franchise is limited to selling only the products included but does utilize the recognition and notoriety accompanying the franchise name and history. Some other support services may be offered the franchisee. Popular names in this group are Pepsi, Exxon, and Ford Motor Company. In the end, franchising is a relationship business with franchiser, customers, other franchisees, suppliers, attorneys, bankers, and family.

Uniform Franchise Offering Circular

For domestic franchises, some of which offer international locations, the exact services franchisees receive are described in the Uniform Franchise Offering Circular (UFOC). Under the Federal Trade Commission (FTC) Franchising and Business Opportunity Ventures Trade Regulation Rules, known as the "FTC rules," franchisers must provide franchisees with full disclosure of all the information they need to make an informed and rational decision about purchasing the franchise in a document called the UFOC. Under the FTC rules, franchisers must supply the complete franchise agreement at least five days before the franchisee signs any forms or issues any money. The terms in this document are uniform and nonnegotiable. Read and understand it thoroughly.

The UFOC contains 23 items of information about the franchise. Key points to identify include when was the company founded and date of incorporation, franchise fees, litigation history, renewal dates, start-up costs, earnings claims, territory rights, and grounds for termination. Much of this same information will be in the Franchise Agreement, but you may want to know these things before you even consider this franchise. Jane Applegate, in *The Entrepreneur's Desk Reference*, lists eight key questions that the franchisees needs to know, such as what are the fees, is the territory you are buying exclusive, can the franchiser bypass the franchisee's outlet, what happens if the franchiser merges with another business, what are the online issues, exactly what training and support are provided, does the franchise sponsor an association of franchisees, and what happens if you die, become disabled, or you want out of the franchise agreement? Be clear about what you want from a franchise before you make any commitments. The citation and description for Applegate's book is listed here:

Applegate, Jane. *The Entrepreneur's Desk Reference*. Bloomberg Press, 2003. 399p. ISBN 1-5766-0086-6.

This easy-to-use guide is an alphabetical compilation of answers, solutions, advice, and ideas for small business owner or managers, covering over 300 topics from the basics like accounting, taxes, marketing, and networking to more advanced concepts like buyout contracts, joint ventures, and employee benefits and problems. Applegate, one of the United States' top small business experts, provides a comprehensive guide which small and medium-sized business owners will refer to often.

If you are buying an international franchise, you will want to be sure that you check the points listed in a UFOC even if the international franchiser is not required to file this document. Get a copy of the franchiser's disclosure document and make sure you understand all of the provisions. Get a clarification or answer to any concerns before you invest. If the agreement is in a foreign language, you will, of course, enlist the aid of a professional translator so you thoroughly understand every detail of the agreement. Disclosure documents should identify the executives of the franchise system and describe their prior experience. Consider how long they have been with the company because investing with an experienced franchiser is usually a safer path to success. The disclosure documents should also report if the franchiser or any of its executives have been convicted of felonies involving fraud or unfair or deceptive practices or are subject to state or federal injunctions involving similar misconduct. Civil actions involving the franchise relationship should also be listed. Financial stability and general business acumen would also be affected by any report of a bankruptcy. Costs, restrictions, and terminations should all be covered as well as training and other assistance. Finally and very important are the names and addresses of current franchisees and franchisees who have left the system within the last year, especially in the country where you are thinking of opening the franchise. Meeting and talking with current and former franchisees is often a reliable way to verify the franchiser claims. Prepare a list of questions and visit several locations if possible. An excellent book to help you prepare for buying a franchise is *Street Smart Franchising* by Joe Mathews, et al., which has many worksheets and checklists to help the new franchisee. See more on this book in the resources list.

Understand before You Sign International Franchise Agreements

Discover and understand the advantages and disadvantages of the typical international franchising arrangements. The most common method employed by domestic U.S. franchisers expanding overseas is "master franchising," wherein the franchiser grants a foreign party the right to establish itself and operate franchised outlets and to license others to do so as well. Direct franchising, wherein the franchiser directly grants to a franchisee the right to operate a franchised outlet, is also used but is typically limited to cases where the franchisee is located in a country geographically close to the United States and where the culture and legal system of the country is similar to that of the United States. Joint ventures are also used, as are various types of licensing and distribution arrangements.

Obviously, numerous legal and business issues present themselves during the course of buying a franchise to operate overseas. To begin such a process and to become more familiar with current events and trends in international franchising, use information from or contact the International Franchise Association at http://www.franchise.org or the American Bar Association's Forum on Franchising at http://www.abanet.org/forums/franchising/home.html. Employ a translator and/or a lawyer whenever you have the slightest bit of doubt about the negotiations or any written agreements or contracts.

Researching Franchise Opportunities

Another outstanding resource for entrepreneurs and new franchisees to begin their research is Franchising: Franchise411 at http://www.franchise 411.com. Franchise411 is the Internet home of Franchise Profiles and Franchise Profiles International. This online library and resources center will help you understand what franchising is and how to take advantage of everything it has to offer. Find here a thorough explanation of UFOCs, the FTC's rules, state registration information, and international franchising. Links to dozens of sites presenting franchise opportunities in the United States and internationally are included, though some need updating. Articles on franchise ratings, franchise politics, global franchising ins and outs, and more are included.

However, the FTC does not require that franchisers register with the Commission in order to conduct business. Some states impose registration rules; check with your Secretary of State office for requirements in your state. States usually grant or deny a franchiser the right to franchise its operations in their state. This state approval only means the state could not find any reason to refuse the franchiser's application. In foreign countries, the requirements for franchises vary even more. Check out the company you are working with as closely as possible in its home country or the country you will be running the franchise in.

Because buying a franchise involves considerable risk on your part, you will want to research a franchise opportunity thoroughly. In order to talk to many different franchisers and industry experts in one location, attend a franchise trade show or exposition. These shows often offer workshops and seminars to teach you about the industry and explore its advantages and disadvantages. Some exhibitors may use hard-sell tactics so it is probably worth your time to do some preliminary investigation before attending one of these shows. Develop a budget or investment range and some business goals. At the show, comparison shop for opportunities that meet the criteria you have developed. Remember you are just investigating possibilities and will need to do a great deal more research before coming to a decision and selecting a franchise to purchase.

Your local chamber of commerce may be aware of trade shows coming to your area or state. Another place to check is FranchiseHandbook.com (http://www.franchise1.com). This site lists shows by date and covers the world. Shows are sponsored by different vendors so if you have several franchises you want to research, see if they will be exhibiting at the show you are thinking of attending. Research beforehand can always save you time and money.

Franchising is a relatively quick, safe way to participate in the new global economy. Find the one that suits your budget, lifestyle, and business needs.

REFERENCES

(Starred titles discussed in the chapter)

Print Resources

Acuff, Frank L. *How to Negotiate Anything with Anyone Anywhere Around the World.* 3rd ed. Amacom, 2008. 307p. ISBN 0-8144-8066-7. $21.95.

This new edition of an established guide to negotiation provides readers with advice on best business practices, transactions, and attitudes throughout the world. Now including 63 countries, topics like foreign outsourcing, multicultural work teams, business entertainment guidelines, and even some factors involved in regional sensitivities are covered thoroughly. Organized by region, this book delivers detailed business profiles of each country with fast facts on monetary units, principal imports and exports, population, cities, language, and religion. Based on his knowledge of local business practices worldwide and familiarity with difference cultures and national psychologies, Acuff uses examples, statistics, and basic guidelines to help businesspeople from the United States negotiate and reduce friction and misunderstandings abroad.

**Applegate, Jane. *Entrepreneur's Desk Reference.* Bloomberg Press, 2003. 399p. ISBN 1-5766-0086-6. $24.95.

This compact guide is an alphabetical compilation of answers, solutions, advice, and ideas for small business owners or managers, covering over 300 topics from the basics like accounting, taxes, management, and networking to more advanced concepts like evaluating a business, partnerships, and human resource issues and so forth. Applegate, one of the U.S.'s top small business experts, provides a comprehensive guide that provides answers to many business problems and challenges.

Bond, Robert E. *Bond's Top 100 Franchises 2008.* 4th ed. Source Book Publications, 2007. 384p. ISBN 1-887137-61-0. $19.95.

Profiles of franchises supply a description of the business with number of operating units and geographic distribution; capital requirements including initial investment and total investment; detailed space needs and staffing levels; initial training and start-up assistance detailed as well as ongoing support; evaluation statements from current franchisees; and specific areas of geographic expansion. His criterion for ranking franchises includes historical performance, competitive advantage, franchisee satisfaction, and financial stability. This directory is one of the first places a prospective franchise buyer should search.

Bosrock, Mary Murray. *European Business Customs & Manners: A Country-by-Country Guide.* Meadowbrook Press (S&S), 2006. 481p. ISBN 0-684-04001-8. $16.00.

This readable comprehensive guide is organized by country and covers all the do's and don'ts of business etiquette. Bosrock covers an amazing array of information on situations businesspeople might encounter, including business attitudes and practices, meetings, negotiations, meals, punctuality, language, gestures, tipping, manners, and gifts. Learn how to avoid unrealistic expectations. This essential tool for anyone entering the international market helps you understand and respect the uniqueness of customers, clients, and employees; success in business around the globe depends on cultural sensitivity.

Clifton, Daphne. *Franchising: Making Franchising Work for You . . . Without Breaking the Bank.* A & C Black, 2007. 128p. ISBN 0-7136-7543-8. $12.95.

Franchising is a popular option for those who want to run their own business but are not sure where to start. Franchising gives you the benefits of branding and reputation of an established enterprise, especially valuable when working in a foreign country, but lets you strike out on your own. Clifton covers issues like understanding the pros and cons, watching costs, finding a potential franchise, understanding the importance of the franchise agreement, and knowing what to do when things go wrong. This title is practical and useful for first-time business owners or entrepreneurs.

deBono, Silvio, et al. *Managing Cultural Diversity.* Meyer & Meyer Sport, Ltd., 2008. 250p. ISBN 1-84126-239-0. $34.00.

Practical and interactive, this manual examines the way teams work, how people are managed in various types of organizations, and how we can understand the impact of organizational and national cultures on day-to-day work. The authors cover a wide range of topics including team dynamics, managing human resources, and managing intercultural diversity. A slight British slant is worth noting for U.S. readers.

Denslow, Lanie, and Nadler, Mary. *World Wise: What To Know Before You Go.* Fairchild Books & Visuals, 2005. 342p. ISBN 1-56367-3592. $31.50.

Written for newcomers and seasoned professionals, Denslow's book is chock full of practical advice on establishing effective working relationships with business people all over the world. Be aware and put into practice the cultural nuances of the host country in which you plan to do business, and you are more likely to have a successful outcome. Brief histories are given for each region of the world and the discussions of trade agreements like the General Agreement on Tariffs and Trade (GATT; now the World Trade Organization) and North American Free Trade Agreement (NAFTA) are also very useful. The cartoons representing the lighter view of global business communications are delightful as well.

Dorsey, Jennifer. *Start Your Own Import/Export Business.* 2nd ed. Entrepreneur Press, 2007. 252p. ISBN 1-59918-108-8. $15.95.

This book contains insights and practical advice for entering global markets. It covers aspects of the start-up process, including collecting money from overseas transactions, using the Internet to simplify your transactions, accessing trade law information to keep your business in compliance, finding contacts in the United States and abroad, using the Internet to simplify your transactions, and choosing a customs broker. Chapters on market research, working online, employees, pricing, and insurance will help run a business efficiently and effectively. A brief appendix on international trade resources may also prove useful. Interviews with successful importers and exporters and an updated resource list will help show the way to success.

Europa World Year Book. Annual. Routledge, Taylor & Francis. 2 v.

This well-respected annual provides a great deal of detailed information on the political, economic, and commercial institutions of the world. Each country is covered by an individual chapter composed of an introductory survey that includes recent history, economic affairs, government, and defense; followed by data on social welfare, finance, telecommunications, trade and industry, utilities, and education. Now also an online product, a free trial electronic subscription is available from the Europa World Web site at http://www .europaworld.com

Exporters' Encyclopaedia. Annual. Dun & Bradstreet.

This comprehensive world reference guide is divided into 220 country-specific sections; firms specializing in international business, laws, and legislation; international trade associations; government agencies; shipping practice; and reference data on weights and measures for overseas ports. Find key contacts, trade and safety regulations, and information on documentation needed. Marketing Data includes legal requirements for importer or agents, procurement standards, environmental protection or pollution control, marking, and labeling. The encyclopedia also provides passport regulations and business etiquette guidelines.

Gesteland, Richard R. *Cross-Cultural Business Behavior.* 4th ed. Copenhagen Business School Press, 2005. 351p. ISBN 8-763-00149-7. $44.49.

This classic compendium of cross-cultural theories is a practical guide for businesspeople on the front lines of global trade. The first section presents the knowledge needed to understand the how-to sections and case studies. Gesteland strives to reduce the confusion and unpredictability of cultural differences by classifying international business customs and practices into logical patterns. Part Two of the book is made up of about 40 negotiator profiles, which are thumbnail sketches of the negotiating behavior a traveler should expect to encounter in the markets covered.

Gundling, Ernest. *Working GlobeSmart: 12 People Skills for Doing Business Across Borders.* Davies-Black Publishing, 2003. 288p. ISBN 0-89-106177-0. $29.95.

Gundling aims to help readers build their global "people skills," because as he believes doing business across borders can be tricky. Cross-border friction is usually caused by underlying cultural difficulties, and in his dense, detailed book he uses anecdotes to help readers understand how to handle a wide variety of situations. At the end of each chapter, Gundling lists a summary and review questions to help the reader think about and apply the skills he just covered. Learn how to establish credibility, obtain information, build a global team, and more. Numerous charts, tables, and appendices are included as well as chapter notes and a bibliography. Find practical, skills-based advice here for developing competence in global negotiations at the organizational and interpersonal levels.

Hinkelman, Edward, et al. *Importers Manual*. Annual. World Trade Press.

Information on how to import virtually any commodity into the United States can be found in this practical reference. It is precisely organized for ease of use and is divided into the major sections of Commodity Index; U.S. Customs Entry and Clearance; International Banking; Legal Considerations of Importing; and Packing, Shipping, and Insurance. The heart of the work, the Commodity Index, contains entry procedures, documentation, restrictions, and prohibitions, marking and labeling requirements, and contact information for regulatory agencies for all products that can be imported into the United States.

Jagoe, John R. *Export Sales and Marketing Manual 2008: The Bible of Exporting*. Annual. Export Institute of the United States. 520p. ISBN 0-943677-66-1. $295.

Having been updated annually for 21 consecutive years, this international trade publication has achieved longevity and global reach. This manual covers all the steps involved in selling products in world markets. Over 120 illustrations, 85 graphs, 40 flow charts, and 60 sample international trade documents lead the user through the process. Jagoe helps users conduct market research through 1200 Web site addresses providing information on various markets and products or services. A lengthy glossary of export terms and detailed index for quick access to important information is also provided.

Keup, Erwin J. *Franchise Bible: How to Buy a Franchise or Franchise Your Business*. 5th ed. McGraw-Hill, 2004. 288p. ISBN 1-932156-62-3. $22.95.

Franchise lawyer Keup explains how to assess your suitability for running a franchise, investigate franchisers, interview existing franchisees, and understand the legal terms and documents associated with franchising. The checklists and worksheets Keup has prepared will be useful to readers as well. The Appendices contain sample franchise documents for Uniform Franchise Offering Circulars, franchise agreements, background data for circulars and agreements, state franchise information guidelines for many states, and UFOC guidelines. The second half of Keup's book tells readers how to franchise their business, but this section is also of interest to new franchisees.

Levonsky, Rieva, and Conley, Maria Anton. *Ultimate Book of Franchises*. Entrepreneur Press, 2004. 540p. ISBN 1-9321-5686-0. $23.95.

Over a thousand companies are listed for the prospective franchisee to survey. The authors provide in-depth facts and figures such as company size, financial ratings, training and support provided, qualifications needed to obtain a franchise, and contact information. Practical, how-to advice on buying your first franchise is presented in an easy-to-understand, organized manner.

Lewis, Richard D. *When Cultures Collide: Leading Across Cultures.* Nicholas Brealey, 2006. 590p. ISBN 1-904-838-022. $35.00.

This guide to working and communicating across cultures explains how your culture and language affect the ways in which you think and respond to situations. Lewis not only helps you understand different cultures but also how to manage in different business cultures. He covers the world, including Asian, Arab, and Eastern European countries. He suggests a broad model you can use to characterize different national characteristics and various traits that shape attitudes toward time, leadership, team building, and organizational structure and behaviors. This exceptional book is a good read for anyone who encounters people of other nationalities and cultures.

**Mathews, Joe, et al. *Street Smart Franchising: Read This Before You Buy a Franchise.* Entrepreneur Press, 2006. 234p. ISBN 1-59918-021-9. $19.95.

Packed with case studies, this book reveals personality types that are most likely to succeed at franchising and alert you to character traits that increase the risk of failure. Part One is "What You Need to Know Before You Start Looking" and Part Two is "Investigating Franchises." Expert advice comes from experienced franchisees and franchisors who work in the real world of everyday business plus definitions, questionnaires, checklists, and acronyms. Taking you through the stages of franchising, The Launch, The Grind, Winning, The Zone, and The Goodbye, authors explain what to avoid or improve on during each phase. Find out what to expect from the company, what to look for as you evaluate them, and even what to watch for while they evaluate you. Also provided are franchising Web sites, franchise brokers, franchise expos, and franchise magazines. Use this resource to develop a proven strategy on how to be a successful franchisee.

Mattock, John. *Cross-Cultural Communication: The Essential Guide to International Business.* Rev. 2nd ed. Kogan Page, 2003. 176p. ISBN 0-7494-3922-X. $24.95.

Mattock's work is full of practical suggestions on how to be more sensitive to the cultural issues of others and how to better communicate in the global world of business. He will help you assess your own attitudes and performance as a partner in an international business venture. He fills the book with examples, opinions, and case studies chosen from his work at Canning, a UK-based company that has training and consulting offices in the United Kingdom, Italy, and Japan and holds seminars in 30 other countries on four continents. The Glossary of Offshore English is very useful as you learn what certain words are likely to mean in an English conversation in the global business world. Well-organized and well-written, this fascinating book will help you learn how to get it right, and how to communicate better when working outside your own culture.

Morrison, Terri. *Kiss, Bow, or Shake Hands: The Bestselling Guide to Doing Business in More than 60 Countries.* Adams Media Corp., 2006. 592p. ISBN 1593373686. $24.95.

This encyclopedic resource presents information for each country on the country history, type of government, languages, religions, business practices, titles and forms of address, for 60 countries. A cultural orientation for each country with negotiation strategies and value systems is included. Well-organized and concise, this newly revised guide will make learning to do business in a foreign country easier.

Mullins, John. *The New Business Road Test: What Entrepreneurs and Executives Should Do Before Writing a Business Plan*. Financial Times/Prentice Hall, 2004. 288p. ISBN 0-273-66356-9. $24.95.

Before writing a business plan or investing any money, use Mullins's seven domains model for assessing your new business ideas. Learn how to run a customer-driven feasibility study to assess that new business opportunity. Case studies use real businesses like Honda, Enterprise Car Rental, and Starbucks to illustrate industry trends and opportunities. What are critical success factors and niche markets? Avoid the "me too" trap and more. Use his practical advice and guidance to help your new business succeed.

Murray, Iain. *The Franchising Handbook: The Complete Guide to Choosing a Franchise*. Kogan Page, Ltd., 2006. 256p. ISBN 0-7494-4541-6.

Franchising is increasing in popularity and profitability as individuals are able to enter the market with a proven brand and established business strategy. Per Murray, in 2005 95 percent of all franchisees reported profitability, making it one of the safest ways to start up a business. This guide offers advice on choosing a franchise and uses real-life examples to illustrate strategies, problems, and successes. Also included is an A–Z directory of franchises arranged by each major market sector.

Norman, Jan. *What No One Ever Tells You about Franchising: Real Life Franchising Advice from 101 Successful Franchisors and Franchisees*. Kaplan Pub., 2006. 193p. ISBN 1-4195-0613-7. $18.95.

Norman is an expert in entrepreneurship and gives readers a look at franchising from the trenches. He covers essentials like identifying the right territories, suppliers, and partners; negotiating terms; evaluating the stability of the franchise; identifying hidden costs; and marketing beyond the franchisor. Combining practical techniques with tips and anecdotes, Norman's book is practical and presents the views of successful franchisers, franchisees, and experts.

Rivoli, Pietra. *The Travels of a T-Shirt in the Global Economy: An Economist Examines the Markets, Power, and Politics of World Trade*. Wiley, 2005. 254p. ISBN 0-4716-4849-3. $16.95.

In order to understand how the global economy really works, readers will follow with Professor Rivoli a T-shirt from Texas cotton-growers to Chinese textile sweatshops, and, finally, to an African used-clothing bazaar. Learn how U.S. farmers teamed with government-sponsored researchers and, using subsidies and trade barriers, have come to dominate the world's cotton production. Explore with Rivoli the history, economics, and politics of world trade.

Rodrigues, Carl. *International Management: A Cultural Approach*. 3rd ed. Sage Publications, Inc., 2008. 544p. ISBN 1-4129-5141-8. $70.00

Rodrigues uses an international cross-cultural context to discuss how different national cultures affect all the functions of management (planning, organizing, staffing, coordinating, and controlling). Anecdotes, exercises, and case studies are used to illustrate and apply the information and theories presented.

International enterprises interested in strategic planning in a multicultural context will find this a very useful volume.

Salacuse, Jeswald W. *The Global Negotiator: Making, Managing, and Mending Deals Around the World in the Twenty-First Century*. Palgrave Macmillan, 2003. 312p. ISBN 0-312-29339-9. $39.95.

This unique, outstanding guidebook breaks down the intricacies of international negotiations into understandable segments and provides the tools to ensure success in the creation, management, and remediation of international deals. Salacuse even explains how to deal with negotiations that go wrong, illustrating how deals may falter and methods to save them. Managers, lawyers, executives, and government officials will use this comprehensive guide to understand the transformations global business has experienced in the last decade.

Seid, Michael, and Thomas, Dave. *Franchising for Dummies*. 2nd ed. Wiley Publishing Inc., 2007. 408p. ISBN 0-470-10957-2. $24.99.

A new and revised edition of this friendly, useful guide that outlines in typical fashion the basics, development procedures, running the business, and moving forward. Learn how to choose and run the right franchise, find the ideal location, manage daily operations, and read through a Uniform Franchise Offering Circular or its international equivalent. One highlight of this practical guide is the approach to franchiser or franchisee disagreements. Seid and Thomas, founder of Wendy's International, suggest sitting down with the franchiser, discussing your concerns, and negotiating a way to settle the problem. This edition includes a CD with sample business plans, forms, training, and legal information to help you get started. This book will help new franchisees make the most of the time and money invested in a franchise.

Small Business Sourcebook (SBS). 2v. Thomson Gale, annual. $405.00.

This directory provides a wealth of information for the small business owner or manager. The Small Business Profiles cover 340 different small businesses. Businesses profiled include catering, cooking schools, fish farms, antique shops, bookstores, and car washes for example. Entries contain as many as 17 subheadings, such as start-up information, educational programs, reference works, sources of supply, statistical sources, trade periodicals, trade shows and conventions, consultants, and franchises and business opportunities. The Small Business Topics section covers general ideas such as retailing, service industry, and franchising. Under restaurants, *SBS* lists nearly 200 franchises. The state listings and federal government assistance sections list programs and offices that provide information and support to small businesses. Check your library for this practical, well-organized source.

Spinelli, Jr., Stephen, et al. *Franchising*. Financial Times/Prentice Hall, 2008. 255p. ISBN 0-7686-8206-1. $34.99.

Learn about every step in franchising from assessing a franchise, developing a franchisee or franchiser relationship, and fine tuning the product or service delivery system. Two of the authors are international franchisers, and they are interviewed and explain their success.

Thomas, David C. and Inkson, Kerr. *Cultural Intelligence: People Skills for Global Business.* Berrett-Koehler Pub., Inc., 2004. 222p. ISBN 1-57675-256-9. $19.95.

These two authors help readers develop a mind-set that applies to a number of countries, cultures, and business situations. You will learn a systematic method of approaching the tremendous variety of interactions and challenges faced in competing in the world of international trade. The three steps presented involve learning the fundamental principles of cross-cultural interactions, practicing mindfulness while paying attention to conversational and body language cues, and developing a repertoire of behavioral skills to use in various situations. Learn how to work and live effectively in a world economy.

Travis, Tom. *Doing Business Anywhere: The Essential Guide to Going Global.* John Wiley & Sons, Inc., 2007. 202p. ISBN 0-470-14961-2. $24.95.

Travis presents his six tenets of global trade and illustrates them in the context of real stories of global trade. He emphasizes the importance of international trade to the economic prosperity of all the world's nations. If you want to start a new venture or expand your present one, Travis helps you organize, plan, operate, and execute with a global mind-set. Learn how to navigate conflicting and confusing laws, deal with different cultures, and operate in different countries. He also explains how to leverage the benefits of free trade agreements to set up and operate a competitive and profitable business. Also highlighted is how to protect your brand through patents, copyrights, and trademarks. Security concerns and measures are also discussed. Travis will convince readers that embracing his six tenets is key to "doing business anywhere."

Tuller, Lawrence. *Doing Business Beyond America's Borders: the Dos, Don'ts, and Other Details of Conducting Business in 40 Different Countries.* Entrepreneur Press, 2008. 304p. ISBN 1-59918-257-2. $21.95.

Covering about 40 countries, this book will allow you to find a new world of customers and empower your business to compete with large transnational corporations. Tuller explains critical steps, tactics, and tools that will help your company navigate the international business landscape. Learn about cultural and interrelational anomalies, negotiations, language barriers, and ways to develop strong overseas relationships. Discover the best ways to sell your products overseas, cost-effective means of transportation, ways to find low-cost production materials and labor, and how to deal with cultural anomalies and foreign languages. Worksheets, anecdotes, and illustrative examples are plentiful.

Weiss, Kenneth D. *Building an Import/Export Business.* 4th ed. John Wiley & Sons, Inc., 2008. 320p. ISBN 0-470-18577-5. $19.95.

Weiss, an entrepreneur and international trade consultant, offers tips and instructions for every aspect of an import/export business. Learn how to get started in the post-9/11 import/export landscape. He explains how to take advantage of GATT, WTO, CAFTA, NAFTA, and other trade agreements. Weiss covers all new and updated regulations, laws, and customs and shipping procedures to help ensure that businesses are in compliance with the Transportation Security Administration (TSA), U.S. Customs and Border Protection (CBP), and U.S. Immigration and Customs Enforcement (ICE). Besides helping importers and exporters plan their business expansion, Weiss describes how to research a raw idea and then successfully launch a stable, profitable business operation. Learn how to find suppliers and the importance of foreign travel. Let the real-life examples presented here help you build your export/import business.

Online Resources

American Association of Exporters and Importers (AAEI): http://www.aaei.org/ accessed Spring 2009).

Begun in 1921, this organization "has been the national voice of American business in support of fair and open trade among nations" with its expertise in custom matters and global trade issues. Members include manufacturers, distributors, and retailers as well as organizations serving carriers, banks, freight forwarders, and brokers. The association works with many U.S. government agencies. Access to news and press releases along with additional information is provided at the Web site.

**American Automobile Association (AAA): http://www.aaa.com (accessed Spring 2009).

Find here many travel resources including the international driving permit application. When traveling overseas, carrying an International Driving Permit even if you are not planning to drive should help you communicate with foreign authorities. This permit is a recognizable form of identification that can help you get on your way more quickly.

**American Bar Association's Forum on Franchising: http://www.abanet.org/ forums/franchising/home.html (accessed Spring 2009).

They publish several print books, *Fundamentals of Franchising* (3rd edition) and the *Franchise Desk Book*. These two references may be available in libraries and cover all aspects of franchising, including registration, disclosure, trademark law, antitrust law, and the like. The table of contents of the quarterly journal, *Franchise Law Journal* is available in PDF from the Web page.

**American Translators Association: http://www.atanet.org/ (accessed Spring 2009).

The American Translators Association can help you find the skilled translator or interpreter you need for a competitive edge. First, take a minute to look through the site and learn how to get your job done right the first time. Then, using the searchable online directory of translator and interpreter services, find what or who you need.

BBC News (Country Profiles) http://news.bbc.co.uk/2/hi/country_profiles/ default.stm (accessed Spring 2009).

BBC's full country profiles include a complete guide to history, politics, and economic background for many countries divided into six major regions of the world. Nineteen international organizations are also profiled, including sections on Facts, Leaders, and Issues. The country profiles also are divided into the Overview, Facts, Leaders, and Media. Related Internet links, and the Related

BBC Links are useful also. The timeline of important events for each country also provide practical, relevant information.

**BEOnline: Business and Economics Online: http://www.loc.gov/rr/business/beonline/ (accessed Spring 2009).

Compiled by the Library of Congress Business Reference Services for researchers, this site has, under Subject Lists, a lengthy list of business topics such as associations, business plans (forms), companies by industry, data sets, e-commerce, franchises, economic indicators, and legal resources. If you click on Associations, you will find an Associations Database that includes contacts, descriptions, addresses, and events data for the organizations listed. Over 10,000 business organizations in the United States are listed. Find here a link to the Herb Growing and Marketing Network or the Association of Bridal Consultants. Under the Title listing, you will find Airlines of the Web, America's Business Funding Directory, American Chambers of Commerce Abroad, American City Business Journals, and more.

Be The Boss: http://www.betheboss.com (accessed Spring 2009).

This international site, with Americas, Europe, and Asia, and Australia included, provides a large franchise directory of franchise opportunities. Franchises can be searches by category and/or investment level. Links are also provided to industry publications and business plans for franchises plus a pre-investment checklist and using your 401(k) for buying a franchise. Franchisees searching for an opportunity will find them here on this easy-to-use and well-organized site.

Bison1.com: http://www.bison.com (accessed Spring 2009).

This well-researched and organized site helps would-be franchisees learn about purchasing a franchise, profiles many franchises in a variety of industries, and even provides a franchise self-test. Franchises are grouped alphabetically, by categories, or premium opportunities. Major sections include the Franchise Directory, Featured Franchises, Ultimate Franchise Opportunities, and Franchise Advice and Commentary. Also available is the Franchise Financing Forum, Franchise News Articles, and the Franchise Expo. Subscribers receive premium content. This worthwhile, useful site is sponsored by a variety of advertisers.

BizMove.com: http://www.bizmove.com (accessed Spring 2009).

The International Section of this site is outstanding. Users will find information on developing an Export Strategy, learning how to sell overseas, writing an international business plan, as well as documentation and pricing for international businesses. Forms and questionnaires for business planning, industry analysis, goal setting, and more are provided. Because it is thorough and written in jargon-free language, small companies aspiring to international expansion will find this site useful.

Business Traveller: **http://www.businesstraveller.com (accessed Spring 2009).**

This leading magazine for the frequent business traveler prints 10 editions worldwide and aims to help corporate travelers save money and make their traveling easier. Find here information on destinations, travel products, cultural hints, and promotions from travel businesses. Leisure travel is also covered.

Canada Business Services for Entrepreneurs: http://www.canadabusiness.ca/ (accessed Spring 2009).

Though this site is aimed at Canadian businesses, you will find help and information here for exporting, importing, e-commerce, selling to the Canadian government and more. The entire Exporting section is a wealth of information for small and medium-sized businesses, from writing the export plan to Business Trip Planning for Exporters. The links under E-Business will help you in many phases of starting or expanding your markets in Canada.

Centre for International Trade: http://www.centretrade.com (accessed Spring 2009).

This membership organization hopes to improve, facilitate, and expand international trade. Members include embassies, trade associations, companies, and individuals. Users will find information on national rules and regulations, tariffs, events, and industry news. Trade opportunities, financing assistance, management help, transportation information, and resources on products, services, training, and Web links are also included. Web links to a wide range of useful sites are current and useful.

ChamberFind.com: http://www.chamberfind.com (accessed Spring 2009).

Easily locate U.S. and world chambers of commerce. Daily Chamber of Commerce Industry updates are also available. Coverage of the world varies including great links for some countries and spotty coverage for others.

CIA World Factbook: https://www.cia.gov/cia/publications/factbook/index.html (accessed Spring 2009).

Prepared by the U.S. Central Intelligence Agency (CIA), this resource is a great beginning research point, with its concise country information such as economic, social, and political profiles. Continually updated, demographics, gross domestic product statistics, membership in international organizations, and diplomatic, communication, and transportation information are all provided.

Country Studies: http://lcweb2.loc.gov/frd/cs/ (accessed Spring 2009).

These in-depth country studies and handbooks were prepared by a team of scholars under the direction of the Federal Research Division of the Library of Congress, as sponsored by the U.S. Army. At present, 102 countries and regions are covered, primarily focusing on lesser-known areas of the world or regions in which U.S. forces might be deployed. One word of warning, however: since funding for the country studies was cancelled in 1999, the studies range in date of preparation from 1988 to 1998. However, the Country Profiles also accessible from this site are being updated. The front page of the Profiles lists when they were updated, mostly in 2006 and 2007. Highlights of the individual studies include photographs, historical and economic backgrounds, tables, glossaries, and bibliographies. The site is searchable by topic.

Economist.com: http://www.economist.com (accessed Spring 2009).

Providing excellent coverage of world news, the Economist.com also contains information on world markets, the latest exchange rates, and country and city guides geared to the business traveler. It is the companion site to the print journal *The Economist*. Although much of the site is free and fully searchable, the Economist.com does charge to view archived articles. Other portions of the site are considered to be premium content viewable by subscription only.

Entrepreneur.com: http://www.entrepreneur.com/ (accessed Spring 2009).

Maintained by *Entrepreneur Magazine*, this site supports new businesses, franchisees, and growing companies. Under First Steps, learn how to evaluate your idea and determine if there is a market for your business. Start Up Topics include location, naming your biz, and business structure. Search on "export" and you will find a wealth of information and articles about all areas of import and export topics. Especially strong in franchising and home-based businesses, this site has expert help on a variety of topics including toolkits for specific kinds of businesses like herb farms, bed and breakfasts, and consulting firms. A unique feature is looking at franchises by the training they offer. Also, search franchises by categories like low cost, top global, and fastest growing. A *Franchise Zone* magazine is available and a Franchise Coach. This useful site has information to share for everyone in small and medium-sized businesses.

Euromonitor International: http://www.euromonitor.com/ (accessed Spring 2009).

Euromonitor International offers quality international market intelligence on industries, countries, and consumers. The have some 30 years of experience publishing market reports, business reference books, online information systems, and bespoke consulting projects. Their Web site has a huge article archive with short articles on topics like trends in retail, food prices, brand growth, in various parts of the world. Many articles are on a specific company, country, or product. Complete company profiles and industry reports can be purchased.

ExecutivePlanet.com: http://www.executiveplanet.com/index.php?title=Main_Page (accessed Spring 2009).

This large site has Cultural Quick Tips to help you learn to work in a multicultural environment. Learn how to question and explore your assumptions in your daily life. Try to understand how your assumptions are impacting your interactions with others. Negotiating tactics, business card protocols, pace of business, thinking styles, and business entertaining tips can all be found here. Find conversation tips and topics, the role of compliments, and business dress, as well as social function dress information and more.

The Export Yellow Pages: http://www.exportyellowpages.com (accessed Spring 2009).

The Export Yellow Pages are administered by the Export Trading Company Affairs of the International Trade Administration in partnership with the U.S. Department of Commerce. Containing information on U.S. business products and suppliers, this site is designed to promote and connect SMEs, improve market visibility, help establish international contacts, simplify sales sourcing, and solve language barriers. This site is often used by foreign buyers as a reference tool to find U.S. goods and services. U.S. firms can register their businesses without charge at http://www.myexports.com. In addition, export intermediaries such as freight forwarders, sales agents, and other service companies that help export businesses can register at no charge in the U.S. Trade Assistance Directory. Find trade leads and other resources here in a wide variety of industries. Products and services are offered by over 27,000 U.S. companies. The U.S. Trade Assistance Directory is available online or in print.

Federation of International Trade Associations (FITA): http://fita.org (accessed Spring 2009).

This huge, very useful site covers all areas of importing and exporting. Users will find help with market research, transportation and logistics, documentation, trade finance and currencies, trade law, directories, trade show calendar, and worldwide trade leads. Find links to Export 1001, a user-friendly introduction to the fundamental aspects of exporting, links to practical sites from other countries, importers' directories, a trade information database, and much more. FITA has a China Business Guide and Trade Software, used to manage international trade enterprises. The Business Travel Mini-Portal provides information on low-cost airfares, MedjetAssist, Travel Advisories, Globafone, Currency Converters, and more. This large site is well organized, annotated, and easy to use.

FindAFranchise.com: http://www.findafranchise.com (accessed Spring 2009).

This user-friendly site calls itself "The Internet Franchise Search Engine" and is sponsored by BizQuest. Here users can browse 1,200 franchises, find the hottest or trendiest franchises, find franchises for sale, or search through a wide variety of categories like Children's Franchises, Educational Franchises, or Home Services Franchises. An alphabetical list is also available. Franchise financing information as well as other franchise resources are also provided. A list of Low Cost Franchises is also available. Lots of well-organized balanced information is presented.

Foreign Government Resources on the Web: http://www.lib.umich.edu/govdocs/foreign.html (accessed Spring 2009).

Maintained by the University of Michigan's Documents Center, this Web site provides an extensive collection of foreign government Web sites. Also accessible from the site are country background information, the text of constitutions and treaties, embassy information, and statistics on demographics, economics, health and military. Many of the links are briefly annotated by the documents center's staff. The center also updates the site frequently: the What's New section is updated weekly and provides annotated links to new resources of interest. Use this site to keep current on foreign government information.

Franchise America: http://www.franchiseamerica.com (accessed Spring 2009).

This huge site opens the door to hundreds of franchise opportunities. Find franchises by categories like Automotive Opportunities, B2B Franchises, China Opportunities, eBusiness, Hot Dog Franchises, Outdoor Travel, Senior Care, Under $20,000, Vending, and more. Lists of International Franchise and Franchisee Associations with contact information are provided. Sign up for a free account to explore thousands of franchises, home-based or conventional.

Franchise Direct: http://www.franchisedirect.com (accessed Spring 2009).

Developed in 1998, this large portal for franchise opportunities operates nine multilingual sites targeting North America and Europe. You can select an industry or a location or search by franchise name. Many industries are available including cleaning, golf, mailing and shipping, restaurant, sports, and travel. Investment needed varies from $15,000 or less to more than $300,000. Lists of new franchises, top franchises, franchises for women, and more are provided. Franchise Success Stories are also available. Easy to navigate, this site is worth a visit when considering a franchise.

FranchiseExpo: http://www.franchiseexpo.com (accessed Spring 2009).

This large directory will help you find the best franchises and franchise business opportunities available. It lists franchises by a lengthy number of categories. You also can find franchises by investment and newest opportunities. Find industry publications and franchise events here as well. Some franchise news and international partners are also included.

**FranchiseHandbook.com: http://www.franchise1.com (accessed Spring 2009).

This online directory lists shows by date and covers the world. Shows are sponsored by different vendors, so if you have several franchises you want to research you can see if they will be exhibiting at the show you are thinking of attending. Franchise opportunities and companies are described with contact information. Franchise industry news and a list of franchises for sale are also available.

Franchise Info Mall: http://www.franchiseinfomall.com (accessed Spring 2009).

Another large franchise directory, Franchise Info Mall is available on the Web. This one has over 100 franchise categories that can be searched. It lists the top 100 franchises, the top 500, and the top 200 international franchises. Franchise expos are listed as well as franchise attorneys and consultants. A few franchise-related articles are also presented.

Franchises.About.com: http://franchises.about.com (accessed Spring 2009).

This well-organized Web site is subtitled All about Franchises, and it is. Find out about the process of buying a franchise, a franchise business plan, choosing a franchise, franchise opportunities, financing, online and book resources, and more. International franchise information is also well covered.

FranchiseSolutions: http://www.franchisesolutions.com (accessed Spring 2009).

This unique site lists Franchise Resales, and allows franchisees to sort franchise opportunities by cash requirements and industry category. Users can also check out Unique Franchises and Home-based Franchises. The Franchise Advice and Resources section includes franchise success stories and advice on starting and managing a successful franchise. Original articles and news on franchising and franchises are also accessible. This site also selects Franchises for Women. A wealth of information is available and nicely organized.

Franchise Times: http://www.franchisetimes.com (accessed Spring 2009).

This monthly online magazine contains useful articles and information on franchises and franchising. Useful free publications and archives of the publication are available and searchable.

**Franchising: Franchise411: http://www.franchise411.com (accessed Spring 2009).

This online library and resources center will help you understand what franchising is and how to take advantage of everything it has to offer. Find here a thorough explanation of UFOCs, the FTC's rules, state registration information, and international franchising. Upcoming franchise seminars and shows and events with dates all over the country are listed. Links to dozens of sites presenting franchise opportunities in the United States and internationally along with information about franchising in general and specific franchises. Articles on franchise ratings, franchise politics, global franchising ins and outs, and more are included. Check out the twenty Red Flags of Franchising to help you consider the advantages and disadvantages of a franchise. Read and analyze the case studies to help your franchise be successful.

The Global Connector: http://www.globalconnector.org (accessed Spring 2009).

Part of Indiana University's Center for International Business Education and Research (CIBER), this gateway leads to thousands of international trade sites. The Global Connector allows searching by either country or by industry. Country data include links to data on government, domestic economy, news and media, entry requirements, transportation, and international trade. Industry specific information can be searched by the type or source of information including trade shows, trade publications, trends and analysis, and regulatory matters.

GlobalEDGE: http://globaledge.msu.edu/ (accessed Spring 2009).

Managed by Michigan State University's Center for International Business Education and Research (MSU_CIBER), this site links to a broad selection of international trade data including economic trends, statistical data sources, government resources, trade portals, journals, and mailing lists. Its Global Resources section provides access to more than 2,000 online resources. Current information on the business climate, news, history, economic landscape, and so forth is provided for 196 countries. Find here a rich collection of country and region specific business links to access a vast collection of information. MSU_CIBER has also contributed its own resources including an interactive forum for business professionals and portions of the information contained in the Knowledge Room, GlobalEDGE's section on the latest issues and trends effecting international business.

Global Trade and Technology Network (GTN): http://www.usgtn.net (accessed Spring 2009).

The GTN, established in 1994 as part of the U.S. Agency for International Development trade facilitation program, focuses on facilitating trade between the United States and foreign countries and helps develop international markets to bolster steady economic growth in the United States and abroad. Now a part of the U.S. Commercial Service, the premier global export business solutions provider of the U.S. Government, this global network of approximately 1800 trade specialists working in 109 domestic offices and in 80 markets worldwide, the Commercial Service helps U.S. companies make international sales with world-class market research, trade events that promote their products or services to qualified buyers, introductions to qualified buyers and distributors, and counseling through every step of the export process. Register here to obtain Import and/or Export assistance.

**International Franchise Association: http://www.franchise.org (accessed Spring 2009).

If you are thinking of or have purchased a franchise, this site contains a comprehensive database with links to over 800 companies. Many details about buying and running an individual franchise are provided. Its publication, *Franchise Opportunities Guide*, is outstanding. IFA's Franchise Discussion Forum allows users to discuss best practices, answer questions and ideas for new and existing franchisees, locate and contact international franchise groups, and exchange ideas and news on technology. Under Franchising Basics, find a free Introduction to Franchising document and Find the Right Franchise for You. Here you can also search franchises by investment dollar amount needed. You will find educational opportunities here as well as news affecting the franchise industry. Under the Events tab users will find a calendar, expos, seminars, and conferences. This easy-to-use, large site spotlights all information related to franchising.

The Internationalist: http://www.internationalist.com (accessed Spring 2009).

This large site is a leading resource for international business and travel. You can find translation services, international maps, world newspapers, currency exchange information, travel advisories, hotels, and more. One whole section is on business information and one on travel. Information on specific countries is complete and covers items like insurance companies, real estate, newspapers, and consultants in addition to country basics.

Journal of Commerce Online: http://www.joc.com (accessed Spring 2009).

This well-respected journal offers links to white papers, research projects, studies and other reference materials related to international logistics, trade, and transportation. Other important sections cover News, Regional News, Tools and Guides, and Resources, plus the digital edition of the journal. A free eNewsletter is available as well as a Career Center and Industry Press Releases. This useful, well-organized site will prove valuable if you are involved in international trade.

KnowThis.com: Marketing Virtual Library http://www.knowthis.com (accessed Spring 2009).

This large site is a smorgasbord of data and guidance on marketing including how to conduct market research, promotion versus advertising, using current technologies, and a large section on Internet marketing, divided into methods and strategies and research. Find guidance on creating marketing plans as well as sample plans. New topics include selling virtual clothes for avatars and reviews of software to enhance small e-commerce sites. Tutorials on managing customers, personal selling, targeting markets, and more are available.

National Association of Export Companies (NEXCO): http://www.nexco.org (accessed Spring 2009).

Dedicated to empowering small to mid-sized companies to build their global commerce efficiently and effectively, this group was founded in 1965. It is a forum for networking, business solutions, and advocacy through its Global Business Roundtable program and sponsors online conferences and an annual trade mission. Its Web site links directly to a comprehensive searchable database maintained by the Federation of International Trade Associations (FITA).

Nations Online Project: http://www.nationsonline.org/oneworld/ (accessed Spring 2009).

This portal is a reference directory and gateway to the countries, cultures, and nations of the world. Improve your cross-cultural understanding and global awareness through the country information presented here. Country profiles include information on geography, government, major cities, the economy, current news, local information, and facts. Find information about country-specific products, banks, companies, and more. Learn about cultural, social, and political issues in any country.

New York Public Library, International Trade Research Guide: http://www.nypl .org/research/sibl/trade/trade.html (accessed Spring 2009).

This wonderful guide produced by the Science, Industry and Business Library (SIBL) will provide invaluable information in learning how to conduct business between the United States and another country. Guides, business directories, periodicals, and trade statistic sources can be located through this large and practical site. It is well organized and easy to navigate; find information grouped under market research, trade leads, shipping and logistics, and cross-cultural business communication.

Nolo Press: http://www.nolo.com (accessed Spring 2009).

This commercial site provides a good collection of free articles, most written by lawyers. Find here information on the legal aspects of buying a franchise. Nolo's legal self-help books, now often accompanied by CD ROMs, are outstanding, and you will find useful information and advice on the site as well as invitations to buy their products. For answers on questions about patents, trademarks and franchising, browse the Small Business Law Center.

TradePort Global Trade Center: http://www.tradeport.org (accessed Spring 2009).

TradePort is a repository of free information and resources for businesses that seek to conduct international trade. Created in 1996, TradePort is backed by an alliance of regional trade associations that assist California export and import businesses, but companies in all states will find plenty of information to assist their export or import efforts. The Export Tutorial as well as the Import Tutorial are full of valuable resources and information. The Market Research section, which has a large Trade Leads section, and the Trade Library, which provides a bibliography of resources, a glossary, and links to trade statistics are current, very practical resources. This useful site is a great place to start researching your export/import adventure.

U.S. Census Bureau: http://www.census.gov (accessed Spring 2009).

This Web page is the best place to start searching for the multitude of data produced by Census programs, publications, and statistics. The home page groups the data under Census 2000, People, Business, Geography, Newsroom, At the Bureau, and Special Topics. Under Business, you can click on the Foreign Trade, Economic Census, NAICS, E-Stats, and Survey of Business Owners. Under Foreign Trade, learn directly from the Census Bureau how to properly classify your products for export and how to file your Shipper's Export Declaration online. The Bureau also processes, tabulates, and releases the data collected by the Bureau of Customs and Border Protection on exports and imports of goods. The catalog, a search feature, and links to related sites are also accessible on the left side of the home page. Another important part of the Census Bureau's Web page is the International Data Base (IDB) at http://www.census.gov/ipc/www/idb/. The IDB presents estimates and projections of basic demographic measures for countries and regions of the world. Country summaries, country rankings, and population pyramids all provide useful data. U.S. export and import statistics by commodity, country, customs district, and method of transportation provide value and quantity on a monthly, year-to-date, and annual history basis. U.S. state export data and port statistics for imports and exports are also available. Use this site frequently to help start and grow your business.

U.S. Chamber of Commerce: http://www.uschamber.com (accessed Spring 2009).

Currently 105 AmChams can be found in 91 countries, affiliated with the U.S. Chamber of Commerce. AmChams advance the interests of U.S. business overseas and are voluntary associations of U.S. companies and individuals doing business in a particular country as well as companies and individuals of that country who operate in the U.S. Information for small businesses and trade issues is provided free to all. Some statistics and directory information is also available.

**U.S. Council for International Business: http://www.uscib.org (accessed Spring 2009).

USCIB and its global network of affiliates offer a wide variety of practical services to help companies, business organizations, and others succeed in the international marketplace. Whether you are exporting overseas, investing abroad, or just want more information on doing business internationally, USCIB has information to help you. Their pages on Carnets are outstanding. USCIB explains what a carnet is, how to register and apply, and how to use it, thoroughly and completely.

U.S. Department of Commerce *Commercial News USA*: http://thinkglobal.us (accessed Spring 2009).

Commercial News USA is the official export promotion magazine of the Department of Commerce and showcases U.S.-made products and services. Users will find lists of companies already exporting grouped in about 15 different industries. Trade show opportunities can also be located here. Issues may be read online for download in PDFs. Franchising information is available, as well as success stories to inspire new exporters.

**U.S. Department of State (DOS): http://www.state.gov (accessed Spring 2009).

With a wealth of country information, including an online version of Background Notes, the site presents basic demographic and economic statistics as well as short narrative descriptions about the people, history, government, and foreign relations. In addition, there is U.S. Embassies and Consulate information as well as a diplomatic list. Listings on the left bar of the home page link to a wealth of topical information including a series of publications that contain factual information on all countries with which the United States has relations. Country Commercial Guides can also be accessed through the site. An important part of this Web site (http://www.travel.state.gov/) provides information on travel advisories, health, and safety. Business travelers can find information on documents necessary for foreign travel like passports and visas as well as current travel warnings. A link to consular information sheets provides detailed information on safety issues for countries around the world.

World Bank: http://www.worldbank.org (accessed Spring 2009).

Established in 1944, the World Bank is composed of five separate organizations all with distinct but related missions, including the International Bank for Reconstruction and Development (IBRD) and the International Development Association (IDA), the International Finance Corporation (IFC), Multilateral Investment Guaranty Agency (MIGA), and the International Centre for Settlement of Investment Disputes (ICSID). Resources provided from its Business Center include World Bank project and program summaries, documents, and reports. The side bar provides links to data and statistics on countries and regions, evaluations, news, and more. Arranged hierarchically, each of these categories allows you to drill down to even more specific information. In addition to providing access to its own collection of resources, the World Bank provides access to each member organization's site. Doing Business (http://www.doingbusiness.org) is a database that provides objective measures of business regulations and enforcement for 175 countries.

World Franchising: http://www.worldfranchising.com (accessed Spring 2009).

This large site organizes over 1,000 North America franchises, which can be searched by Industry Type, Average Total Investment, Average Franchise Fee, Average, Royalty Fee, and Total Operating Units. The Top 100 Franchises, Hottest New Franchises, UFOCS, and Franchisee Resources are also available. Linked under International is the portal to the European Franchise Industry (http://www.franchisingeu.com). Here you will find comprehensive, detailed information about many of the leading European franchises, which can be sorted by Industry and Total Operating Units.

World Trade Magazine: http://www.worldtrademag.com/ (accessed Spring 2009).

This large site is a treasure trove of information for individuals and companies either involved in international trade or wanting to enter the global market and understand supply chains. Besides print information, you can find Webinars on supply chains, buyers and suppliers, financial supply chains, and more. Find a global supply chain buyers guide, currency calculator, white papers, eNewsletter, and more. Industry news such as FedEx Post First Loss in 11 Years, and Logistics Costs Higher in Russia, is also provided.

World Trade Organization (WTO): http://www.wto.org (accessed Spring 2009).

Established in 1995, the WTO is composed of more than 140 countries that cooperate on global economic policymaking and provides the ground rules for international commerce. The organization's world-renown annual report *International Trade Statistics* is available on its Web site via the Resources link. Also available are documents published by the WTO, information on trade topics, and links to publications of many member countries, news, and international trade resources.

Yahoo! Directory, Business and Economy/Trade: http://dir.yahoo.com/Business _and_Economy/Trade/ (accessed Spring 2009).

Especially important categories on this site are organizations, e-commerce, software, and use tax issues. This large site includes a wealth of information with good international coverage on a wide variety of topics. Under International Trade Organizations, users will find listings for 148 useful organizations involved in global trade. Under its small business site (http://smallbusiness.yahoo.com/) the e-commerce section covers online shopping centers, privacy seal programs, and digital money. For industries it covers manufacturing as well as the retail industry. Check this site for current, accurate business information.

Yahoo! Small Business Resources: http://smallbusiness.yahoo.com (accessed Spring 2009).

Under Getting Started on the far right side of this large site, the section on Franchises contains a great many useful links to articles on purchasing a franchise, questions to ask other franchisees in the chain, franchise funding sources, and researching a franchise opportunity. In addition, under Business Tools, there is a Franchise Search option that allows the user to search by category and/or investment dollar amount ranges. If you are just considering the franchise option, this site will help you get started learning about the world of the franchise.

In the particular area of Franchising, I have found another type of Web site. I am not recommending these sites but they might be helpful to some users.

FranChoice: http://www.franchoice.com (accessed Spring 2009).

The FranChoice program is a consultation program that is like working with a realtor when you buy a house. An industry expert works with the prospective franchisee to find a good match in terms of the type of franchise to buy and run. Fees are paid by franchisers. Franchise consultants help you select and evaluate a franchise opportunity, including reviewing and explaining the UFOC.

FranNet: http://www.frannet.com (accessed Spring 2009).

A service similar to FranChoice is FranNet. This site is a bit larger with testimonials, events, helpful tips, news, and links to other sites. If you want to use one of these services, it is probably good to shop around on the Internet and find the best deal you can for the service you need.

7

Sustaining and Managing International Trade Ventures

Chapter Highlights:

Principles of Management
Action Plans
Organization Chart
Technology
Web Site
Time Management and Organization

Management is responsible for the accomplishment of the mission of an organization and its new initiatives. Managers decide such matters as what and how much to produce, which markets to serve and pursue, how much to advertise, and what prices to charge. An owner or manager is the person responsible for planning and directing the work of a group of people, checking their work, and taking corrective action if necessary. In a global business, you often plan and direct the work of outside sources or contractors in order to accomplish delivery of the product or service. To manage for success, develop international tactical plans that implement your overall strategic plan, such as a market entry point and a sales approach. Motivate your personnel by emphasizing team work. Remember keeping better track of your money, staff, and paperwork will result in a more successful international business.

PRINCIPLES OF MANAGEMENT

The major principles of management are planning, organizing, leading, and controlling. Good managers accomplish the entire management process efficiently and effectively. Remember that your business will be the accumulation of the management decisions you make. Your business will accomplish its work under the guidelines that you set up. You need a vision of what you want your international business or organization to be and accomplish. Plan, plan, plan, but do not treat international trade as a stand-alone process. Also remember that your customers are the real judges of how good your management decisions are. Base your decisions on how you want all your customers to view your products or services.

Let's run through each principle of management to understand it a bit more clearly:

1. *Planning* is the intellectual process that determines the anticipated use of resources, methodology, and projected outcome on a given time line. Based on an organization's mission, planning begins with setting goals and objectives. An international business develops and uses its business plan to begin the challenge of managing its business. Look at the goals and plan how to achieve them.

2. *Organizing* involves decisions concerning the best allocation and utilization of resources for implementing the business or strategic plan. Managers coordinate the use of capital, information, physical resources, and people as part of this process. Choosing an organizational model is important and can determine the success or failure of your business. Are you ready to move your business into the international arena? Make lists and make sure everything is in place and ready to run your global expansion or entrance.

3. *Leading* involves the people of the organization or staffing and therefore is a complex function. Managers with leadership ability get employees to willingly follow in the achievement of the organization's goals. Motivation is extremely important. Building a team is one method of leading an organization effectively. Good managers lead by example, so organize your work and keep everyone involved in your business informed about the business needs and decisions. Communication skills are vital to good leadership. Leadership is sometimes considered an art, but it involves skills that can be learned.

4. *Controlling* involves monitoring, evaluating, and correcting whatever is necessary to achieve the established goals. Planning and controlling are closely linked, and controlling involves comparing accomplishments at different intervals of time against the set goals and taking corrective action if necessary. When things are not going according to your plan, you need to step back and adjust. Problems will occur. Supplies will not be delivered on time or someone will get sick. Learn to improvise and revise, continue monitoring your business functions, and make changes to improve how it works.

An especially good Web site to help new managers is the Free Management Library at http://www.managementhelp.org. This large collection of articles and books is arranged alphabetically by subjects like Customer Service, Finances, Growing Organizations, Marketing, Planning, and Taxation.

ACTION PLANS

If you are a new importer/exporter, how do you accomplish all the above and do you need to? Three action plans can help build a framework or strategy for you to operate and manage your business by organizing the necessary activities like obtaining and working with suppliers and other vendors to get necessary supplies, materials and services; filling orders; providing customer support and service after the sale; and dealing with unexpected occurrences.

These action plans explain what you, the owner or manager, need to do to get the new phases of your business working smoothly. As the business evolves, you will move from doing things yourself to doing things through others. The success of your business may depend on how well you can make this transition.

1. Set up an *Operations Plan*. Figure out how you will create and deliver your product or service to your foreign customers. What materials, software, hardware, equipment, and other supplies do you need? Where will it be set up? Does it work? Do you need more than one phone line? Do you need a fax machine? What type and how many PCs do you need? Do you or others need new skills or expertise? Do you need a high-speed or DSL Internet connection? Locate and sign up for workshops or classes. As thoroughly as you can, plan every step of the operation from raw material or product location to delivery to the local and virtual customers.

2. The next action plan is your *Management Plan*. Part of this plan will be managing employee, and you need to consider what employees you need to start your international venture and what jobs they will perform. As we learned above, part of managing is organizing. Delivery of products or services must be kept on schedule or customers will not return, and business will decline instead of grow. A good manager monitors all the diverse activities of the business and intervenes if things are not happening or are not happening in a timely fashion. Set up processes for getting things from accounting, payroll, deliveries, and other departments done. Recognize if some activities are a major drain on your time and resources, preventing you from getting more important things done. Value your time as your most valuable asset; you can always make more money but not more time. We will talk more about time management later in this chapter.

3. The final action plan is your *Contingency Plan*. Though careful planning is necessary, Murphy's Law (if anything can go wrong, it will) may intervene. Your Contingency Plan will help you avoid disruptions in your operation when industry, economic, or business conditions here in the United States or

in the market you are targeting change beyond what you have prepared to handle—perhaps you will have more customers than you had dreamed possible or your supplier cannot provide the materials you need or goes out of business completely. Basically, here you try to identify the areas in your business that are susceptible to variable factors. Contingency planning is a prearranged method of changing the direction of your business or retrenching in the face of less-than-hoped-for results. So if things go much better or worse than expected, you have considered your responses and are prepared to react, perhaps more quickly than your competitors, thus presenting you with an opportunity or competitive advantage.

Action plans can also be part of strategic planning or developing a strategy for your business to grow and develop.

ORGANIZATION CHART

The management process is a key ingredient throughout the business life cycle, and related to the organizational structure is another management tool used to further the organization's goals, the Organization Chart, or Org Chart for short. Org Charts illustrate the intended structure of the organization or company and reflect the power structure of the company. Your business may need to incorporate strong working relationships with outside consultants into the structure of everyday operations to form a management team for the organization or business. This team should be shown on your Org Chart and might consist of an accountant, lawyer, import/export adviser, banker, and other consultants who provide needed expertise to assist in running the business. Develop an Org Chart that reflects where you want the organization to go and how it will grow rather than simply reflecting how it is now. For more help on building an Org Chart, take a look at the topics Organization Charts as a Management Tool and How to Build an Org Chart on the Web site http://management.about.com. Here you will find advice and examples representing different types of small and larger businesses.

Along with the Org Chart, develop a list of key personnel with a job description listing responsibilities and authority level. Planning in advance will help you grow your business in an organized manner resulting in less last-minute decision-making. When an organization has structure, employees will feel they know where the company is going and what their role is in getting there. A structured organization has a better chance at success.

TECHNOLOGY

A Web site today often functions much like a business card. It is virtually impossible for most companies to function in many industries without a

Web presence. To many young people, using the Internet is as natural as using the telephone, or cell phone today. Conducting business using the Internet is also taken for granted, especially in the global economy. As we have discussed, you will want to use the Internet to gather information about the industry, market, and competitors and to exchange e-mail to facilitate networking with customers, suppliers, or advisers and mentors. Decide how using the Internet will benefit your particular business daily. See the next chapter for more in-depth coverage of issues concerning e-commerce, technology, and the Internet.

The personal computer (PC), hardware, sits at the center of this technology. Purchase the best desktop PC that you can afford and some software will be available with the purchase or at reduced cost. Purchase software that can help you with your managerial duties such as word processing, a spreadsheet or bookkeeping or accounting package recommended by your accountant, a fast modem, wireless card, and perhaps software to manage the communications connection to the server computer. Your telephone company, cable or satellite TV company, or a local Internet company can explain ways to connect and costs. Be sure to read the small print as there are many restrictions in the services offered by any company and talking to other business owners who have used the service is as important here as in other areas of doing business. Once you begin using a PC and the Internet for business functions, you will find a myriad of tasks it can help manage, including but not limited to managing your inventory, tracking customer accounts and communications, monitoring your competition and your industry, and keeping in touch with business associates and customers. The SBA's Small Business Development Center network has a large site on e-commerce beginning with overviews and tutorials at http://sbdcnet.org/SBIC/e-com.php. This large site contains online training, discusses how e-commerce fits with your business, and covers building a Web site, finding a Web host, taxes and e-commerce, and more. Start your research on how to use a PC and the Internet to expand your business globally here.

The following pages start the discussion on Web sites, and the next chapter will more thoroughly cover e-commerce.

WEB SITE

Most companies are developing Web sites to enlarge their customer base and boost profits. If you do not already have one, clearly define why you need a Web site and determine how much you can spend on getting it developed and then maintained. Or, if you have a Web site, what do you need to add or change to help attract international business or more international business. Study Web sites of businesses similar to yours and make note of what you like and do not like about them. How are they organized, how

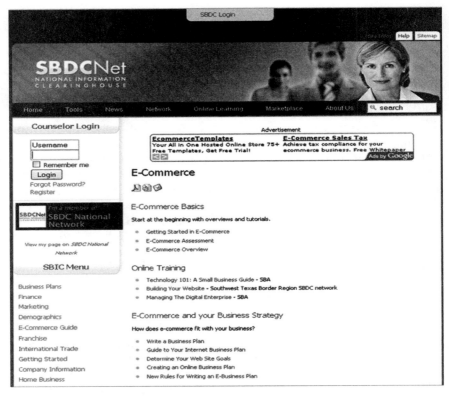

E-Commerce page. SBDC.Net National Information Clearinghouse.

Source: http://sbdcnet.org/SBIC/e-com.php

do you contact someone with a question, and can you place an order quickly, if you are planning to offer that service on your site? Can you have your site or at least part of it translated into another language? Then, you will want to research locally and on the Internet different companies that can help in its design, development, and implementation. Have they developed other sites that service international customers? Like other phases of starting a business, research and preparation will help make your Web site project a success. On the Export.gov site (http://export.gov) you will find in the E-Commerce Toolbox, in the left frame, Guide to Going Online. This useful page walks you through the steps you need to follow. In this toolbox, you will find an abundance of information on identifying your markets, developing your markets, payments, pricing, and more. As mentioned above another great source of help for developing your e-commerce business is the National SBDC Information Clearinghouse at http://sbdcnet.org/SBIC/e-com.php.

However, use the same type of criteria for hiring a professional Web site developer, if you go that route, as you do when hiring an accountant or lawyer. Study their work, check references, talk to colleagues, ask for bids, and shop around for the best price without sacrificing quality. Remember that you only have one chance on the Internet to make a good first impression. In your contract with a Web designer, be sure to specify a work schedule, desired results, and payment terms as well as a termination clause.

Now that you have a Web site, you need a Web-hosting service. Work with your Web designer to find a Web host that works for you. Again, this will probably be a long-term relationship, and you will want to keep that in mind too. Another good book for helping you learn the basics about Web sites and e-commerce is the following:

Belew, Shannon and Elad, Joel. *Starting an Online Business All-in-One Desk Reference for Dummies*. Wiley Publishing, Inc., 2006. 814p. ISBN 978-0-7645-9929-3. $29.99.

As in other titles in this series, you find the basics of starting a business on the Internet. E-commerce survival stories, best practices, and other resources to help you expand your international business are provided. Find out how to select an online host, understand Web site design, establish a graphic identity, provide outstanding customer service, and provide various payment options. Sections on Niche E-Commerce and E-Commerce Advances will prove very useful, along with the chapters "Crossing Borders and Selling Internationally" and "Seeking Out the Next Level of Your Business." The authors' advice on understanding your competition is always very practical.

Again, see the next chapter for more on e-commerce.

TIME MANAGEMENT AND ORGANIZATION

If you do not manage your time, time will manage you. There are never enough hours in the day to complete all the work associated with your growing and expanding business, so you need to learn some time-management solutions. Efficiency is vital to any business. The following are major areas to help you save time and use it wisely:

1. *Track your time usage.* Make a copy of a page from your day planner and record the time you spend doing things for a week. Now you will see the pattern of how you are spending your time.

2. *Allocate and prioritize your time.* This step is very personal. Identify your most productive time. If you are a morning person, you want to start the day with the most difficult or worrisome task and then mix in easy tasks as breaks. Or if it takes you awhile to get going in the a.m., you may want to return phone calls, check e-mail, etc., until you are wide awake and ready to tackle difficult tasks. Whenever possible, complete projects with deadlines

first as this will please your customer, win you repeat business, and get positive reinforcement for you and your business.

3. *Stick to the schedule and control your agenda.* Take time each afternoon to write a prioritized list of the next day's tasks and projects so you can start your day in a productive manner. Often by lunch time, your plans may be shattered; but try to complete as many tasks on the list as possible, and then move what cannot be finished to the next day's list. Also make "To Do" lists for the week and one for things to do during the month. As you finish these items, cross them off for a feeling of accomplishment and moving forward. If you are constantly interrupted, you must make it clear that you can only be interrupted by dire emergencies which you define. Turn on the answering machine; do not answer the door, whatever it takes. If you are unable to do this in your workplace, take a day or an afternoon away from the workplace each week to catch up on whatever is being pushed aside or what needs your entire concentration to finish. If you are still having trouble, investigate day timer software to help you organize and manage your time.

4. *Stay or get organized.* This item is extremely important. Keep your desk and work space tidy. Completed projects should be filed. Answered phone messages filed or tossed. New orders filed. A neat space allows you to concentrate on the task at hand. A good filing system allows you to retrieve information you need quickly, without wasting time looking for things. Set aside time for planning and when planning, also schedule time for organizing.

5. *Delegate what you can.* You must delegate work to others in your organization who may have more time or more skill in a particular area. Delegate routine administrative tasks, special projects, and tasks that an employee has a special talent for accomplishing. Explain fully what is expected of the employee and encourage him/her to ask questions at any time. Once the task or project has been completed, do not forget to evaluate the final product and discuss the results with the employee. As your business grows, you will spend more time strategizing and less time on the daily components of running a business.

Remember to avoid the big "day wasters." Talking on the telephone, surfing the Web, and e-mail are all great things when used in moderation, but you can seriously lose hours and hours of your day with all of them. Limit your day wasters to your least productive hour or so each day. In addition, do not forget that saying "no" can help you from being overburdened.

Managing paperwork is another daunting task. Every day it accumulates, but strive to handle each piece of paper only once. File paperwork as diligently as you schedule meetings and appointments. Buy a weekly or daily planner and write things down. Have an address book or contact management software on your PC where you record contact information and toss piles of business cards. Buy different color folders for different topics, subjects, segments of your business. U.S. Customs forms and paperwork will require regular attention and completion to be sure shipments can come into and/or leave the country. Retire files as soon as possible but separate and retain any information needed for verification, tax purposes, or other financial matters. Most importantly, purge files at the end of every year. Most business tax forms should be kept indefinitely in case of an audit.

Consistent timely decision-making is essential to good management and good time-management skills can assist in achieving that goal. Make timely decisions and communicate them to employees and customers alike in order to have a successful international business. Because of time differences, it is more essential than ever to communicate in a timely manner to customers and suppliers in other time zones.

REFERENCES

(Starred titles discussed in the chapter)

Print Resources

**Belew, Shannon and Elad, Joel. *Starting an Online Business All-in-One Desk Reference for Dummies*. Wiley Publishing, Inc., 2006. 814p. ISBN 978-0-7645-9929-3. $29.99.

Readers will find the basics of starting a business on the Internet. E-commerce survival stories, best practices, and other resources to help you develop your new business are provided. Good tips on selecting an online host, understanding Web site design, establishing a graphic identity, providing customer service, and providing various payment options are clearly outlined. The chapters on Niche E-Commerce and E-Commerce Advances are especially useful. Some coverage of legal matters, Internet security, trademarks, copyrighting, and taxes are included.

Berger, Suzanne. *How We Compete: What Companies Around the World Are Doing to Make It in Today's Global Economy*. Currency Doubleday, 2006. 334p. ISBN 0385513593.

Berger and the MIT Industrial Performance Center looked at over 500 international companies to discover which practices are working in today's global economy. They compared strategies and successes of companies in various industries. For example, in electronics and software, they compared Intel and Sony who make their own products to Cisco and Dell who rely on outsourcing. Readers will find their conclusions fascinating, instructive, and surprising, and will learn the many ways to win in the global economy.

Capela, John J. *Import/Export for Dummies*. Wiley Publishing, Inc., 2008. ISBN 978-0-470-26094-4. 338p. $19.99.

Capela is an international business consultant, and this practical guide covers how to evaluate import/export opportunities, expand your global operations, identify target markets, find customers, follow the rules and regulations of different countries, and develop a marketing strategy. The introductory discussion of what environmental forces make international business different is essential reading before you start or begin managing an international adventure. Another important section discusses the selection of products and suppliers. Learn about the various approaches to exporting and importing and some of the qualities you need to possess to be successful.

De Beer, A. A. et al. *Management for Entrepreneurs.* 2nd ed. Juta Academic, 2004. 224p. ISBN 0-7021-5543-8. $24.95.

The authors focus on eight business functions including management, finance, marketing, operations, purchasing, human resources, administration, and public relations. Each of these functions is described in terms of increasing profitability and ensuring the success of your business or company. Many activities and examples including self-evaluation quizzes are included with each chapter. Learn how to apply management ideas, techniques, and theories to your business.

Hatten, Timothy S. *Small Business Management: Text with Goventure CD-Rom.* 2nd ed. Houghton Mifflin, 2004. 660p. ISBN 0-618-25815-9. $90.27.

GoVenture—Live the Life of an Entrepreneur is a management simulation program on CD-Rom that is packaged with this copy of *Small Business Management.* Over 6,000 graphics, audio, and video clips immerse users in the day-to-day challenges of being an entrepreneur. Each chapter contains "What Would You Do" scenarios to allow users to make decisions and solve problems from real-life situations. The book includes a full chapter on business plans with sample plans for a service business and one for a retail business. Other chapters or sections cover franchising, including selecting an international franchise, marketing, human resources, and management. The section called Financial and Legal Management is outstanding. Additionally, e-commerce is thoroughly covered, including online marketing. Although it is expensive, this package is definitely a useful tool for the new entrepreneur.

International Trade Centre. *Export Quality Management: An Answer Book for Small- and Medium-Sized Exporters.* International Trade Centre (UN Publications), 2005. 252p. ISBN 92-9137-214-5. $50.00.

Using a question and answer format, exporters or importers can learn how to navigate the world of international standards, mandatory technical regulations, metrology, ISO 9000 series standards, accreditation, conformity assessment procedures and more. Organized in sections, each section is comprehensive and well written. This work covers various aspects of quality requirements, quality assurance, conformity assessment and certification, and trade-related environmental issues. This guide is especially helpful in trading with developing countries and transitional economies.

Lauer, Chris. *The Management Gurus.* Penguin Group, 2008. 278p. ISBN 978-1-59184-208-8. $24.95.

Lauer and Soundview Executive Book Summaries brought together summaries of 15 management classics and contemporary hits in one easy-to-digest volume that will help you learn about management and leadership. Begin to learn about Winning with People, how to be an influencer, how national borders have given way to a global economy and marketplace, the "cybercontinent," crisis management, and more.

Lewis, Richard D. *When Cultures Collide: Leading Across Cultures*. Nicholas Brealey, 2006. 590p. ISBN 1-904-838-022.

This guide to working and communicating across cultures explains how your culture and language affect the ways in which you think and respond to situations. Lewis not only helps you understand different cultures but also how to manage in different business cultures. He covers the world including Asian, Arab, and Eastern European countries. He suggests a broad model you can use to characterize different national characteristics and various traits that shape attitudes toward time, leadership, team building, and organizational structure and behaviors. This exceptional book is a good read for anyone who encounters people of other nationalities and cultures.

Magos, Alice. *Business Plans That Work*. 3rd edition. Toolkit Media Group, 2008. 244p. ISBN 0-8080-0858-7. $19.95.

The essential elements of a professional business plan have been updated in accordance with new laws and regulations in this revised edition, which translates complicated marketing and financial concepts into down-to-earth, practical guidance. The major highlight of this title is the five updated sample business plans that include a wealth of detailed information about the operation of a successful small business. Plans are presented for simple one-person companies, as well as for corporations with numerous employees. Learn how to create a professional plan, describe the international mission and objectives, analyze the competition, target market(s), create sales and marketing plans, and generate financial statements. Use the business plan as a management tool long after it is completed.

Mattock, John. *Cross-Cultural Communication: The Essential Guide to International Business*. Rev. 2nd ed. Kogan Page, 2003. 176p. ISBN 0-7494-3922-X. $24.95.

Mattock's work is full of practical suggestions on how to be more sensitive to the cultural issues of others and how to better communicate in the global world of business. He will help you assess your own attitudes and performance as a partner in an international business venture. He fills the book with examples, opinions, and case studies chosen from his work at Canning, a UK-based company that has training and consulting offices in the United Kingdom, Italy, and Japan and holds seminars in 30 other countries on four continents. The Glossary of Offshore English is very useful as you learn what certain words are likely to mean in an English conversation in the global business world. Well-organized and well-written, this fascinating book will help you learn how to get it right, and how to communicate better when working outside your own culture.

Parks, Ronald K. and Parks, Judith Stolz. *Manager's Mentor: A Guide for Small Business*. Prairie Sky Publishing Co., 2003. 256p. ISBN 0-9729165-0-4. $19.95.

This complete guide to starting and running your small business emphasizes the importance of management principles and their practical applications. Each chapter begins with a real-life story from Ron's childhood on a farm in Nebraska to illustrate his values, thought processes, and strategies used to run his successful business. An entire chapter is devoted to efficiency and finding and developing ways to work more efficiently. Two chapters are devoted to

"Creating a Workforce" and "Taking Care of Employees" because hiring and keeping good employees is so essential to a small business. Discover how to develop a company culture; develop good communication skills; manage capital assets, manage customers, vendors, and consultants; and improve your management skills. As the title says, if you need a mentor to help in managing your small business, the Parks can help you.

Salacuse, Jeswald W. *The Global Negotiator: Making, Managing, and Mending Deals Around the World in the Twenty-First Century.* Palgrave Macmillan, 2003. 312p. ISBN 0-312-29339-9. $29.99.

This unique, outstanding guidebook breaks down the intricacies of international negotiations into understandable segments and provides the tools to ensure success in the creation, management, and remediation of international deals. Salacuse even explains how to deal with negotiations that go wrong, illustrating how deals may falter and methods to save them. Managers, lawyers, executives, and government officials will use this comprehensive guide to understand the transformations global business has experienced in the last decade.

Travis, Tom. *Doing Business Anywhere: The Essential Guide to Going Global.* John Wiley & Sons, Inc., 2007. 202p. ISBN 0-470-14961-2. $24.95.

Travis presents his six tenets of global trade and illustrates them in the context of real stories of global trade. He emphasizes the importance of international trade to the economic prosperity of all the world's nations. If you want to start a new venture or expand your present one, Travis helps you organize, plan, operate, and execute with a global mind-set. Learn how to navigate conflicting and confusing laws, deal with different cultures, and operate in different countries. He also explains how to leverage the benefits of free trade agreements to set up and operate a competitive and profitable business. Also highlighted is how to protect your brand through patents, copyrights, and trademarks. Security concerns and measures are also discussed. Travis will convince readers that embracing his six tenets is key to "doing business anywhere."

Tuller, Lawrence. *Doing Business Beyond America's Borders: the Dos, Don'ts, and Other Details of Conducting Business in 40 Different Countries.* Entrepreneur Press, 2008. 304p. ISBN 1-59918-257-2. $21.95.

Covering about 40 countries, this book will allow you to find a new world of customers and empower your business to compete with the large transnational corporations. Tuller explains critical steps, tactics, and tools that will help your company navigate the international business landscape. Learn about cultural and interrelation anomalies, negotiations, language barriers, and ways to develop strong overseas relationships. Discover the best ways to sell your products overseas, cost-effective means of transportation, ways to find low-cost production materials and labor, and how to deal with cultural anomalies and foreign languages. Worksheets, anecdotes, and illustrative examples are plentiful.

The Ultimate Small Business Guide; a Resource for Startups and Growing Businesses. Basic Books, 2004. 501p. ISBN 0-7382-0913-9. $19.95.

This large collection of how-to's, step-by-step objective lists, and enlightening FAQs covers all aspects of planning, launching, managing, and growing your small business. Sections cover "Refining and Protecting Your Idea," "Communicating with Your Customers," "Selling Online," and "Managing Yourself and Others." Financing, pricing, cash flow, ratios, and assets are thoroughly and carefully covered in a section called "Figuring It Out."

Walsh, Ciaran. *Key Management Ratios: Master the Management Metrics that Drive and Control Your Business.* 3rd ed. Financial Times/Prentice Hall, 2003. 400p. ISBN 0-273-66345-3. $24.95.

Business ratios are the standards and targets that help owners and managers work toward achieving their goals in running a successful business. Fully international, using companies in the United Kingdom, United States, European Union, and Japan, Walsh proceeds to teach readers everything needed to know about key business ratios, linking them to day-to-day operations. He also covers financial statements, balance sheets, cash flow, liquidity, and cost, volume and price relationships. You will take some knowledge away from studying this thorough and well-organized book.

Weiss, Kenneth D. *Building an Import/Export Business.* 4th ed. John Wiley & Sons, Inc., 2008. 320p. ISBN 0-470-18577-5. $19.95.

Weiss, an entrepreneur and international trade consultant, offers tips and instructions for every aspect of an import/export business. Learn how to get started in the post-9/11 import/export landscape. He explains how to take advantage of GATT, WTO, CAFTA, NAFTA, and other trade agreements. Weiss covers all new and updated regulations, laws, and customs and shipping procedures to help ensure that businesses are in compliance with the Transportation Security Administration (TSA), U.S. Customs and Border Protection (CBP), and U.S. Immigration and Customs Enforcement (ICE). Besides helping importers and exporters plan their business expansion, Weiss describes how to research a raw idea and then successfully launch a stable, profitable business operation. Learn from the real-life examples presented here.

Yerkes, Leslie, and Decker, Charles. *Beans: Four Principles for Running a Business in Good Times and Bad.* John Wiley & Sons, Inc., 2003. 176p. ISBN 0-7879-6764-5. $19.95.

From the true story of a small Seattle coffee bar, the authors distill universal business truths such as maintain a consistent, quality product; view both customers and employees as friends; and be passionate about what you do. Each chapter is divided into scenes and contains lots of dialogue. Also stressed is the importance of intention in striving for and achieving success: you have achieved success when your results match your intentions. Learn good management skills by example.

Zeigler, Kenneth. *Getting Organized at Work: 24 Lessons for Setting Goals, Establishing Priorities, and Managing Your Time.* 128p. ISBN 0-07-159138-9. $12.95.

This useful, well-written guide demonstrates how to uncover and eliminate nonessential activities that consume time. Learn how to move past the clutter to expedite unprecedented efficiency and productivity. As Zeigler states, "the key is action." Two dozen easy-to-implement tactics will help you set realistic goals, end procrastination, control and manage your desk, manage your e-mail, and plan meetings wisely. Zeigler also suggests that, at the end of each week, you ask yourself what you could do better next week. Discover the use of a master list to keep your mind focused and your work flowing. Zeigler's hints will keep help you prioritize and manage.

Zodl, Joseph A. *Export Import: Everything You and Your Company Need to Know to Compete in World Markets.* 4th ed. IIEI Press, 2005. ISBN 0-9773098-0-0. $39.95.

In easy-to-understand language and writing style, Zodl leads the reader into the world of international business, dispels the myths, simplifies tasks and processes, and illustrates important points with real-world examples. Zodl defines the vocabulary and terminology needed to understand the world of international business and points out sources for expert advice. This title provides the information the exporter needs to take a U.S.-manufactured product, sell it to a foreign buyer, make the shipment correctly, and get paid in U.S. dollars. It shows a middleman how to buy a product made by someone else and resell it at a profit to an overseas customer. Zodl also has a Web site users may be interested in checking out at http://www.zodl.net/firstpage.htm.

Online Resources

**About.com: http://management.about.com (accessed Spring 2009).

Clearly management and management skills are huge topics and vitally important to a successful business. This site about the art and science of management provides a treasure trove of information, links, books, and other assorted help in learning new management skills and improving those an entrepreneur has already developed. Find sections called Management 101, Management Tips, How to Manage, and more. Learn best business practices and leadership skills from experts. A related area of the site is Human Resources, which helps users learn about HR issues and managing employees. Project Management and Work/Life Balance are also covered by this useful site.

BEOnline: http://www.loc.gov/rr/business/beonline/ (accessed Spring 2009).

Compiled by the Library of Congress Business Reference Services for researchers, this site has, under Subject Lists, a lengthy list of business topics such as associations, business plans (forms), companies by industry, data sets, e-commerce, franchises, economic indicators, and legal resources. If you click on Associations, you will find an Associations database that includes contacts, descriptions, addresses, and events data for the organizations listed. Over 10,000 business organizations in the United States are included. Find here a link to the Herb Growing and Marketing Network or the Association of Bridal Consultants. Under the Title listing, you will find Airlines of the Web, America's Business Funding Directory, American Chambers of Commerce Abroad, American City Business Journals, and more.

BizMove.com: http://www.bizmove.com (accessed Spring 2009).

The wealth of information covers a variety of topics including General Management, Small Business Marketing, Internet Business, and International Trade. Worksheets and sample plans will help guide you. Very valuable too is the Small Business General Management section, which covers strategic planning, productivity management, stock control, business survival tips, and more. Growing a Business on the Internet covers topics such as Search Engine Positioning, Website Promotion, and Email Marketing Methods. International Trade centers on Exporting but covers many diverse topics including How to Export a Service and How to Sell Overseas.

Business.gov: http://www.business.gov (accessed Spring 2009).

Business.gov is another government site developed to help businesses find the information they need and want. The Market Research section of this site is especially noteworthy. Links to information on major industries, population and demographic resources, plus Rural America Facts provide users with a multitude of useful resources. International trade connections are useful for global or Internet businesses too. Major categories include Laws and Regulations, Buying and Selling, Financial Assistance, Taxes, etc. Also find workplace issue information on interviewing, working environments, training, hiring procedures, and employing minors. The site map works like a table of contents and gets you where you want to go quickly and easily.

Business Owners Idea Café: http://www.businessownersideacafe.com (accessed Spring 2009).

Developed by successful entrepreneurs and authors of published guides on starting a business, this large site presents short articles on all aspects of small business or entrepreneurial life. The main divisions include CyberSchmooz, Starting your Biz, Running Your Biz, Take Out Info, Classifieds, The "You" in your Biz, De-Stress and Have Fun, About Idea Café, and Join Idea Café. The large Running Your Biz: eCommerce section has excellent coverage on all things e-commerce plus links to outside information on e-commerce. Here you can find experts to answer your questions or discuss your current business crisis. You will find sample business plans, financing help, business forms, and business news.

Centers for International Trade Development: http://www.citd.org/StartupKit/index.cfm (accessed Spring 2009).

This very useful site has a guide for new exporters, an export readiness assessment tool, and an excellent Export FAQ for companies just getting into international trade. Their Trade Information Database includes U.S. and world trade and economic data, trade contacts and leads, trade reference tools, foreign market research, trade/investment regulations, trade documentation, and finance and insurance sections. A trade resources directory provides information on numerous trade associations and organizations. A trade show calendar is also available, as are booklets on best markets for various U.S. industries. Start gathering import/export information here.

Economist.com: http://www.economist.com (accessed Spring 2009).

Providing excellent coverage of world news, the Economist.com also contains information on world markets, the latest exchange rates, and country and city guides geared to the business traveler. It is the companion site to the print journal *The Economist*. Although much of the site is free and fully searchable, the Economist.com does charge to view archived articles. Other portions of the site are considered to be premium content viewable by subscription only.

Entrepreneur.com: http://www.entrepreneur.com (accessed Spring 2009).

Entrepreneur Magazine provides a wealth of information and assistance to the new entrepreneur. A thorough understanding of the need for the right type of marketing plan to fit your business and your style of planning and working is very important; and this site guides you through the process of discovering the right type for you. Learn how to determine your marketing goals and objectives and how a plan will help you achieve them. Under Marketing and Sales, you will also find tips on building buzz, branding, word-of-mouth advertising, and marketing materials. Learn about the "9 Tools for Building Customer Loyalty," for example. Discover how to create an ad budget and create great ads and direct mail pieces. The E-business section explains legal issues, setting up an e-commerce site, e-mail marketing, Internet security, and more. International marketing research is well covered in the Marketing section. Use this outstanding site often during the planning and opening of your global business.

Entrepreneurship: http://entrepreneurship.org/ (accessed Spring 2009).

The Ewing Marion Kauffman Foundation is the entrepreneur's trusted guide to high growth. This large site is filled with relevant, practical, and timely information on how to manage and expand your business. Included are original articles written for the site by entrepreneurs drawing on their own experiences and an aggregation of the "best of the best" existing articles and tools to guide you on the path to high growth. Topics are arranged around eight key subject areas: Accounting and Finance, Human Resources, Marketing and Sales, Products and Services, Business Operations, The Entrepreneur, Public Policy, and Entrepreneurship Law. The Sales and Marketing section includes a section on Global Markets. Search on Global and find articles like Eleven Pitfalls to Avoid in Going Global and Entrepreneurs, Manage Your Global Growth.

Export America. **U.S. Department of Commerce: http://www.trade.gov/ exportamerica/ (accessed Spring 2009).**

The official magazine of the International Trade Administration (ITA) of the U.S. Department of Commerce, this publication offers practical export advice and is very valuable to small and mid-sized exporters. It includes country- and industry-specific opportunities, trade events, online marketing tips, and export statistics. Articles cover such topics as export documentation, market research, U.S. customs, and success stories, which are available at the Web site. Selected articles from current journal issues can be viewed at this

Web site. Although not globally searchable, full text of past journal issues from November 1999 through the most current completed year are also available.

**Export.gov: http://www.export.gov (accessed Spring 2009).

Created as a Government to Business initiative, Export.gov is the government's portal to exporting and trade services. It is designed to simplify the exporting process by being a single point of access to export-related services and thus reducing the need to view multiple government sources. Over 19 U.S. departments and agencies contribute to the information it provides including the U.S. International Trade Administration, the U.S. Commercial Service, the Department of Commerce, the Export-Import Bank, the Agency for International Development, and the U.S. Trade and Development Agency. Export.gov is fully searchable and allows you to search globally the contents of all of its contributing entities.

EXPORT911.com: http://www.export911.com/ (accessed Spring 2009).

This business and educational Web site focuses on international business. It provides in-depth information on export/import marketing, management, letters of credit, export cargo insurance, shipping, logistics, manufacturing, purchasing, bar codes, and more. Major sections include Gateways to Global Markets, Purchasing Department, Production Department, and Product Coding (bar codes). Business Tools include Conversion Tables, Abbreviations, Acronyms, and Symbols, and General References. Case studies and samples are also provided. This large site provides a plethora of educational and informational articles and data.

Federal Trade Commission (FTC): http://www.ftc.gov/bcp/business.shtm (accessed Spring 2009).

The FTC provides business information for consumers and businesses. One section is entitled E-Commerce and the Internet and provides you with rules and information about Internet advertising and marketing, a code of online business practices, online privacy needs, regulations of Internet auctions, securing your server, selling on the Internet, and more. Economic and legislation information related to the Internet is also provided.

Federation of International Trade Associations (FITA): http://www.fita.org (accessed Spring 2009).

Founded in 1984, FITA has more than 450 affiliates, which are independent international associations that fall into one of the following categories: world trade clubs, associations or chambers of commerce with regional/bilateral interests, associations focused on international logistics, associations supporting international trade, associations supporting exporters, or professional associations. More than 400,000 groups are linked here. Neither individuals nor companies can become members but can join the member organizations. FITA provides an outstanding linking site, which is searchable, has annotated links, and is available in languages other than English. The organization also publishes the e-mail newsletter *Really Useful Sites for International Trade Professionals*.

**Free Management Library: http://www.managementhelp.org/ (accessed Spring 2009).

The Library provides easy-to-access, clutter-free, comprehensive resources regarding the leadership and management of yourself, other individuals, groups, and organizations. Content is relevant to most small and medium-sized organizations. Over the past 10 years, the Library has grown to be one of the world's largest well-organized collections of these types of resources. Approximately 650 topics are included here, spanning 5,000 links. Topics include the most important practices to start, develop, operate, evaluate and resolve problems in for-profit and nonprofit organizations. Each topic has additionally recommended books and related articles. Grouped alphabetically by subject, the E-Commerce collection is particularly noteworthy.

GlobalEDGE: http://globaledge.msu.edu/ (accessed Spring 2009).

Managed by Michigan State University's Center for International Business Education and Research (MSU_CIBER), this site links to a broad selection of international trade data including economic trends, statistical data sources, government resources, trade portals, journals, and mailing lists. Its Global Resources section provides access to more than 2,000 online resources. MSU_CIBER has also contributed its own resources including an interactive forum for business professionals and portions of the information contained in the Knowledge Room, GlobalEDGE's section on the latest issues and trends effecting international business.

International Trade Administration (ITA): http://trade.gov/index.asp (accessed Spring 2009).

Part of the Department of Commerce, the ITA has set up this site to strengthen the U.S.'s competitiveness, promote trade and investment, and encourage fair trade and compliance with trade laws and agreements. Find statistics through its TradeStats Express and some PDFs of free publications, though many are only available for purchase. *A Basic Guide to Exporting* is probably the most thorough and useful publication as it provides practical help for exporters/ importers. Find trade events and missions and get export counseling through this site. The FAQ section has many links to more information for exporters and importers. The ITA conducts analytical studies of individual industries and of foreign countries, and this huge site has many industry and gross domestic products statistics. All of the agency and related Web sites comprising the large DOC organization are globally searchable from the DOC site including the Economic and Statistics Administration. A Spanish version of the site is also available.

Market Research, Industry Research, Business Research: http://www.virtualpet.com /industry (accessed Spring 2009).

This major portal for researching companies and industries presents a step-by-step process to begin researching an industry. Here you can find sources to help you learn about legal issues, regulatory issues, competition, markets, and even history of the industry for your new business. Additional links to Industry Portals are also available. Three other linked sites offer help on How to Learn about a Company by Examining its Products, How to Review, Evaluate, Critique a Web Site, and How to Conduct a Patent Search.

MoreBusiness.com: http://www.morebusiness.com (accessed Spring 2009).

Sections on this site include Startup, Running SmallBiz, Templates, and Tools. The Templates section provides sample business contracts and agreements, business and marketing plans, press releases, and business checklists. A large collection of articles and advice under Business Technology will help you understand the Internet, online shopping, Web site technology, hacking, and even laptop issues. The section Build Your Own Website is very useful. Many of the articles are lengthy and thorough. Use this site to help improve your marketing and management skills.

Quick MBA: http://www.quickmba.com/entre/bplan/ (accessed Spring 2009).

For those new to business plans and SWOT analysis, this site is thorough and practical. Learn the basics of both these concepts and many more here. Management and marketing articles are useful and helpful to new owner/managers as well as experienced ones. A political, economic, social, technical (PEST) analysis is presented, why to use it, and how it relates to SWOT. Often articles include recommended readings.

**SBDCNET: http://sbdcnet.utsa.edu (accessed Spring 2009).

The Small Business Development Center National Information Clearinghouse provides timely, Web-based information to entrepreneurs. Small Business Development Centers (SBDC) are located in all 50 states. SBDCs offer free, confidential business counseling. This Web site provides information on business start-up, international trade, e-commerce, industry research, marketing, trends, and more. The International Trade section has many links to more information and more help in moving into exporting or importing. Templates for business plans and marketing tools are also available. A free newsletter will help you keep up on trends in small business. Entrepreneurs will find plenty of links and information here to help plan, expand, and run a new business.

Small Business Administration: http://www.sba.gov (accessed Spring 2009).

This official government site offers a wealth of resources and programs for starting and growing a small business. In the library of the SBA site, the Small Business Management Series contains a group of publications like planning and goal setting for small business and inventory management. In addition, the Emerging Business Series covers topics like strategic planning, management issues, and human resource management. Other major sections of the site cover business planning, financing, managing, marketing, employees, taxes, legal aspects, and business opportunities. Under Financing you will find articles on Breakeven Analysis, Estimating Costs, and Cash Management. Find here online forms, business plans, and loan information. Some content is available in Spanish.

USA.gov: http://www.USA.gov (accessed Spring 2009).

Information by Topic will interest and amaze first-timer visitors. Topics include Defense and International, Environment, Energy and Agriculture, Money and Taxes, Reference and General Government, and Science and Technology. Tabs at the top of the page include one for Businesses and Nonprofits, which has a section on International Trade. Clicking on Data and Statistics brings up an alphabetical list of links to resources chock full of statistics. Economic Indicators is the Web site of the Economics and Statistics Administration, part of the U.S. Department of Commerce (http://www.economicindicators.gov), and it provides timely access to the daily releases of key economic indicators from the Bureau of Economic Analysis (BEA) and the Census Bureau. In addition, under Businesses and Nonprofits is a section titled Foreign Businesses Doing Business in the U.S. Under Frequently Asked Foreign Business Questions is a section called Doing Business Abroad. Spanish translation of the site is also available. You can e-mail questions about the site and the statistics or telephone for help too. Your taxes pay for the collection, compiling, and publishing of these statistics, and they are available for your use.

U.S. Customs and Border Protection (CBP): http://www.cbp.gov/ (accessed Spring 2009).

Under the Department of Homeland Security, the CBP unifies and integrates the work of several separate government entities including functions of the U.S. Customs Service, the Immigration and Naturalization Service, and the Agricultural Department's Animal and Plant Health Protection Service. It provides protection, advice, and control of merchandise shipped into the country as well as enforcement and compliance with many diverse regulations concerning homeland security, the flow of trade, inspections at ports of entry, and seizures of illegal drugs and contraband. The Importing and Exporting sections of the CBP Web site contain a wealth of information on current trade issues, export licenses and fees, news on specific products, the Harmonized Tariff Schedule, pertinent statutes and regulations, and other publications, forms, and videos.

VIBES: Virtual International Business and Economic Sources: http://library.uncc .edu/display/?dept=reference&format=open&page=68 (accessed Spring 2009).

The more than 1,600 links to free sources of information at this site were selected by Jeanie Welch of the University of North Carolina Charlotte. The table of contents breaks the sites into three groups: comprehensive, regional, and national. The comprehensive section organizes its links by category, including banking and finance, business practices and company information, emerging markets, and international trade law. Research and tables and graphs are highlights of this site. The regional section allows searching devoted to a single region or continent such as Europe or the Middle East. The national section links to sites devoted to a particular country.

Yahoo! Small Business Resources—Online Business—Ecommerce http://small business.yahoo.com/ecommerce/ (accessed Spring 2009).

This large site is packed with articles and links to information on all aspects of starting, marketing, and running an online business. Fully searchable and easy to navigate, this site provides information and help on Web connectivity, domain names, and even an eBay Center. The annotated links lead users to other well-respected sites like Entrepreneur.com, AllBusiness.com (http://www.all business.com/), and Inc.com (http://inc.com/), for example, and are divided by subject area. Also check out Reaching Beyond Borders for international business suggestions and additional insights in implementing a successful e-commerce site.

The Internet and Selling Globally

Expanding your operations outside your home country is a proposition that is obviously exciting and scary. Worldwide, the total number of people using the Internet will soon reach 1.5 billion. China itself will have the world's highest number of Internet users, already surpassing India. U.S. homes and businesses with broadband access now total over 100 million.

We now take for granted the role of technology and the Internet and its impact on communication. The fundamental issue that separates the Internet from other support tools used to build international trade is that time and distance do not matter or impact costs. In other words, businesses no longer have to worry about how far away a customer is or what time of day it is in the local time zone. With the Internet, all communication is immediate and distance has no impact on cost. Internet-enabled cell phones are easy to use and becoming less expensive every day. The duration of the communication does not impact costs either. The full impact of the advantages of the Internet over other forms of communication is just being understood by international and domestic companies. The Web is uniting the world. Today product manuals, price lists, software patches, training materials, and audio-video materials are all only a click away for users. Information is available on demand.

Therefore, one way to ease the stress of expanding into international business is to use the Internet and e-commerce to test the waters and not risk investing in hiring staff, international travel, capital, time, etc. Selling wares globally is a growing niche for many e-commerce sites. Now you can serve customers directly and bypass the middle of the supply chain—distributors, wholesalers, and "brick-and-mortar" stores—to reach potential customers in every nook and cranny of the world. A partner who has experience in working outside the United States or using the Internet for international business would also make this leap less scary and risky. The return on investment in going international can be lucrative especially as the ever-competitive U.S. market becomes oversaturated with products and services. Overseas the product may be relatively new and sought-after with few, if any, distributors; and you may find untapped markets in dozens of countries.

Looking just at retail sales in 2007, many retailers struggled with weak store and catalog sales. By contrast, e-commerce was the retailing industry's growth engine. In 2007, the business-to-consumer e-commerce market grew nearly six times faster than total retail sales. In 2007, online retail sales reached $165.9 billion, an increase of 21.8 percent from $136.2 billion a year earlier. Meanwhile, total retail sales grew by 3.9 percent to $2.41 trillion from $2.32 trillion in 2006, according to the National Retail Federation. In early 2008, Amazon.com's North American sales were up 35 percent from 2007 to $2.17 billion, while international sales were up 47 percent, to $189 billion. But adjusting for the effect of exchange rates, international sales grew only 34 percent. The economic downturn in the fall of 2008 greatly impacted retail sales in all sectors.

Therefore, looking at the pros and cons of taking your e-commerce business international, you may find the pros are the following:

- More opportunity for growth in customer base and increased sales in foreign countries;
- Global name recognition and inexpensive advertising;
- Low financial investment;
- An opportunity to move ahead of your competition;
- Inexpensive and immediate translation; and
- Full control over information flow.

While the cons may include:

- Language barriers that may complicate the process;
- Selling products on a large scale, which may require setting up foreign distributors and manufacturing plants;

- Laws and regulations vary by country, which adds another layer of compliance and complexity.

GETTING STARTED

The Internet connects buyers and sellers in the majority of countries around the world. Experts believe that international markets are growing at nearly twice the rate of domestic markets and that this trend will continue for some time to come. When you start selling on the Internet, you become part of the global e-commerce market; and international customers may seek you out whether you are ready for them or not. Remember that international trade rules are complicated and even accidental violations of policy can get you in trouble. Consult with government agencies, trade organizations, or a lawyer who practices international law before you make your first international sale. A great Web site to start at is the Business Owners Idea Café at http://www.businessownersideacafe.com/business/ecommerce.php.

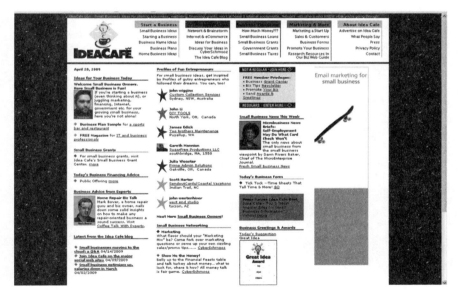

Home page. Idea Café.

Source: http://www.businessownersideacafe.com/business/ecommerce.php

Here you will learn about the current technologies to use, companies that can design a commercial Web site, and more.

QUICK CHECKLIST FOR MAKING THE E-COMMERCE DECISION

If what you have learned so far makes you hesitate, here is a list of questions to make you consider more details and implications:

1. *Level of Experience*: Have you already done business in another country? Have you received inquiries from other countries? Make a list of potential buyers by product for each country. Is there a trend, and who are your domestic and/or foreign competitors?

2. *Management and Personnel*: Who will be responsible for e-commerce exports? What are the expected outcomes? What changes in the organization are needed to ensure export sales are adequately serviced, and who will lead the follow through after the planning stage?

3. *Production Capability*: Is there a commitment to international sales for the long term, not just as a short term measure to boost a domestic downturn or slump in sales? Will filling export orders negatively affect domestic sales? What are the new costs? What about employment affects, and what design, packaging, and/or labeling changes are needed?

4. *Financial Capacity*: What capital is available for developing an international market? Are there operating costs? List the initial expenses, and is there a deadline for making this business expansion become self-supporting?

INVESTIGATE MORE POSSIBILITIES

Use the Internet to perform the following business functions for expanding into international trade: market research, identifying, profiling and communicating with potential agents and distributors, customer and market support services, advertising, trade leads, and logistics such as tracking package status, pricing freight movements, routine communications with customers, and more.

One of the keys to successfully using the power of the Internet is to plan properly the whole company's Internet effort. Go back to Chapter 5 to work through developing a business plan keeping the needs and limitations of foreign Internet buyers in mind. Other questions to consider include: What training is needed for company staff to ensure the use of the Internet is appropriate and efficient? How will our needs for the Internet change as our international business changes? Is there a need for an intranet Web site for internal users?

Sometimes there is confusion between the roles of outside companies when providing Internet solutions. Your Internet Service Provider (ISP) is the company that supplies your company with connectivity to the Internet, arranging for equipment and special phone lines to ensure that the company's computers can access the Internet. Many companies have a third party host their Web sites. This company may be the same company that designs the Web site, or it may be the company that provides access to the Internet, or there may be three separate companies. The company that is paid to store the data and images of the Web site is the host.

Involve the Webmaster early in the initial stages of planning the company's Web site; his/her responsibility is to turn your ideas and goals for your company into reality. Be sure he/she is aware of the international component as these international needs will impact decisions about the technical specifications for the Web site. Find and visit the Web sites of companies who have the function and design that you believe will fit your requirements, and share your list of sites with the Webmaster to help ensure that he/she understands your vision for your site. The Webmaster may be a company employee or an outside contractor; however, an employee in the company should be trained in updating and making simple changes to the Web site. Be sure to maintain your site and keep it current, with the latest product or service support information so foreign agents and distributors can consult it for information and assistance. Make it a priority to keep your site up to date by continually changing the product and company information.

OTHER TECHNICAL CONSIDERATIONS

Besides implementation and Web site development issues, discuss the following issues with your Webmaster:

- The lower speed Internet connections or connections through older software in some countries. These conditions are changing but remember them and take into consideration that some foreign customers will have lower modem speeds and/or lower quality phone connections. The connection between the ISP and the Internet network itself can also affect Internet performance. Minimizing the use of graphics can help sites load faster, and users can navigate more quickly to the information they need.

- User statistics. Data about who accessed your Web site and when will help you understand your customers better and provide the service needed. This data may help track the effectiveness of your advertising or marketing campaigns and measure the interest in your products overseas.

- Site registration. Asking visitors to register prior to providing full product or service details is a well-known method for tracking visitors' interests.

- Site security. If your company wants to protect sensitive information such as pricing or technical manuals, ask the Webmaster to use some type of security to block unauthorized visitors from parts of the site. Passwords are one option. Remember that anything online can probably make its way into the hands of a competitor.

THE LANGUAGE BARRIER

This most obvious cultural distinction is the first one you will need to overcome to do business in a non-English-speaking country or region. While English is the recognized language of business in many countries, not

everyone speaks it. Look back to the Barriers to Cross-Cultural Communications topic in Chapter 6 for more detail. Chapter 6 also deals
with cultural differences. Using graphic features can be difficult as they
may only make sense for users who read left to right. For populations that
read right to left, the graphics meaning may be changed or incompre-
hensible. The choice of colors for your site is also difficult. Understand that
different colors mean different things in different cultures and research
before you design your Web pages. Current estimates are that only about
57 percent of Internet users speak English. Obviously, if you can communicate in the local language, you will have a distinct advantage. The most
basic detail of online business involves understanding the written word.
What will you do if you receive an e-mail from a customer in a language
you did not understand? You actually have several possible solutions to this
dilemma:

1. Translation Software: One popular solution is to purchase a good software
   program that lets you convert standard business applications into a foreign a
   language. These software packages may translate just one language or a more
   comprehensive program includes multiple languages, and they generally are
   as easy to operate as a common word processing program. Translation.net
   has been in business since 1994 on the Internet, so has a long history of
   helping people communicate. SysTran Software Inc. (http://www.systran
   soft.com) is another well-established company.

2. Web-based translations: The Internet expedites many things including the
   availability of real-time translation services and products. You and/or your
   customers can translate information by using a Web browser. Pricing is generally based on the size of your company or number of users, number of transactions monthly or yearly, or on the product type itself. To find out more
   about these services, try Applied Language Solutions at http://www.applied
   language.com/ or Translation Experts at http://www.tranexp.com.

3. Free Online Translation Tools: Several companies offer free translation software
   through the Internet. FreeTranslation.com (http://www.freetranslation.com/) is
   a powerful instant translation service powered by SDL's Enterprise Translation
   Server and is a very popular site. The translation is generated by a computer and
   is displayed instantly. Affiliated with Click2Translate, this site dynamically
   shows the cost of having the same text professionally translated too. PROMPT
   from Smartlink Corporation (www.online-translator.com/site_Translation.aspx
   ?prmtlang=en) is another free online translation service, and it also provides
   automated translation software.

Whether every business should have their entire Web site translated into
other languages is an issue still up for debate. Most companies thinking of
involving themselves in international trade should consider translating a
welcome or introductory page into three or four most important languages
such as German, French, and Spanish or depending on the products or

services Chinese, Japanese, or Hindi. At least provide a link to Yahoo's Babel fish (free online Web page translation service: http://babelfish .yahoo.com/) to help foreign visitors. Let potential customers know if you offer a translation service locally to translate their e-mails into English. If you have forms on the Web site, be sure the form conforms to the conventions of international addresses, titles, surnames, postal codes, etc. Be careful about making too many fields obligatory as they may not apply. Do not forget the country field. Keep your target market in mind when developing forms. Remember that often companies new to international e-commerce cannot fill international orders simply because their systems cannot register international addresses or price total delivery costs.

Another important step after you have invested in a Web site is to make sure customers know it exists and how to find it—marketing. Put your URL and e-mail address on all brochures, flyers, billboards, ads in many types of publications, stationery, and business cards. Get your Web address listed in Internet business directories and possibly join a virtual mall. Last but definitely not least, be certain to get your address on as many search engines as you possibly can.

EXPANDING YOUR BUSINESS ONLINE

You may be very happy to keep your company small, but for some the challenge of growth is irresistible, and often e-commerce really makes a company "take off." Remember the key to successful expansion in any business is planning, as I often emphasize. Before moving your small e-commerce business to the next level you need to determine what that level is. Start by closely analyzing your options and determine the advantages and disadvantages of the common paths.

1. A very obvious way to expand your business is to offer more products or services on your existing site, which will attract a wider customer base and bring in larger revenues. This strategy is implemented by many companies regularly whether they realize it or not. However, if you consciously identify it as your first growth strategy, your actions will be more targeted and aggressive.
   Here is a start on identifying pros for expanding your e-commerce business by adding products or services:
   - You continue to retain full control of your company.
   - The exploration of different areas, products, services, markets, etc. may increase your enthusiasm for the business.

   And of course, the cons include:
   - It takes time to see results.
   - It make take a larger financial investment to support back-end systems for added inventory or providing expanding services.

2. Another way to expand your e-commerce business is to acquire other sites. Start by identifying competitor sites that may prove profitable for your company. Also look at complementary business sites as they may offer products and services that are different but still a good fit for your business. Pros of acquiring other sites include:

- It is a quick way to expand and/or diversify.
- Other sites expand your site's customer base easily.

On the other hand, cons include:

- Expansion requires an infusion of cash.
- Negotiations for the sale may drag on and be a drain on time and resources.

3. Another well recognized way to expand your company is to partner opportunities for affiliate programs. Partnerships could be with a national organization to provide a product or service or partnerships with other businesses that will expand your product line and customer base. Pros of affiliate or partnerships include:

- Another entity shares the financial burden and associated risks.
- More staff and business knowledge may be available.
- There may be tax or legal advantages.

Cons may include:

- You must share the profits.
- You lose some control and power in making decisions.
- Negotiations take time and slow decision-making.
- Raising funds may be more difficult.

E-COMMERCE PITFALLS

Although there are many benefits offered by the Internet and all companies need to use it to enhance their international expansion, potential downsides and concerns do exist:

- Do not use it as a substitute for all foreign travel. Ultimately travel should still be included in your company's overall international business plan.
- Remember that not everyone in the world has as much access to the Internet as we in the United States do. We accept it as reliable, inexpensive, and accessible to all, but some regions of the world remain shut out or at least limited, while others, like most of the population of South Korea, enjoy high-speed access and financial transactions are most often conducted via a PC or cell phone.
- Be wary and keep security measures current and active. All companies as well as individuals should maintain a certain level of scrutiny and suspicion about

Internet correspondence especially in relation to financial issues as a strong potential for fraud does exist.

• Remain vigilant about information posted on the company Web site. The more competitors know about your products or pricing details, the easier it is to compete against your company. Security and control on the Internet is important for a variety of reasons.

As you have learned after reading this chapter, e-commerce is rapidly growing and rapidly expanding through the world; this often profitable type of business is also available to more entrepreneurs than ever before. The world is shrinking and consumers are enthusiastically embracing the possibilities of getting the products and services when they need them, at a price they can afford, and when they want them. Planning as in any new business venture is still the key to success. Leap into the e-commerce world, but plan for success.

REFERENCES

(Starred titles discussed in the chapter)

Print Resources

Addison, Doug. *Small Websites, Great Results: The Blueprint for Creating Websites that Really Work.* Paraglyph, Inc., 2004. 352p. ISBN 1-932111-90-5. $29.99.

If you want a simple, well-designed, highly focused Web site, Addison's approach will work for your small business. Design ideas and marketing techniques are showcased in profiles of 20 small businesses. You will discover new approaches to creating sites, find out what really makes small sites work, learn about strategies for getting, keeping, and satisfying customers, and pick up tips on how to work with professional designers to get the results you want and need. Learn how to create an update or editorial calendar and how to organize the files on your Web site so that your business site is always different, current, and easy to change. Discover what to leave off your site to keep it simple and uncluttered. Addison will convince you that quality is much better than quantity.

A Basic Guide to Exporting: Official Government Resource for Small and Medium-sized Businesses. 10th ed. U.S. Department of Commerce, 2007. 190pp. ISBN 0-16079-20-4-5. $19.95. Also available online is the 1998 edition: http://www .unzco.com/basicguide/index.html.

Conventional wisdom once held that U.S. businesses should be content selling within their domestic market as international markets were too difficult and too expensive to penetrate. However, in the past decade, barriers to trade have been lowered and advances in communications technology have been and are tremendous. Now exporting is seen as a prime growth area, and this title describes the costs and risks associated with exporting, how to develop a strategy for success, and where to get the knowledge to enter exporting. Assistance from the federal and state government is also discussed.

Belew, Shannon and Elad, Joel. *Starting an Online Business All-in-One Desk Reference for Dummies*. Wiley Publishing, Inc., 2006. 814p. ISBN 978-0-7645-9929-3. $29.99.

As in other books of this series, readers find the basics of starting a business on the Internet. E-commerce survival stories, best practices, and other resources to help you develop your new business are provided. Find good tips on selecting an online host, understanding Web site design, establishing a graphic identity, providing customer service, and providing various payment options. The chapters Niche E-Commerce and E-Commerce Advances are especially useful. Some coverage of legal matters, Internet security, trademarks, copyrighting, and taxes are included.

Brown, Bruce C. *The Ultimate Guide to Search Engine Marketing: Pay Per Click Advertising Secrets Revealed*. Atlantic Publishing Group, Inc., 2007. 288p. ISBN 0-910627-99-3. $24.95.

You can increase your Web site traffic with Pay Per Click (PPC) Advertising. PPC brings you fast results and you can reach your target audience with the most cost-effective method on the Internet today. Brown shows you the secrets of executing a successful, cost-effective campaign. PPC, is an advertising technique that uses search engines where you can display your text ads throughout the Internet keyed to the type of business you have or the type of products you are promoting. The key to success in PPC advertising is to know what you are doing, devise a comprehensive and well-crafted advertising plan, and know the relationships between your Web site, search engines, and PPC advertising campaign methodology. Brown will teach you the six steps to a successful campaign: Keyword Research; Copy Editing, Setup, and Implementation; Bid Management; Performance Analysis; Return on Investment; and Reporting and Avoiding PPC Fraud.

Cyr, Donald, and Gray, Douglas. *Marketing Your Product*. 4th ed. Self-Counsel Press, Inc., 2004. 200p. ISBN 1-55180-394-1. $18.95.

Covering all the essentials of marketing, this expanded edition of a marketing classic demonstrates how your business can carve a niche for its products or services. Learn about market researching, market positioning, planning a marketing strategy, product launching, and competitor awareness. Cyr and Gray help readers answer questions like what you should know about global marketing and why people choose one product over another. One highlight in this edition is a chapter on the value of the Internet as a marketing tool in the global marketplace. Good worksheets help entrepreneurs and new small business owners develop their own marketing plan.

Damani, Chetan, and Damani, Neil Sait Ravi. *7 Habits of Successful Ecommerce Companies*. Imano PLC, 2004. 105p. ISBN 0-95-4905512. $49.95.

The Damanis succinctly cover everything you need to know when setting up an e-commerce operation to make it a success. Key elements are cover in a well-organized, practical manner. Sections cover the seven habits, which include conduct return on investment marketing; measure, analyze, optimize; and value the customer relationship.

Dorsey, Jennifer. *Start Your Own Import/Export Business*. 2nd ed. Entrepreneur Press, 2007. 252p. ISBN 1-59918-108-8. $15.95.

This book contains insights and practical advice for entering global markets. It covers aspects of the startup process, including collecting money from overseas transactions, using the Internet to simplify your transactions, accessing trade law information to keep your business in compliance, how to find contacts in the United States and abroad, using the Internet to simplify your transactions, and choosing a customs broker. Chapters on market research, working online, employees, pricing, and insurance will help run a business efficiently and effectively. A brief appendix on international trade resources may also prove useful. Interviews with successful importers and exporters and an updated resource list will help show the way to success.

Exporters' Encyclopaedia. Annual. Dun & Bradstreet.

A comprehensive world reference guide, this encyclopedia is divided into 220 country-specific sections; firms specializing in international business, laws, and legislation; international trade associations; government agencies; shipping practice; and reference data on weights and measures for overseas ports. Find key contacts, trade and safety regulations, and information on documentation needed. Marketing Data includes legal requirements for importer/agents, procurement standards, environmental protection and pollution control, marking, and labeling. The encyclopedia also provides passport regulations and business etiquette guidelines.

Fuhrman, John. *The Electronic Dream: Essential Ingredients for Growing a People Business in an e-Commerce World*. Markowski International Publishers, 2004. 144p. ISBN 0938716611. $11.95.

Fuhrman explains the opportunities available in e-commerce. Learn how to move more products and use the new quality tools available to help become successful. Chapters cover leadership, trends, importance of growth and energy, and the basics of selling and marketing on the Internet.

Funk, Tom. *Web 2.0 and Beyond: Understanding the New Online Business Models, Trends, and Technologies*. Greenwood Publishing Group, Inc., 2008. 192p. ISBN 0-313-35187-2. $34.95.

Because "Web 2.0" is now a buzzword, it can describe many things including Web sites, cultural trends like social networking, blogging, or podcasting, or the technology underlying today's newest and coolest Web applications—so it is really a series of trends, not a collection of things. With the trends pioneered by giants like Amazon, YouTube, and Google, even the smallest companies can take advantage of new, open-source programming tools, new social software, and new networks. The Web 2.0 landscape is really about users controlling their online experience and influencing the experiences of others. Small companies can gain customers and competitive advantage by putting these new technologies to work for them. This nontechnical guide will help you understand recent developments in the online world and put them to practical business uses.

Gendron, Michael P. *Creating the New E-Commerce Company*. South-Western, 2005. 304p. ISBN 0-324-22485-0. $34.95.

Gendron discusses how emerging technologies should be viewed in a total corporate context as an intrinsic part of the organization's structure and mission. Learn how new technologies will revamp the way we do business every day and learn to use them to maximize your company's potential. Management in all sizes of businesses will have to think about how organizations and industries can adapt to the electronic future. E-thinking in day-to-day business tactics and strategic plans is essential. Discover how this conversion to e-commerce thinking can boost the bottom line.

Hanson, Ward. *The Principles of Internet Marketing*. 2nd ed. South-Western College Publishing, 2005. 467p. ISBN: 0-32-407477-8. $120.00.

This popular introduction to e-commerce explores Internet-based marketing as part of an overall marketing program and discusses techniques that work and those that do not. Stanford professor Ward Hanson incorporates pricing, brand building, new product development, online communities, and personalization into this discussion. This second edition illustrates leading practices by industry leaders, demonstrates how the use of research supports conclusions, and pays special attention to the uniqueness of online marketing. Hanson includes a useful glossary.

Haugtvedt, Curtis P. et al. *Online Consumer Psychology: Understanding and Influencing Consumer Behavior in the Virtual World*. Lawrence ErlbaumAssoc., Inc., 2005. 416p. ISBN 0-805-85154-2. $54.95.

Issues created by the Web including customization, psychological effects of site design, word of mouth processes, and the study of consumer decision-making online are addressed. The advantages of the Internet are as follows: bringing like-minded individuals together; using customization and understanding why consumers customize products and services; advertising and marketing; empowering consumers to make better decisions; using online research tools; and gaining insight into how consumers think.

Hinkelman, Edward, et al. *Importers Manual*. Annual. World Trade Press. 960p.

Information on how to import virtually any commodity into the United States can be found in this practical reference. It is precisely organized for ease of use and is divided into the major sections of Commodity Index; U.S. Customs Entry and Clearance; International Banking; Legal Considerations of Importing; and Packing, Shipping, and Insurance. The heart of the work, the Commodity Index, contains entry procedures, documentation, restrictions, and prohibitions, marking and labeling requirements, and contact information for regulatory agencies for all products that can be imported into the United States.

Jagoe, John R. *Export Sales and Marketing Manual 2008: The Bible of Exporting*. Annual. Export Institute of the United States. 520p. ISBN 0-943677-66-1. $295.00.

Having been updated annually for 21 consecutive years, this international trade publication has achieved longevity and global reach. This manual covers all the steps involved in selling products in world markets. Over 120 illustrations,

85 graphs, 40 flow charts, and 60 sample international trade documents lead the user through the process. Jagoe helps users conduct market research through 1200 Web site addresses providing information on various markets and products and services. A lengthy glossary of export terms and detailed index for quick access to important information is also provided.

Karavdic, Munib. *E-Commerce and Export Performance*. Cambria Press, 2006. 321p. ISBN 1-934043-18-9. $89.95.

Karavdic investigates how e-commerce impacts export marketing and performance in terms of product design and global promotion and distribution. He uses a comprehensive survey of 340 Australian exporters to advance his e-commerce marketing theory. Interviews with senior management are also part of this study. Practitioners as well as marketing students and faculty will find a wealth of information here on business environment export marketing strategy and e-commerce activities.

Levine, Michael. *Guerrilla PR Wired: Waging a Successful Publicity Campaign Online, Offline, and Everywhere In Between*. McGraw-Hill, 2003. 288p. ISBN 0-07-138232-1. $15.95.

This collection of cutting-edge, low-cost publicity techniques includes sample press releases and attention-getting strategies targeted for the wired environment. Focused on the Web or Internet, the chapters on Internet PR and "The Web and How to Unweave It," are particularly informative to those new to using the Internet for marketing. Levine has many years of experience in PR, and entrepreneurs will benefit from this discussion and hints gathered from his experiences.

Levinson, Jay Conrad, et al. *Guerilla Marketing on the Internet: The Definitive Guide from the Father of Guerilla Marketing*. Entrepreneur Press, 2008. 304p. ISBN 1-599-1819-43. $21.95.

These authors demonstrate how to use unconventional "guerilla marketing" techniques to utilize today's ultimate marketing weapon, the Internet. Find here case studies, low-cost tactics for maximizing traffic to your Web site, tips to avoid the 12 biggest Internet marketing mistakes, and creative tactics and cutting-edge tools to inspire your customers to take action. Capture and keep your market share.

McFadyen, Thomas. *Ecommerce Best Practices: How to Market, Sell, and Service Customers with Internet Technologies*. McFadyen Solutions, 2008. 366p. ISBN 0-9815951-0-3. $34.95.

This title provides tools for companies in any stage of developing a Web presence to market and sell their products or services to global customers. McFadyen is a frequent speaker and consultant on e-commerce matters. Learn how to make navigation easy for your customers, use the latest in shopping carts, and make visitors into buyers. Well-written and well-organized, this resource can improve your Web site.

Meyerson, Mitch, and Scarborough, Mary Eule. *Mastering Online Marketing*. Entrepreneur Press, 2007. 211p. ISBN 1-59918-151-7. $21.95.

This 12-step system teaches readers how to build and sustain a thriving e-commerce business. These strategies and tactics will help you get targeted traffic to your Web site, turn visitors into buyers, and generally help build a successful business on the Internet. Find help in understanding why your Web site is under-performing. Worksheets, resources, and case studies from successful businesses are highlights of Meyerson and Scarborough's bible for online marketing.

Morrison, Terri. *Kiss, Bow, or Shake Hands: The Bestselling Guide to Doing Business in More than 60 Countries.* Adams Media Corp., 2006. 592p. ISBN 1-59-33736-86. $24.95.

This encyclopedic resource presents information for each country on the country history, type of government, languages, religions, business practices, titles and forms of address for 60 countries. A cultural orientation for each country with negotiation strategies and value systems is included. Well-organized and concise, this newly revised guide will make learning to do business in a foreign country easier.

Murphy, Christopher. *Competitive Intelligence: Gathering, Analyzing, and Putting It to Work.* Gower Publishing, Division of Ashgate Pub., Ltd., 2005. 304p. ISBN 0-566-08537-2. $120.00.

Businesses need intelligence to find suppliers, mobilize capital, win customers, and beat the competition. Murphy advocates a conscious, systematic approach to getting intelligence and using it to recognize and seize opportunities. Learn how companies try to stay ahead of their rivals, about difference methods of research and sources of information, and about analytical techniques that transform facts and opinions into a platform of knowledge to support informed business decision-making. Learn how to read between the lines of company reports and press releases, how to understand corporate cultures, and how to research industries and companies in other countries. While focused on the British business world, the lessons presented have universal application and examples are taken from across the globe. The final chapter, "Intelligence Countersteps," will help you protect your company from the practices of unscrupulous researchers and investigators.

Nelson, Carl A. *Import/Export: How to Take Your Business Across Borders.* 4th ed. McGraw-Hill Companies, 2008. 352p. ISBN 0-07-148255-5. $21.95.

As in previous editions, Nelson demystifies international trade including basics such as writing the business plan, choosing a product/service, sample for customs and duties, and financing international transactions. He uses examples and success stories to illustrate his points. Hot-button issues such as the WTO, doing business with NAFTA, Africa, India, China, and the EU, and the changing world of e-commerce are explored. His step-by-step guidance will help entrepreneurs succeed in international ventures and use the Internet to advantage.

Olsen, Kai A. *The Internet, the Web, and EBusiness: Formalizing Applications for the Real World.* Scarecrow Press, 2005. 432p. ISBN 0-810-85167-9. $57.00.

This introductory book to the online world includes case studies and exercises about the human-computer interface and presents a concise overview of the fundamental principles of computer applications on the Internet. Learn the distinction between formal and informal processes and their relationship to virtual environments. Tables and graphics illustrate Olsen's ideas in an easy-to-understand manner. This basic knowledge will help you understand and utilize the online environment to the best of your ability.

Parasuraman, A. and Colby, Charles L. *Techno-Ready Marketing: How and Why Your Customers Adopt Technology*. The Free Press, 2001. 240p. ISBN 7-806-84864-945. $27.00.

Presented here is a compelling framework for measuring the propensity of customers to welcome and use technology-intensive products and services. Learn how to determine each customer's technology readiness, how to motivate customers to use new technology, why people either embrace or resist technology, and divide your consumers into five distinct groups. CEOs, small business owners or managers, and marketing professionals will learn how to succeed in the technology-driven future.

Phillips, Michael and Rasberry, Salli. *Marketing Without Advertising*. 4th ed. Nolo Press, 2003. 240p. ISBN 0-87337-930-6. $24.00.

This book takes readers on an in-depth, practical journey through marketing strategies. One valuable section illustrates how to design and implement a marketing plan. Other topics include updating the physical appearance of your business, educating and helping prospective customers find your business, and using the Internet to market your business internationally. Sections on the importance of good relations with your employees and how they influence the perception of your business are interesting and informative. Questionnaires, checklists, and worksheets help readers understand important points and make decisions about expanding their marketing efforts by using the Internet.

Plunkett, Jack W. et al. *Plunkett's E-Commerce and Internet Business Almanac 2010*. Annual. Plunkett Research, Limited, 2010. 623p. ISBN 1-59392-163-2 $299.99.

Over 400 in-depth profiles of e-commerce and Internet companies are provided. This edition includes overviews through easy-to-use tables on all facets of business on the Internet including e-commerce revenues, access and usage trends, and global Internet user data in the industry analysis section. Find data on Internet growth companies, online services and markets, online retailing strategies, emerging e-commerce technologies, manufacturers of software and equipment for Internet communications, and much more. Information is indexed and cross-referenced. Use *Plunkett's* to plan your global expansion.

Regnerus, Bob. *Big Ticket Ecommerce: How to Sell High-Priced Products and Services Using the Internet*. Innovation Press, 2008. 181p. ISBN 0-9764624-9-4. $16.95.

Learn techniques and methods of selling high-priced products and services through the new technologies available to e-commerce leaders and innovators. Regnerus describes how to plan and market these products to the clients who need them.

Reynolds, Janice. *The Complete E-Commerce Book: Design, Build & Maintain a Successful Web-based Business*. 2nd ed. Publishers Group West, 2004. 374p. ISBN 1-57-82031-20. $24.95.

This basic book explores important considerations in starting and building any business including customer satisfaction, marketing, and planning for growth. For e-commerce, effective Web site design, cutting-edge programming, building traffic, choosing reliable vendors, and superior hardware are essential for efficient business operations. Reynolds use real-world examples from the Web to gain ideas and insight to help readers solve business and technical dilemmas.

Rich, Jason R. *Design and Launch Your eCommerce Business in a Week*. Entrepreneur Press, 2008. 260p. ISBN 1-59918-183-5. $15.95.

This step-by-step guide will help you build a Web site quickly and with little frustration. Using inexpensive, turnkey solutions like Yahoo!, GoDaddy, Google, and eBay, beginners can design and build a professional, easy-to-navigate e-commerce site. Learn how to reach potential customers, accept payments from all over the world, and process simple orders. Discover ideas on how to keep customers coming back.

Ricks, David A. *Blunders in International Business*. 4th ed. Blackwell Pub., 2006. 182p. ISBN 1-4051-3492-5. $19.95.

This new edition is significantly updated and revised. The anecdotes and lessons are divided into chapters on production, names, marketing, translation, management, and more. Under Insufficient Market, Ricks gives examples of companies trying to sell corn flakes in Japan (generally the Japanese are not interested in breakfast cereals), fried chicken in Brazil (where their own charcoal-broiled chicken is cheaper and tastier), and frozen food in France (where the French prefer fresh foods). Learn about mistakes international companies like AOL, Toyota, and McDonald's have made and avoid them. Valuable lessons and strategies for coping with similar situations make Ricks's book an entertaining and useful read.

Risdahl, Aliza. *Streetwise eCommerce: Establish Your Online Business, Expand Your Reach, and Watach Your Profits Soar!* Adams Media Corporation, 2007. 371p. ISBN 1-59869-144-9. $19.95.

This handy guide teaches readers how to create and manage an e-mail list, design a Web site, build an online community, and market and sell online. Early chapters discuss the uses of various online communication tools like e-mail, blogs, and message boards and compares online marketing to traditional marketing efforts. Risdahl, an author of several books on entrepreneurship and Internet marketing, discusses building and maintaining your online presence, how to sell online, and evaluating techniques for your successes. Learn how to develop company policies, negotiate a Web deal, and understand the basics of Web design. Well-organized and user friendly, this resource will help you discover strategies and tools useful for developing and expanding your e-commerce business.

Small Business Sourcebook. 2v. Thomson Gale, annual. $405.00.

This directory provides a wealth of information for the small business owner or manager. The Small Business Profiles cover 340 different small businesses.

Businesses profiled include catering, cooking schools, fish farms, antique shops, bookstores, and car washes. Entries contain as many as 17 subheadings, such as start-up information, educational programs, reference works, sources of supply, statistical sources, trade periodicals, trade shows and conventions, consultants, and franchises and business opportunities. The chapter on import/export services will prove very useful along with the section on trade shows and exhibiting, which lists publications to help you get more out of exhibiting. The Small Business Topics section covers general ideas such as budgets and budgeting, retailing, service industry, franchising, insurance, and seasonal business. Like the small business profiles, these entries have the same 17 subheadings and lead users to many resources relating to the topics. The state listings and federal government assistance sections list programs and offices that provide information and support to businesses. Check your library for this practical, well-organized source.

Strange, C. A. *How to Start and Run an Internet Business.* How to Books, 2008. 222p. ISBN 1-84528-202-7. $26.00.

Strange has written a practical guide to establishing a profitable online business. She includes case studies, business ideas, ways to create a visible and usable Web presence, and tips for gaining and keeping a good customer base. She provides checklists and hints on secrets for online business success. Learn how to create an appealing virtual shop window for retail sales. She covers many aspects of selling to the international market too. If you have the right idea, Internet access, and enthusiasm for working until you get it right, a career as an Internet entrepreneur may be right for you.

Sweeney, Susan and MacLellan, Andy. *Advanced Marketing on the Internet.* 7th ed. Maximum Press, 2006. 452p. ISBN 1-93164-437-3. $35.95.

The authors teach business owners the techniques and methods to increase the effectiveness and growth of new or existing e-businesses. Discussed are proven online marketing techniques like link strategy, mail lists, content site advertising, viral marketing, RSS, blogvertising, and behavioral advertising. Learn about creating the right interface, identifying design and brand integrity, writing quality copy and content, and analyzing Web statistics. This new edition covers cutting-edge technologies.

Travis, Tom. *Doing Business Anywhere: The Essential Guide to Going Global.* John Wiley & Sons, Inc., 2007. 202p. ISBN 0-470-14961-2. $24.95.

Travis presents his six tenets of global trade and illustrates them in the context of real stories of global trade. He emphasizes the importance of international trade to the economic prosperity of all the world's nations. If you want to start a new venture or expand your present one, Travis helps you organize, plan, operate, and execute with a global mind-set. Learn how to navigate conflicting and confusing laws, deal with different cultures, and operate in different countries. He also explains how to leverage the benefits of free trade agreements to set up and operate a competitive and profitable business. Also highlighted is how to protect your brand through patents, copyrights, and trademarks. Security concerns and measures are also discussed. Travis will convince readers that embracing his six tenets is key to "doing business anywhere."

Zodl, Joseph A. *Export Import: Everything You and Your Company Need to Know to Compete in World Markets*. 4th ed. IIEI Press, 2005. 174p. ISBN 0-9773098-0-0. $39.95.

In easy-to-understand language and writing style, Zodl leads the reader into the world of international business, dispels the myths, simplifies tasks and processes, and illustrates important points with real-world examples. Zodl defines the vocabulary and terminology needed to understand the world of international business and points out sources for expert advice. This title provides the information the exporter needs to take a U.S.-manufactured product, sell it to a foreign buyer, make the shipment correctly, and get paid in U.S. dollars. It shows a middleman how to buy a product made by someone else and resell it at a profit to an overseas customer. Zodl also has a Web site users may be interested in checking out at http://www.zodl.net/firstpage.htm.

Online Resources

BEOnline: Business and Economics Online: http://www.loc.gov/rr/business/beonline/ (accessed Spring 2009).

Compiled by the Library of Congress Business Reference Services for researchers, this site has, under Subject Lists, a lengthy list of business topics such as associations, business plans (forms), companies by industry, data sets, e-commerce, economic indicators, international trade, and legal resources. If you click on Associations, you will find a short list of associations. Clicking on an association name takes you to its Web site. Under the International Trade Listing, you will find Foreign Trade Statistics, the Trade Compliance Center.

BizMove.com: http://www.bizmove.com (accessed Spring 2009).

The wealth of information on this site covers a variety of topics including general management, small business marketing, Internet business, and international trade. Worksheets and sample plans will help guide users. Growing a Business on the Internet covers topics like search engine positioning, Web site promotion, and e-mail marketing methods. International trade centers on exporting but covers many diverse topics including how to export a service and how to sell overseas.

Bplans.com: http://www.bplans.com (accessed Spring 2009).

This well-established, frequently updated site, sponsored by Palo Alton Software, Inc., is the best for help in writing your business plan. The section entitled Write a Business Plan, contains articles, calculators on cash flow, starting costs, break even and more, a business plan template, and executive summary and mission statement help plus access to Expert Advice. Currently 60 free plans are viewable online for free. On this fully searchable site, you can quickly find topics that you need, such as getting your plan funded and business plan legalities. Another nice feature is that they offer a Business Planning Audio for auditory learners. The section called Running an Online Business includes great articles for setting up and running an e-commerce site; find ideas on marketing your site and how to improve sales as well as measuring key performance factors. Other sections include finance and capital, marketing and advertising, buying a business, market research, and a monthly newsletter. Bplans.com is a useful, practical site that also offers fee-based experts and assistance.

Business.gov: http://www.business.gov (accessed Spring 2009).

Business.gov is another government site developed to help businesses find the information they need and want. The Advertising and Marketing section is especially useful. Links to information on major industries, population and demographic resources, plus Rural America Facts provide users with a multitude of useful resources. International trade connections are outstanding for global or Internet businesses too. You will find links to International Economic Trends, Import and Export Statistics, and Foreign Trade Statistics. Check out the section on e-commerce for more information from the Federal Trade Commission (FTC).

Business Owners Idea Café: http://www.businessownersideacafe.com (accessed Spring 2009).

Developed by successful entrepreneurs and authors of published guides on starting a business, this large site presents short articles on all aspects of small business or entrepreneurial life. The main divisions include CyberSchmooz, Starting your Biz, Running Your Biz, Take Out Info, Classifieds, The "You" in your Biz, De-Stress and Have Fun, About Idea Café, and Join Idea Café. The large Running Your Biz: eCommerce section has excellent coverage on all things e-commerce plus links to outside information on e-commerce. Here you can find experts to answer your questions or discuss your current business crisis. You will find sample business plans, financing help, business forms, and business news.

Buyusa.gov: http://www.buyusa.gov/home/export.html (accessed Spring 2009).

This simple-to-use government Web site offers to help businesses get into international sales through market research, trade events, introductions to buyers and distributors, and counseling for any and every step of the export process. One part of the Web site helps importers to the United States, and another helps exporters from the United States, and both parts cover products and services. When you click on a country, you get the Country Commercial Guide (CCG), a calendar of events, employment opportunities, market information, and services for U.S. exporters/suppliers. Also part of this site is *Commercial News USA*, the "official export promotion magazine of the U.S. Department of Commerce." This online publication also contains a wealth of information including franchising, trade shows, a company index, and more. Part of the Web site, AsiaNow, promotes trade with 14 Asia-Pacific markets and provides single point access to regional trade events, extensive services, and research covering Asian markets. Access Eastern Mediterranean provides U.S. companies with information on the region's markets and its 180 million consumers. The Americas and Showcase Europe provide information and services to those areas of the globe.

Canada Business Services for Entrepreneurs: http://www.canadabusiness.ca/ (accessed Spring 2009).

Though this site is aimed at Canadian businesses, you will find help and information here for exporting, importing, e-commerce, selling to the Canadian government, and more. The links under E-Business will help you in many phases of starting or expanding your markets in Canada.

ClickZ Stats: http://www.clickz.com/stats (accessed Spring 2009).

This large site has sectors for statistics on B2B, Demographics, Government/ Politics, Hardware, Search Tools, Security Issues, and Geographics. Categorized by month, year, and subsection, the Statistics Toolbox was set up as a resource that lets users to find statistics, numbers, and tables that have been incorporated into ClickZ Stats articles. The Web Worldwide is a look at current and projected Internet users with links to some related articles on different countries. Use the information here to understand the Internet business environment and make informed business decisions.

**_Commercial News USA_: http://www.export.gov/cnusa (accessed Spring 2009).

Commercial News USA is the official export promotion magazine of the U.S. Department of Commerce, and it showcases U.S.-made products and services. You will find lists of companies already exporting grouped in about 15 different industries. Trade show opportunities are highlighted and described, often letting businesses know who attends and who should attend. This publication is also an excellent source for trade leads and to advertise your products or services to find customers or partners; subscribe online or by mail. Issues may be read online for download in PDFs. Franchising information is available as well as success stories to inspire new exporters.

E-Business Research Center: http://www.cio.com/forums/ec/ (accessed Spring 2009).

From the publisher of _CIO_ magazine, this site is a gateway to recent full-text e-commerce articles in CIO.com publications. Links to case studies include date and one-sentence summary. Other topics covered are: customer service, demographics and market research, e-banking, billing and payment systems, electronic data interchange (EDI), industry associations, legal and government, marketing and sales, retailing, return on investment (ROI) and management, and security and infrastructure. Case studies, surveys, discussion forums, and events are also included. Each section provides relevant non-_CIO_ links, including publications.

E-Commerce Guidebook: http://www.online-commerce.com (accessed Spring 2009).

This site offers a good introduction to online payment. It is maintained by Net-Nation, a Canadian site-hosting provider, and the directory provides links to leading companies in online payment transactions. The tutorial provides a simple step-by-step explanation of how online payment works.

E-Commerce Guide—SBDCNet: http://sbdcnet.org/SBIC/e-com.php (accessed Spring 2009).

The Small Business Development Center National Information Clearinghouse provides timely, Web-based information to entrepreneurs. Small Business Development Centers (SBDC) are located in all 50 states. SBDCs offer free, confidential business counseling. This Web site provides information on business start-up, international trade, e-commerce, industry research, marketing, trends, and more. The E-Commerce Guide contains online training in building your Web site, managing a digital business, writing an Internet business plan, and more. A free newsletter will help you keep up on trends in small business. Small and medium-sized business owners will find plenty of links and information here to help plan, expand, and run a new business.

Ecommerce-Guide to Building a Successful Ecommerce Site: http://www. ecommerce-guide.com (accessed Spring 2009).

Jupiter Corporation's large e-commerce site has different channels for News & Trends, Solutions, Resources, Forums, Products, Glossary, and Events. In the section on building a successful site, users will find advertising and marketing, technology, affiliate, payment, Web design, and customer relation areas to help build a better, growing business. White papers and case studies are also available. Trends and product reviews are provided as well as company information. Videos are also provided for visual information. The articles on international e-commerce are practical and informative. Additionally, the E-Commerce Webopedia provides definitions of old, new, and upcoming terms, like cookies, Netcheque, and key fob, related to e-commerce. The eBiz FAQ is a particularly useful section.

eCommerce Info Center: http://www.ecominfocenter.com/ (accessed Spring 2009).

With over 40,000 selected links, the wide range of resources included in this site cover information sources, services for e-merchants and e-shoppers as well as electronic commerce professionals, technology updates, international and government data, nonprofit sector information, and a glossary and tutorial. Small Business and B2B areas are particularly well covered. The Global section provides links on all aspects of international industries, trade, and travel. Use this large list of links to get to the information you need quickly and easily.

Ecommerce Times: http://www.ecommercetimes.com (accessed Spring 2009).

This commercial Web site sponsored by the Triad Commerce Group offers short news articles, columns, products and service guide, TechNewsWorld, MacNewsWorld, and LinuxInsider in an easy-to-read format. Under Ecommerce Times Archives, you will find news items dating from 1999. White papers and case studies are also available. When you click on a particular article, related articles are listed below it. Several other channels present many news options.

Entrepreneur.com: http://www.entrepreneur.com (accessed Spring 2009).

Entrepreneur Magazine provides a wealth of information and assistance to the new entrepreneur. A thorough understanding of the need for the right type of marketing plan to fit your business and your style of planning and working is very important; and this site guides you through the process of discovering the right type for you. Learn how to determine your marketing goals and objectives and how a plan will help you achieve them. Under Marketing & Sales, you will also find tips on building buzz, branding, word-of-mouth advertising, and marketing materials. Learn about the "9 Tools for Building Customer

Loyalty," for example. Discover how to create an ad budget and create great ads and direct mail pieces. The E-business section explains legal issues, setting up an e-commerce site, e-mail marketing, Internet security, and more. International marketing research is well covered in the Marketing section. Use this outstanding site often during the planning and opening of your global business.

Entrepreneurs.About.com: http://entrepreneurs.about.com/ (accessed Spring 2009).

This large site has many different parts and is at times a bit difficult to navigate. Use the search feature if you have trouble. On the left side of this main page, you will find Business Ideas on a Budget, Choosing a Business to Start, Business Plan Outline, Step-by-Step, Business Legal Organizational Structures, and "How to" Library. Further down, topics like Financing, Case Studies and Interviews, and Resources also provide more links to information. The About.com large Web site also covers the Biotech/Biomedical, Composites/Plastics, Metal, Insurance, and Retail industries. The Retail Industry (http://retailindustry.about.com/), for which it is notoriously difficult to locate information, is especially well done; articles provide information on current retail trends, retail statistics, retail industry profile, apparel trends, consumer trends, and more. The entire site is fully searchable, so put in keywords and find information. Under Business and Finance, you will also find articles on, for example, various industries, selling to the government, store operations, retail trends, advertising costs, branding and more. International information on global trade shows and industry trends is also available through a simple search.

Export.gov: http://www.export.gov (accessed Spring 2009).

Created as a government-to-business initiative, Export.gov is the government's portal to exporting and trade services. It is designed to simplify the exporting process by being a single point of access to export-related services and thus reducing the need to view multiple government sources. Over 19 U.S. departments and agencies contribute to the information it provides including the U.S. International Trade Administration, the U.S. Commercial Service, the Department of Commerce, the Export-Import Bank, the Agency for International Development, and the U.S. Trade and Development Agency. Companies new to exporting will find step-by-step help through the export process. To facilitate international trade, companies can also find references on foreign tariff and tax information, search foreign and domestic trade events, subscribe to receive trade leads and industry specific market intelligence as well as gain access to federal export assistance and financing. The National Trade Data Bank (NTDB) provides access to Country Commercial Guides, market research reports, best market reports and other programs. Find Global Business Opportunity Leads as well as Market and Country Research. FedBizOpps (formerly known as Commerce Business Daily) is linked here too. Also linked is the TradeStats Express page for National and State Export data. Export.gov is fully searchable and allows you to globally search the contents of all of its contributing entities. Use this site to start market research, international statistics searches, and for getting advice and counseling.

ExportHelp, your online export helpdesk: http://www.exporthelp.co.za/index.html (accessed Spring 2009).

This large export assistance site from South Africa has an abundance of information and advice for new exporters. Find information on documentation, marketing, an initial SWOT analysis, country selection, and more. A lengthy article on trade fairs and getting the most out of them is also a highlight. The section on e-commerce is also practical.

The Export Yellow Pages: http://www.exportyellowpages.com (accessed Spring 2009).

The Export Yellow Pages are administered by the Export Trading Company Affairs of the International Trade Administration in partnership with the U.S. Department of Commerce. Containing information on U.S. business products and suppliers, this site is designed to promote and connect SMEs, improve market visibility, help establish international contacts, simplify sales sourcing, and solve language barriers. This site is often used by foreign buyers as a reference tool to find U.S. goods and services. U.S. firms can register their businesses without charge at http://www.myexports.com. In addition, export intermediaries such as freight forwarders, sales agents, and other service companies that help export businesses can register at no charge in the U.S. Trade Assistance Directory. Find trade leads and other resources here in a wide variety of industries. Products and services are offered by over 27,000 U.S. companies. The U.S. Trade Assistance Directory is available online or in print.

Federal Trade Commission (FTC): http://www.ftc.gov/bcp/business.shtm (accessed Spring 2009).

The FTC provides business information for consumers and businesses. One section is entitled E-Commerce and the Internet and provides businesses with rules and information about Internet advertising and marketing, a code of online business practices, online privacy needs, regulations of Internet auctions, securing your server, selling on the Internet, and more. Economic and legislation information related to the Internet is also provided.

Federation of International Trade Associations (FITA): http://www.fita.org (accessed Spring 2009).

This huge, very useful site covers all areas of importing and exporting. Users will find help with market research, transportation and logistics, documentation, trade finance and currencies, trade law, directories, trade show calendar, and worldwide trade leads. Find links to Export 1001, a user-friendly introduction to the fundamental aspects of exporting, links to practical sites from other countries, importers' directories, a trade information database, and much more. FITA has a China Business Guide and Trade Software, used to manage international trade enterprises. This large site is well organized, annotated, and easy to use.

FedStats: http://www.fedstats.gov (accessed Spring 2009).

The official Web site of the Federal Interagency Council on Statistical Policy is a gateway to statistics from over 100 U.S. federal agencies and is well organized and easy to use. Users can find under Links to Statistics, Topic Links A–Z, Map-Stats, and Statistics By Geography from U.S. Agencies. MapStats provides statistical profiles of states, counties, cities, congressional districts, and federal judicial districts. The Statistical Reference Shelf, a bit further down on the home page, is a large collection of online reference sources like the *Statistical Abstract of the United States*. You will find a variety of other sources such as the *State and Metropolitan Area Data Book* and *Digest of Education Statistics*, which will provide statistics on many topics of interest to entrepreneurs. On the other half of the page, Links to Statistical Agencies, under Agencies by Subject, click Economic on the drop-down arrow to lead you to a list of Periodic Economic Censuses. Below this area, you will find Data Access Tools, which link users to agency online databases.

Free Management Library: http://www.managementhelp.org/ (accessed Spring 2009).

The Library provides easy-to-access, clutter-free, comprehensive resources regarding the leadership and management of yourself, other individuals, groups, and organizations. Content is relevant to most small and medium-sized organizations. Over the past 10 years, the Library has grown to be one of the world's largest well-organized collections of these types of resources. Approximately 650 topics are included here, spanning 5,000 links. Topics include the most important practices to start, develop, operate, evaluate and resolve problems in for-profit and nonprofit organizations. Each topic has additionally recommended books and related articles. Grouped alphabetically by subject, the E-Commerce collection is particularly noteworthy.

The Global Connector: http://www.globalconnector.org (accessed Spring 2009).

Part of Indiana University's Center for International Business Education and Research (CIBER), this gateway leads to thousands of international trade sites. The Global Connector allows searching by either country or by industry. Country data include links to data on government, domestic economy, news and media, entry requirements, transportation, and international trade. Industry-specific information can be searched by the type or source of information including trade shows, trade publications, trends and analysis, and regulatory matters.

GlobalEDGE: http://globaledge.msu.edu (accessed Spring 2009).

Managed by Michigan State University's Center for International Business Education and Research (MSU_CIBER), this site links to a broad selection of international trade data including economic trends, statistical data sources, government resources, trade portals, journals, and mailing lists. Its Global Resources section provides access to more than 2,000 online resources. MSU _CIBER has also contributed its own resources including an interactive forum for business professionals and portions of the information contained in the Knowledge Room, GlobalEDGE's section on the latest issues and trends effecting international business.

Global Technology Forum: http://www.ebusinessforum.com (accessed Spring 2009).

This excellent site from *The Economist* Intelligence Unit targets senior executives and offers an international selection of e-commerce news. Global News Analysis, updated daily, is organized by region of the world and links to recent, full-text articles from a variety of respected sources. See Best Practices for company-focused discussions organized by telecommunications, pharmaceuticals, media/entertainment, professional services, consumer products, energy/chemicals/utilities, and more. The Research module is chock full of in-depth material from respected analysts in market trends and benchmarking and features a Web site of the week. This superb, searchable site is cosponsored by leaders in the Internet economy, including HP, Dimension Data, Nortel Networks, and Oracle.

The Industry Standard: http://www.thestandard.com (accessed Spring 2009).

This site provides complete coverage of the news, analysis, trends, and events that shape the Internet economy every day. Companies, people, products, and technologies that impact the direction of the e-economy are covered. The News section looks at technology news and trends along with products. The Media part covers the major players that capitalize on using the Internet providing music, video, games, content, marketing, and publishing. The Money part details mergers, venture capital activities, bankruptcies, and IPOs, while Politics covers government regulations and laws domestically and internationally. The Metrics section tracks key data points and statistics. The Opinion section provides daily blogs from the best journalists to keep up with daily news events, market trends, and the future of the Internet economy.

KnowThis.com: Marketing Virtual Library: http://www.knowthis.com (accessed Spring 2009).

This large site is a smorgasbord of data and guidance on marketing including how to conduct market research, promotion versus advertising, using current technologies, and a large section on Internet marketing, divided into methods and strategies and research. Find guidance on creating marketing plans as well as sample plans. New topics include selling virtual clothes for avatars and reviews of software to enhance small e-commerce sites. Tutorials on managing customers, personal selling, targeting markets, and more are available.

The List: the Definitive ISP Buyer's Guide: http://www.thelist.com/ (accessed Spring 2009).

This large commercial site will help you find an ISP, find a broadband ISP, find a Web host, find a Web designer, and even find an ASP or a tech job. It covers the entire United States and Canada, letting you search by area code or location. It provides FAQs on various items and also leads users to other business information.

Marketer Digital Intelligence: http://www.emarketer.com/ (accessed Spring 2009).

This excellent site for Internet economy statistics is large and frequently updated. While eMarketer's purpose is to sell expensive competitive business reports, it also provides a good amount of free, browsable information, including a free newsletter. The eMarketer Daily Newsletter provides current information every business day. Under the Reports tab, you will find statistical reports for sale, but under Articles there are links to current and past articles with some statistical breakdown on specific markets and emerging technologies.

MoreBusiness.com: http://www.morebusiness.com (accessed Spring 2009).

Sections on this site include Startup, Running SmallBiz, Templates, and Tools. The Templates section provides sample business contracts and agreements, business and marketing plans, press releases, and business checklists. A large collection of articles and advice under Business Technology will help you understand the Internet, online shopping, Web site technology, hacking, and even laptop issues. The section called Build Your Own Website is very useful. Many of the articles are lengthy and thorough. Use this site to help improve your marketing and management skills.

New York Public Library, International Trade Research Guide: http://www.nypl .org/research/sibl/trade/trade.html (accessed Spring 2009).

This wonderful guide produced by the Science, Industry and Business Library (SIBL) will provide invaluable information in learning how to conduct business between the United States and another country. Guides, business directories, periodicals, and trade statistic sources can be located through this large and practical site. It is well organized, and easy to navigate; find information grouped under market research, trade leads, shipping and logistics, and cross-cultural business communication.

OnlineBusiness.About.com: http://onlinebusiness.about.com/ (accessed Spring 2009).

Part of the large About.com collection of useful Web sites, the Online Business/ Hosting site covers the basics like Online Business 101, Building Your Website, Getting Traffic/Marketing, Daily Operations, Blogging, Search Engines, and Selling Goods Online. Find articles about improving your ranking in search engines, hiring a Web designer, marketing offline, and more. Use the Google-like search box to find articles. Look for subjects like Starting Up, Web Hosting, Auctions, Search Engines, and Success Stories. Find Web site guides, newsletters, FAQs, discussion forums, and chat, plus build a Web store, or learn about banner advertising or portal sites. Other topics include associations, business issues, broadcasting, domain registration, history of the Internet, innovations, legal resources, news resources, online journals, reference services and trading, trade fairs and statistics. Learn about all aspects of e-commerce on this constantly updated and growing site.

Open Directory Project: E-Commerce http://dmoz.org/Business/E-Commerce (accessed Spring 2009).

This excellent gateway page provides entry points to current articles, periodicals specializing in e-commerce and related fields, government and standards information sites, and organizations. It is updated frequently and most links are active. Some of the sites linked to may have costs. Links cover a wide variety of topics such as Web site promotion, sales agents, shopping carts, technology vendors, and Internet law. Links are not annotated.

Quick MBA: http://www.quickmba.com/entre/bplan/ (accessed Spring 2009).

For those new to business plans and SWOT analysis, this site is thorough and practical. Learn the basics of both these concepts and many more here. Management and marketing articles are useful and helpful to new owners and managers as well as experienced ones. A political, economic, social, technical (PEST) analysis is presented, why to use it, and how it relates to SWOT. Often articles include recommended readings.

Red Herring: http://www.redherring.com/ (accessed Spring 2009).

Red Herring, a media company, covers innovation, entrepreneurial activity, the business of technology, and venture capital and capital markets worldwide. By analyzing all of these areas, it evaluates the probable success or failure of companies and technologies. Each major area is divided into subtopics; for instance, Capital is further subdivided into Economy & Policy, Public Markets, Venture Capital, and Private Markets. The site publishes profiles of notable companies, briefings, metrics and statistics, and opinions. Free registration is required to access much of the content.

SBDCNET: http://sbdcnet.utsa.edu (accessed Spring 2009).

The Small Business Development Center National Information Clearinghouse provides timely, Web-based information to entrepreneurs. Small Business Development Centers (SBDC) are located in all 50 states. SBDCs offer free, confidential business counseling. This Web site provides information on business start-up, international trade, e-commerce, industry research, marketing, trends, and more. The International Trade section has many links to more information and more help in moving into exporting or importing. Templates for business plans and marketing tools are also available. A free newsletter will help you keep up on trends in small business. Entrepreneurs will find plenty of links and information here to help plan, expand and run a new business.

Small Business Administration: http://www.sba.gov (accessed Spring 2009).

This official government site offers a wealth of resources and programs for starting and growing a small business. Under Startup Basics, check out the areas you need help with while doing your business planning. Other major sections cover business planning, financing, international trade, managing, marketing, employees, taxes, legal aspects, and business opportunities. Find here online forms, sample business plans, loan information, and many publications. The *Export Library* contains titles like Breaking into the Trade Game, Export Working Capital Program, Export Financing for Small Businesses, and SBA & Ex-Im Bank Co-Guarantee Program. Some content is available in Spanish. Also part of the SBA program are the Small Business Development Centers (SBDC) at http://www.sba.gov/sbdc. SBDCs are located in every state and deliver counseling and training for small businesses in the areas of management, marketing, financing, and feasibility studies.

TechWeb: E-Business http://www.techweb.com/tech/ebiz (accessed Spring 2009).

TechWeb has lots of advertising but, beyond that, the latest in e-business news, trends and analysis, and product reviews. e-Business white papers and reports are also available. Users have access to a huge variety of information by using difference Pipelines, for example, InternetWeek, Small Business, Web Services, and many more. Each Pipeline has trends, a blog, security issues, a glossary, newsletter, services, and more.

USA.gov: http://www.usa.gov (accessed Spring 2009).

Information by Topic will interest and amaze first-timer visitors. Topics include Defense and International, Environment, Energy and Agriculture, Money and Taxes, Reference and General Government, and Science and Technology. Tabs at the top of the page include one for Businesses and Nonprofits, which has a section on International Trade. Clicking on Data and Statistics brings up an alphabetical list of links to resources chock full of statistics. Economic Indicators is the Web site of the Economics and Statistics Administration, part of the U.S. Department of Commerce (http://www.economicindicators.gov), and it provides timely access to the daily releases of key economic indicators from the Bureau of Economic Analysis (BEA) and the Census Bureau. In addition, under Businesses and Nonprofits is a section titled Foreign Businesses Doing Business in the U.S. Under Frequently Asked Foreign Business Questions is a section called Doing Business Abroad. Spanish translation of the site is also available. You can e-mail questions about the site and the statistics or telephone for help too. Your taxes pay for the collection, compiling, and publishing of these statistics, and they are available for your use.

U.S. Bureau of Industry and Security: http://www.bis.doc.gov (accessed Spring 2009).

This agency of the Department of Commerce is responsible for advancing U.S. national security, foreign policy, and economic objectives by ensuring an effective export control and treaty compliance system and promoting continued U.S. strategic technology leadership. It issues export licenses, prosecutes violators of export control policies, and implements the Export Administration Act's anti-boycott provisions. Export license requirements are triggered by the actual item (commodity, software, or technology) being exported, where it is going, who is going to use it, and what they will be using it for. The Web page's FAQs on Export Licensing will answer many questions. Another important section, entitled E-Commerce, is where you will find regulations on orders processed using the Internet, intangible downloads, the transfer of funds to certain entities, prohibited activities, and more. Check this site before you fill your first Internet order.

**U.S. Census Bureau: http://www.census.gov (accessed Spring 2009).

This Web page is the best place to start searching for the multitude of data produced by census programs, publications, and statistics. The home page groups the data under Census 2000, People, Business, Geography, Newsroom, At the Bureau, and Special Topics. Under Business, you can click on the Foreign Trade, Economic Census, NAICS, E-Stats, and Survey of Business Owners. Under Foreign Trade, learn directly from the Census Bureau how to properly classify your products for export and how to file your Shipper's Export Declaration online. The Bureau also processes, tabulates, and releases the data collected by the Bureau of Customs and Border Protection on exports and imports of goods. The catalog, a search feature, and links to related sites are also accessible on the left side of the home page. Another important part of the Census Bureau's Web page is the International Data Base (IDB) at http://www.census.gov.ipc/www/idb/ The IDB presents estimates and projections of basic demographic measures for countries and regions of the world. country summaries, country rankings, and population pyramids all provide useful data. U.S. export and import statistics by commodity, country, customs district, and method of transportation provide value and quantity on a monthly, year-to-date, and annual history basis. U.S. state export data and port statistics for imports and exports are also available. Use this site frequently to help start and grow your business.

VIBES: Virtual International Business and Economic Sources: http://library .uncc.edu/display/?dept=reference&format=open&page=68 (accessed Spring 2009).

The more than 1,600 links to free sources of information at this site were selected by Jeanie Welch of the University of North Carolina Charlotte. The table of contents breaks the sites into three groups: comprehensive, regional, and national. The comprehensive section organizes its links by category, including banking and finance, business practices and company information, emerging markets, international trade law, and more. Research and tables and graphs are highlights of this site. The regional section allows searching devoted to a single region or continent such as Europe or the Middle East. The national section links to sites devoted to a particular country.

Web Monkey E-Commerce Tutorial http://www.webmonkey.com/tutorial/tag/ business (accessed Spring 2009).

This resource for Web developers includes several "how-to" sections. E-business how-tos include marketing a site and tracking usage. Learn how to gather user data. The site is searchable by keyword and topic. Find here excellent, practical, hands-on information.

WebSite MarketingPlan: http://www.websitemarketingplan.com (accessed Spring 2009).

This large site contains a wealth of information for small businesses. A large assortment of articles and sample marketing plans are available as well as sample business plans, a newsletter, Internet marketing articles, marketing strategy articles, and more. Featured tabs include Marketing/Planning, Marketing & Management, Marketing Techniques, Internet Marketing, Ecommerce, and Public Relations. Learn about the four seasons of public relations. Lengthy articles on advertising, using PR for communicating to customers and finding new ones, and customer retention are outstanding. There are many commercial links but plenty of free help for the new entrepreneur too. This site is especially helpful for those interested in e-commerce. Easy to navigate, this site will help you develop a marketing plan that you can use.

WorkZ: http://www.workz.com/content/view_content.html?section_id=480 (accessed Spring 2009).

Hot topics on this large site include e-mail marketing, Web design, podcasting, blogs, e-commerce, and more. You will also find Forms and Templates and Web Techniques very useful. The Run Your Business section includes a wealth of articles of good business practices for all areas of your business. Ecommerce covers many facets of selling and marketing online and offline. The Trade Show section includes many hints on how to make good use of your time attending and making use of the contacts after the show.

Yahoo! Small Business Resources—Online Business—Ecommerce: http:// smallbusiness.yahoo.com/ecommerce/ (accessed Spring 2009).

This large site is packed with articles and links to information on all aspects of starting, marketing, and running an online business. Fully searchable and easy to navigate, this site provides information and help on Web connectivity, domain names, and even an eBay Center. The annotated links lead users to other well-respected sites like Entrepreneur.com, AllBusiness.com, and Inc.com, for example, and are divided by subject area. Also check out Reaching Beyond Borders for international business suggestions and additional insights in implementing a successful e-commerce site.

Appendix

This appendix is organized into two sections. The World contains resources that apply generally to the import/export business or to multiple regions. The Regions of the World covers resources specific to North America, South America, Europe, Asia/Pacific, and Africa/Middle East.

THE WORLD

Print Resources

Acuff, Frank L. *How to Negotiate Anything with Anyone Anywhere Around the World*. 3rd ed. Amacom, 2008. 307p. ISBN 0-8144-8066-7. $21.95.

This new edition of an established guide to negotiation provides readers with advice on best business practices, transactions, and attitudes throughout the world. Now including 63 countries, topics like foreign outsourcing, multicultural work teams, business entertainment guidelines, and even some factors involved in regional sensitivities are covered thoroughly. Organized by region, this book delivers detailed business profiles of each country with fast facts on monetary units, principal imports and exports, population, cities, language, and religion. Based on his knowledge of local business practices worldwide and familiarity with difference cultures and national psychologies, Acuff uses examples, statistics, and basic guidelines to help businesspeople from the United States negotiate and reduce friction and misunderstandings abroad.

Denslow, Lanie, and Nadler, Mary. *World Wise: What To Know Before You Go*. Fairchild Books & Visuals, 2005. 342p. ISBN 1-56367-3592. $31.50.

Written for newcomers and seasoned professionals, Denslow's book is chock full of practical advice on establishing effective working relationships with businesspeople all over the world. Be aware and put into practice the cultural nuances of the host country in which you plan to do business, and you are more likely to have a successful outcome. Brief histories are given for each region of the world and the discussions of trade agreements like the General Agreement on Tariffs and Trade (GATT), now the World Trade Organization, and North American Free Trade Agreement (NAFTA) are also very useful. The cartoons representing the lighter view of global business communications are delightful as well.

Europa World Year Book. Annual. Routledge, Taylor & Francis. 2 v.

This well-respected annual provides a great deal of detailed information on the political, economic, and commercial institutions of the world. Each country is covered by an individual chapter composed of an introductory survey that includes recent history, economic affairs, government, and defense; followed by data on social welfare, finance, telecommunications, trade and industry, utilities, and education. Now also an online product, a free trial electronic subscription is available from the Europa World Web site at http://www.europa world.com.

Exporters' Encyclopaedia. Annual. Dun & Bradstreet.

A comprehensive world reference guide, this encyclopedia is divided into 220 country-specific sections; firms specializing in international business, laws, and legislation; international trade associations; government agencies; shipping practice; and reference data on weights and measures for overseas ports. Find key contacts, trade and safety regulations, and information on documentation needed. Marketing data includes legal requirements for importer or agents, procurement standards, environmental protection and pollution control, marking, and labeling. The encyclopedia also provides passport regulations and business etiquette guidelines.

Hinkelman, Edward, et al. *Importers Manual*. Annual. World Trade Press. 960p.

Information on how to import virtually any commodity into the United States can be found in this practical reference. It is precisely organized for ease of use and is divided into the major sections of Commodity Index; U.S. Customs Entry and Clearance; International Banking; Legal Considerations of Importing; and Packing, Shipping, and Insurance. The heart of the work, the Commodity Index, contains entry procedures, documentation, restrictions, and prohibitions, marking and labeling requirements, and contact information for regulatory agencies for all products that can be imported into the United States.

Jagoe, John R. *Export Sales and Marketing Manual 2008: The Bible of Exporting*. Annual. Export Institute of the United States. 520p. ISBN 0-943677-66-1. $295.

Having been updated annually for 21 consecutive years, this international trade publication has achieved longevity and global reach. This manual covers all the steps involved in selling products in world markets. Over 120 illustrations, 85 graphs, 40 flow charts, and 60 sample international trade documents lead the user through the process. Jagoe helps users conduct market research through 1200 Web site addresses providing information on various markets and products and services. A lengthy glossary of export terms and detailed index for quick access to important information is also provided.

Lewis, Richard D. *When Cultures Collide: Leading Across Cultures*. Nicholas Brealey, 2006. 590p. ISBN 1-904-838-022. $35.00.

This guide to working and communicating across cultures explains how your culture and language affect the ways in which you think and respond to situations. Lewis not only helps you understand different cultures but also how to manage in different business cultures. He covers the world, including Asian, Arab, and Eastern European countries. He suggests a broad model you can use to characterize different national characteristics and various traits that shape attitudes toward time, leadership, team building, and organizational structure and behaviors. This exceptional book is a good read for anyone who encounters people of other nationalities and cultures.

Morrison, Terri. *Kiss, Bow, or Shake Hands: The Bestselling Guide to Doing Business in More than 60 Countries*. Adams Media Corp., 2006. 592p. ISBN 1-59-337368-6. $24.95.

This encyclopedic resource presents information for each country on the country history, type of government, languages, religions, business practices, and titles and forms of address for 60 countries. A cultural orientation for each country with negotiation strategies and value systems is included. Learning to do business in a foreign country will be easier using this newly revised, well-organized and concise guide.

Nelson, Carl A. *Import/Export: How to Take Your Business Across Borders*. 4th ed. McGraw-Hill Companies, 2008. ISBN 0-07-148255-5. $21.95.

As in previous editions, Nelson demystifies international trade including basics like writing the business plan, choosing a product or service, providing samples for customs and duties, and financing international transactions. He uses examples and success stories to illustrate his points. Hot-button issues such as the WTO, doing business with NAFTA, Africa, India, China, and the EU, and the changing world of e-commerce are explored. His step-by-step guidance will help entrepreneurs succeed in international ventures and use the Internet to their advantage.

Tuller, Lawrence. *Doing Business Beyond America's Borders: the Do's, Don'ts, and Other Details of Conducting Business in 40 Different Countries*. Entrepreneur Press, 2008. 304p. ISBN 1-59918-257-2. $21.95.

Covering about 40 countries, find a new world of customers and empower your business to compete with the large transnational corporations. Tuller explains critical steps, tactics, and tools that will help your company navigate the international business landscape. Learn about cultural and interrelational anomalies, negotiations, language barriers, and ways to develop strong overseas relationships. Discover the best ways to sell your products overseas, cost-effective means of transportation, ways to find low-cost production materials and labor, and how to deal with cultural anomalies and foreign languages. Worksheets, anecdotes, and illustrative examples are plentiful.

Online Resources

BBC News (Country Profiles): http://news.bbc.co.uk/2/hi/country_profiles/ default.stm (Accessed Spring 2009).

BBC's full country profiles include a complete guide to history, politics, and economic background for many countries, divided into six major regions of the world. Nineteen International Organizations are also profiled, many including sections called Facts, Leaders, and Issues. The country profiles also are divided into the Overview, Facts, Leaders, and Media. Related Internet Links, and Related BBC Links are useful also. The timeline of important events for each country also provide practical, relevant information. Also includes audio and video clips from the BBC archives.

Business Directories for Americans Abroad: http://www.embassy.org/ibc/usabroad (Accessed Spring 2009).

Find information to help with foreign travel, import, export, immigration, etc. Companies listed here are providers of goods and services to Americans working, traveling, or investing overseas. This large portal will help you find the information you need.

Business Traveller: http://www.businesstraveller.com (Accessed Spring 2009).

This leading magazine for the frequent business traveler prints ten editions worldwide and aims to help corporate travelers save money and make their traveling easier. Find here information on destinations, travel products, cultural hints, and promotions from travel businesses. Leisure travel is also covered.

Centre for International Trade: http://www.centretrade.com (Accessed Spring 2009).

This membership organization hopes to improve, facilitate, and expand international trade. Members include embassies, trade associations, companies, and individuals. Users will find information on national rules and regulations, tariffs, events, and industry news. Trade opportunities, financing assistance, management help, transportation information, and resources on products, services, training, and Web links are also included. Web links to a wide range of useful sites are current and useful.

CIA World Factbook: https://www.cia.gov/cia/publications/factbook/index.html (Accessed Spring 2009).

Prepared by the U.S. Central Intelligence Agency (CIA), this resource is a great beginning research point, with its concise country information such as economic, social, and political profiles. Continually updated, demographics, gross domestic product statistics, membership in international organizations, and diplomatic, communication, and transportation information are all provided.

Country Studies: http://lcweb2.loc.gov/frd/cs/cshome.html (Accessed Spring 2009).

These in-depth country studies and handbooks were prepared by a team of scholars under the direction of the Federal Research Division of the Library of Congress, as sponsored by the U.S. Army. At present, 102 countries and regions are covered, primarily focusing on lesser-known areas of the world or regions in which U.S. forces might be deployed. One word of warning, however: since funding for the country studies was cancelled in 1999, the studies range in date of preparation from 1988 to 1998. However, some country profiles also accessible from this site are being updated. Highlights of the individual studies include photographs, historical and economic backgrounds, tables, glossaries, and bibliographies. The site is searchable by topic.

Economist.com: http://www.economist.com (Accessed Spring 2009).

Providing excellent coverage of world news, the Economist.com also contains information on world markets, the latest exchange rates, and country and city guides geared to the business traveler. It is the companion site to the print journal *The Economist*. Although much of the site is free and fully searchable, the Economist.com does charge to view archived articles. Other portions of the site are considered to be premium content viewable by subscription only.

Euromonitor International: http://www.euromonitor.com/ (Accessed Spring 2009).

Euromonitor International offers quality international market intelligence on industries, countries, and consumers. The have some 30 years of experience publishing market reports, business reference books, online information systems and bespoke consulting projects. Their Web site has a huge article archive with short articles on topics such as trends in retail, food prices, and brand growth in various parts of the world. Many articles are on a specific company, country, or product. Complete company profiles and industry reports can be purchased.

ExecutivePlanet.com: http://www.executiveplanet.com (Accessed Spring 2009).

This large site has Cultural Quick Tips to help you learn to work in a multicultural environment. Learn how to question and explore your assumptions in your daily life. Try to understand how your assumptions are impacting your interactions with others. Negotiating tactics, business card protocols, pace of business, thinking styles, and business entertaining tips can all be found here. Find conversation tips and topics, the role of compliments, business dress as well as social function dress information and more.

Export.gov: http://www.export.gov (Accessed Spring 2009).

Created as a government-to-business initiative, Export.gov is the government's portal to exporting and trade services. It is designed to simplify the exporting process by being a single point of access to export-related services and thus reducing the need to view multiple government sources. Over 19 U.S. departments and agencies contribute to the information it provides including the U.S. International Trade Administration, the U.S. Commercial Service, the Department of Commerce, the Export-Import Bank, the Agency for International Development, and the U.S. Trade and Development Agency. Companies new to exporting will find step-by-step help through the export process. To facilitate international trade, companies can also find references on foreign tariff and tax information, search foreign and domestic trade events, subscribe to receive trade leads and industry-specific market intelligence as well as gain access to federal export assistance and financing. The China Business Information Center is especially useful. Export.gov is fully searchable and allows you to search globally the contents of all of its contributing entities.

The Export Yellow Pages: http://www.exportyellowpages.com (Accessed Spring 2009).

The Export Yellow Pages are administered by the Export Trading Company Affairs of the International Trade Administration in partnership with the U.S. Department of Commerce. Containing information on U.S. business products and suppliers, this site is designed to promote and connect SMEs, improve market visibility, help establish international contacts, simplify sales sourcing, and solve language barriers. This site is often used by foreign buyers as a reference tool to find U.S. goods and services. U.S. firms can register their businesses without charge at http://www.myexports.com. Also, export intermediaries such as freight forwarders, sales agents, and other service companies that help export businesses can register at no charge in the U.S. Trade Assistance Directory. Find trade leads and other resources here in a wide variety of industries. Products and services are offered by over 27,000 U.S. companies. The U.S. Trade Assistance Directory is available online or in print.

Federation of International Trade Associations (FITA): http://www.fita.org (Accessed Spring 2009).

This huge, very useful site covers all areas of importing and exporting. Users will find help with market research, transportation and logistics, documentation, trade finance & currencies, trade law, directories, trade show calendar, and worldwide trade leads. Find links to Export 1001, a user-friendly introduction to the fundamental aspects of exporting, links to practical sites from other countries, importers' directories, a trade information database and much more. FITA has a *China Business Guide and Trade Software*, used to manage international trade enterprises. The Business Travel Mini-Portal provides information on low-cost airfares, MedjetAssist, Travel Advisories, Globafone, Currency Converters, and more. This large site is well organized, annotated, and easy to use.

Foreign Government Resources on the Web: http://www.lib.umich.edu/govdocs/foreign.html (Accessed Spring 2009).

Maintained by the University of Michigan's Documents Center, this Web site provides an extensive collection of foreign government Web sites. Also accessible from the site are country background information, the text of constitutions and treaties, embassy information, and statistics on demographics, economics, health and military. Many of the links are briefly annotated by the documents center's staff. The center also updates the site frequently: the What's New section is updated weekly and provides annotated links to new resources of interest. Use this site to keep current on foreign government information.

Foreign Information by Country: http://ucblibraries.colorado.edu/govpubs/for/foreigngovt.htm (Accessed Spring 2009).

Developed and maintained by the University of Colorado Government Publications Library, this huge site provides a wide array of country information. Country information is compiled by international organizations, governments, the U.S. government, and more. Statistics from many sources and even travel information is included. Start your country information search here.

The Global Connector: http://www.globalconnector.org (Accessed, Spring 2009).

Part of Indiana University's Center for International Business Education and Research (CIBER), this gateway leads to thousands of international trade sites. The Global Connector allows searching by either country or by industry. Country data include links to data on government, domestic economy, news and media, entry requirements, transportation, international trade, and more. Industry-specific information can be searched by the type or source of information including trade shows, trade publications, trends and analysis, and regulatory matters.

GlobalEDGE: http://globaledge.msu.edu/(Accessed Spring 2009).

Managed by Michigan State University's Center for International Business Education and Research (MSU_CIBER), this site links to a broad selection of international trade data including economic trends, statistical data sources, government resources, trade portals, journals, and mailing lists. Its Global Resources section provides access to more than 2,000 online resources. Current information on the business climate, news, history, economic landscape, etc. is provided for 196 countries. Find here a rich collection of country- and region-specific business links to access a vast collection of information. MSU _CIBER has also contributed its own resources including an interactive forum for business professionals and portions of the information contained in the Knowledge Room, GlobalEDGE's section on the latest issues and trends effecting international business.

International Data Base (IDB): http://www.census.gov.ipc/www/idb (Accessed Spring 2009).

The IDB presents estimates and projections of basic demographic measures for countries and regions of the world. Country summaries, country rankings, and population pyramids all provide useful data. U.S. export and import statistics by commodity, country, customs district, and method of transportation provide value and quantity on a monthly, year-to-date, and annual history basis. U.S. state export data and port statistics for imports and exports are also available. Use this site frequently to help start and grow your business.

International Monetary Fund (IMF): http://www.imf.org/external/index.htm (Accessed Spring 2009).

The IMF database contains approximately 32,000 time series covering more than 200 countries and areas and includes all series appearing on the International Financial Statistics (IFS) Country Pages, exchange rate series for all Fund member countries, plus Aruba and the Netherlands Antilles, and most other world, area, and country series from the IFS World Tables. Find here the *Export and Import Price Index Manual.* Under the Country Information tab, you will find detailed, current information about the economic situation in the country. The site is fully searchable and easy to use. The complete text of the *World Economic Outlook* is also available online; learn how the economic slowdown in the United States in 2007 affected other areas of the world and continues to affect the global economy.

The Internationalist: http://www.internationalist.com (Accessed Spring 2009).

This large site is a leading resource for international business and travel. You can find translation services, international maps, world newspapers, currency exchange information, travel advisories, hotels, and more. One whole section is on business information and one on travel. Information on specific countries is complete and covers items like insurance companies, real estate, newspapers, and consultants in addition to country basics.

Nations Online Project: http://www.nationsonline.org/oneworld/ (Accessed Spring 2009).

This portal is a reference directory and gateway to the countries, cultures, and nations of the world. Country profiles include information on geography, government, major cities, the economy, current news, local information, facts, and more. Find information about country-specific products, banks, companies, and more. Learn about cultural, social, and political issues in any country.

New York Public Library, International Trade Research Guide: http://www .nypl.org/research/sibl/trade/trade.html (Accessed Spring 2009).

This wonderful guide produced by the Science, Industry and Business Library (SIBL) will provide invaluable information in learning how to conduct business between the United States and another country. Guides, business directories, periodicals, and trade statistic sources can be located through this large and practical site. Find information grouped under market research, trade leads, shipping and logistics, and cross-cultural business communication on this well-organized and easy-to-navigate site.

Portals to the World from the Library of Congress: http://www.loc.gov/rr/ international/portals.html (Accessed Spring 2009).

This comprehensive site contains selective links providing authoritative, in-depth information about nations and areas of the world. They are arranged by country or area with the links for each sorted into a wide range of broad categories. Information about each country is grouped under subjects like Business, Commerce, Economy, and Media and Communications as well as Government, Politics, and Law.

STAT-USA/Internet: http://www.stat-usa.gov/ (Accessed Spring 2009).

This service of the U.S. Department of Commerce is a single point of access to authoritative business, trade, and economic information from across the federal government. An important part of this resource is http://www.stat-usa.gov/ tradtest.nsf—Obtain current and historical trade-related releases, international market research, trade opportunities, country analysis, and our trade library from the National Trade Data Bank (NTDB). The NTDB provides access to Country Commercial Guides, market research reports, best market reports and other programs. USA Trade *Online* provides current and historical import and export statistics for over 18,000 commodities traded worldwide, as well as the most current merchandise trade statistics available in a spreadsheet format. The **International Trade Library** is a comprehensive collection of over 40,000 documents related to international trade. All are full text searchable, as well as keyword searchable by country or product.

TradePort Global Trade Center: http://www.tradeport.org (Accessed Spring 2009).

TradePort is a repository of free information and resources for businesses that seek to conduct international trade. Created in 1996, TradePort is backed by an alliance of regional trade associations that assist California export and import businesses, but companies in all states will find plenty of information to assist their export or import efforts. The Export Tutorial as well as the Import Tutorial are full of valuable resources and information. The Market Research section, which has a large Trade Leads section, and the Trade Library, which provides a bibliography of resources, a glossary, and links to trade statistics are current, very practical resources. This useful site is a great place to start researching your export/import adventure.

University of Colorado at Boulder, Foreign Information by Country: http:// ucblibraries.colorado.edu/govpubs/for/foreigngovt.htm (Accessed Spring 2009).

This very large and very well-organized site is a gateway to country guides and information. Select the Country or Territory you are interested and choose from information on topics like government information, country profile, or diplomatic relations. Find here links to information from international organizations too. Further down the main page you will find a link to the Library of Congress Portals to the World (http://www.loc.gov/rr/international/portals.html) where librarians have organized more resources on topics like business, commerce, economy, and culture as well as recreation and travel. Both these terrific sites provide practical information to the new exporter/importer.

U.S. Census Bureau: http://www.census.gov (Accessed Spring 2009).

Under the heading Business and Industry, you can click on the Foreign Trade, Economic Census, NAICS, E-Stats, and Survey of Business Owners. Under Foreign Trade, learn directly from the Census Bureau how to properly classify your products for export and how to file your Shipper's Export Declaration online. The Bureau also processes, tabulates, and releases the data collected by the Bureau of Customs and Border Protection on exports and imports of goods. The catalog, a search feature, and links to related sites are also accessible on the left side of the home page. Another important part of the Census Bureau's Web page is the International Data Base (IDB) at http://www .census.gov.ipc/www/idb. The IDB presents estimates and projections of basic demographic measures for countries and regions of the world. Country summaries, country rankings, and population pyramids all provide useful data. U.S. export and import statistics by commodity, country, customs district, and method of transportation provide value and quantity on a monthly, year-to-date, and annual history basis. U.S. state export data and port statistics for imports and exports are also available. Use this site frequently to help start and grow your business.

U.S. Chamber of Commerce: http://www.uschamber.com (Accessed Spring 2009).

Currently 105 AmChams can be found in 91 countries, affiliated with the U.S. Chamber of Commerce. AmChams advance the interests of U.S. business overseas and are voluntary associations of U.S. companies and individuals doing business in a particular country as well as companies and individuals of that country who operate in the U.S. Information for small businesses and trade issues is provided free to all. Some statistics and directory information is also available.

U.S. Department of State (DOS): http://www.state.gov (Accessed Spring 2009).

A wealth of country information, including an online version of Background Notes, the site presents basic demographic and economic statistics as well as short narrative descriptions about the people, history, government, and foreign relations. In addition, there is U.S. Embassies and Consulate information as well as a diplomatic list. Listings on the left bar of the home page link to a wealth of topical information including a series of publications that contain factual information on all countries with which the United States has relations. Country Commercial Guides can also be accessed through the site. An important part of this Web site (http://www.travel.state.gov/) provides information on travel advisories, health, and safety. Business travelers can find information on documents necessary for foreign travel like passports and visas as well as current travel warnings. A link to consular information sheets provides detailed information on safety issues for countries around the world.

VIBES: Virtual International Business and Economic Sources: http://library.uncc .edu/display/?dept=reference&format=open&page=68 (Accessed Spring 2009).

The more than 1,600 links to free sources of information at this site were selected by Jeanie Welch of the University of North Carolina Charlotte. The table of contents breaks the sites into three groups: comprehensive, regional, and national. The comprehensive section organizes its links by category, including banking and finance, business practices and company information, emerging markets, and international trade law. Research and tables and graphs are highlights of this site. The regional section allows searching devoted to a single region or continent such as Europe or the Middle East. The national section links to sites devoted to a particular country.

World Bank: http://www.worldbank.org (Accessed Spring 2009).

Established in 1944, the World Bank is composed of five separate organizations all with distinct but related missions including the International Bank for Reconstruction and Development (IBRD) and the International Development Association (IDA), the International Finance Corporation (IFC), Multilateral Investment Guaranty Agency (MIGA), and the International Centre for Settlement of Investment Disputes (ICSID). Resources provided from its Business Center include World Bank project and program summaries, documents, and reports. The side bar provides links to data and statistics on countries and regions, evaluations, news, and more. Arranged hierarchically, each of these categories allows you to drill down to even more specific information. In addition to providing access to its own collection of resources, the World Bank provides access to each member organization's site. *Doing Business* (http://www.doing business.org) is a database that provides objective measures of business regulations and enforcement for 175 countries.

World Trade Magazine:http://www.worldtrademag.com/(Accessed Spring 2009).

This large site is a treasure trove of information for individuals and companies either involved in international trade or wanting to enter the global market and understand supply chains. Besides print information, find Webinars on supply chains, buyers/suppliers, financial supply chains, and more. Find a global supply chain buyers guide, currency calculator, white papers, e-Newsletter, and more. Industry news such as FedEx Post First Loss in 11 Years, Logistics Costs Higher in Russia, is also provided.

World Trade Organization (WTO): http://www.wto.org(Accessed Spring 2009).

Established in 1995, the WTO is comprised of more than 140 countries that cooperate on global economic policy making and provides the ground rules for international commerce. The organization's world-renown annual report *International Trade Statistics* is available on its Web site via the Resources link. Also available are documents published by the WTO, information on trade topics, and links to publications of many member countries, news, and international trade resources.

World Wide Chamber of Commerce Guide:http://www.chamberfind.com (Accessed Spring 2009).

The local Chamber of Commerce has long been the best source for community data, local businesses, attractions, festivals, relocation data, tourist information, and more. This site can be searched by U.S. chambers by state, world chambers by regions, or keywords. Local businesses that are chamber members can also be located here. Chamber sites vary but most can be very useful before visiting an area. Many of the foreign site provide at least some information in English by clicking on a U.S. or British flag.

Yahoo! Directory, National Governments: http://dir.yahoo.com/government (Accessed Spring 2009).

This site is a quick way to find links to governments around the world. Countries from Brunei, Burkina Faso, and Moldova to Oman and Vanuatu are listed. Some countries have few links under their category at this time, but many, like Australia, are a gateway to departments, documents, local governments, research labs, statistics, taxes, and more. Links are often briefly annotated.

REGIONS OF THE WORLD

Africa/Middle East

Print Resources

Al-Sabt, Mohammad. *Arabian Business and Cultural Guide.* TradersCity.com, 2006. 208p. ISBN 0-9790311-1-7. $35.00.

This practical resource for exporters and international traders will help you understand the business culture, the culture, and how to do business with countries like Saudi Arabia, Kuwait, Qatar, and Bahrain. Find tips on how to get connected to the Arabian market, how to make your literature effective, how to negotiate and price, and how to get market data. Food products, electronics and electrical goods, and jewelry are top imports for these countries. Find here ways to break into these lucrative markets.

Mahajan, Vijay. *Africa Rising: How 900 Million African Consumers Offer More Than You Think.* Wharton School of Publishing, 2008. 288p. ISBN 0-13-233942-0. $19.79.

According to Mahajan, Africa, like many emerging markets, has been long overlooked but is poised for explosive growth and opportunity, in this guide for executives and anyone with an interest in global business. He presents arguments for the idea that Africa is richer than you think, and currently presents an opportunity as large as China and India, so it is a good idea to get in on the ground level. Mahajan describes a burgeoning middle class and illustrates how successful companies are organizing the marketplace and creating infrastructure. He illustrates how to identify these problems and overcome the obstacles. This well-written overview of the market provides a tremendous insight into Africa's wealth.

Rehman, Aamir A. *Dubai and Co.: Global Strategies for Doing Business in the Gulf States.* McGraw-Hill, 2007. 288p. ISBN 0-071-4941-38. $27.95.

Rehman illustrates how to approach this region of the world with savvy strategies for managing risks and challenges while crafting business models and strategies designed for this unique market. He will help change your perceptions about the Gulf states and the broader Middle East and explain how to expand your international business to make it faster, bigger, and better. Access Gulf capital more effectively and enable your business to expand and generate both local and global profits.

Online Resources

Africa Business Pages: http://www.africa-business.com/index.html(Accessed Spring 2009).

The Business Guide is one highlight of this large site designed to encourage international business with African countries; the guide provides suggestions on how to do business successfully with African countries. In addition, find information, news, reports, and analysis on the business scene as well as a comprehensive listing of products and services currently in demand in the emerging markets here. Reliable suppliers from and distributors in African markets can also be found

AME Info: http://www.ameinfo.com (Accessed Spring 2009).

The ultimate Middle East business resource, this large site includes Middle East business and financial news, country guides, and industry reports. The country guides provide a business and a social profile, health information, passport and visa information, travel, and history and government data. Also included is a business directory of more than 300,000 companies in 14 Middle East countries.

Mbendi: http://www.mbendi.com/index.htm(Accessed Spring 2009).

This large site is Africa's leading business Web site and is used each month by a large international business audience to identify and research business opportunities in Africa and in the resources sector worldwide. You can subscribe to a free e-mail newsletter to be alerted to business opportunities and to advertise your services to a large audience of international businesses.

Asia/Pacific

This booming area of the world is generally regarded as encompassing littoral East Asia, Southeast Asia, and Australasia near the Pacific Ocean, plus the states in the ocean itself (Australia and New Zealand) and also includes South Asia.

Print Resources

Ambler, Tim, et al. *Doing Business in China.* 3rd ed. Routledge, 2008. 304p. ISBN 0-415-43632-x. $39.95.

> Presented here is a theoretical framework for understanding Chinese business culture plus a basic, practical guide to business practices, market conditions, negotiations, organizations, and the business environment of China. Case studies and examples of business ventures as diverse as car washes, sausages, and outdoor clothing are discussed, along with the issues surrounding products, pricing, distribution, and advertising. The authors conclude with a five pillars model of building a successful business in greater China.

Bijapurkar, Rama. *Winning in the Indian Market: Understanding the Transformation of Consumer India.* Wiley, 2007. 250p. ISBN 978-0-470-82199-2. $19.95.

> Bijapurkar illustrates how India is on the brink of a consumer revolution. Because the government is implementing increasingly laissez-faire policies to open up the domestic market and because the middle-class population is exploding, the long-term potential is spectacular. However, India's complex consumer structure and characteristics are proving to be a challenge to many successful global companies. Bijapurkar writes an insightful and entertaining book that provides thought-provoking answers to problems like what are the cultural traps and minefields in entering India's market, what are the opportunities, and what assumptions should global companies make about this market. Learn about the diversity and complexity of Indian consumers before you do business in India.

Brahm, Laurence J. *Doing Business in China: The Sun Tzu Way.* Tuttle, 2004. 160p. ISBN 0-80-4835-314. $14.95.

> This humorous but practical handbook on mastering the art of negotiating with the Chinese will help business managers plan their strategies for entering the huge Chinese market. Learn how to bridge the cultural gaps in the process of closing deals.

Chee, Harold, and West, Chris. *Myths about Doing Business in China.* Palgrave Macmillan, 2005. 200p. ISBN 1-403-94458-X. $36.95.

> This well-written cross-cultural guide to doing business in China provides fresh, clear material. The authors paint a realistic and pragmatic picture of what the

"real" situation is in China and how western businesspeople can best position themselves to meet the challenges of entering its growing market. The book is arranged along 10 popular myths about China and the Chinese, and they are debunked using solid evidence and prescient insight. If you are looking for a realistic view of China, its people, its growing economy, in order to understand how to work and communicate with them effectively, read this charming work.

Collins, Robert, and Block, Carson. *Doing Business in China for Dummies*. Wiley Publishing Inc., 2007. 364p. ISBN 0-470-20920-8. $21.99.

Learn how to navigate Chinese business culture and etiquette with this authoritative guide. Collins and Block start with the basics and continue through helping you negotiate the Chinese bureaucracy. Travel tips are also included. Find help here to understand the Chinese markets, develop a strong business plan, find employees, work through currency controls and the Chinese banking system, and more. Get tips on advertising and deciding where to set up shop. Also find useful top-ten lists and tear-out cheat sheets.

Dallas, Nick. *How to Do Business in China*. McGraw-Hill, 2008. 128p. ISBN 0-07-1597-239. $12.95.

Dallas highlights 24 lessons that can facilitate a corporation's entry into China. Bristling with amazing opportunities and considerable risks, engaging with China is inescapable and will definitely be profitable for many firms. Tips on avoiding common mishaps and enhancing company preparedness are outlined here. From culture cues and negotiating style to assessing risk and protecting your copyrights and trademarks, you will learn the basic steps needed to plan effectively and efficiently to trade with China.

Davies, Paul. *New Business in India: The 21st Century Opportunity*. World Scientific Publishing Co., 2008. 200p. ISBN 98-127-9042-X. $30.00.

This comprehensive introduction to entering the Indian market will take business planners and developers working in SMEs through the procedures that they must address in order to establish any successful business relationships now when there is a early entry advantage. Learn how to enter the Indian domestic market from Davies, who has firsthand experience and practical insights into the Indian market.

Dossani, Rafiq. *India Arriving: How this Economic Powerhouse is Redefining Global Business*. AMACOM, 2008. 304p. ISBN 0-8144-7424-1. $24.00.

Dossani takes the reader on a tour through India's recent cultural, political, and economic transformations to show how India will surpass China as the World's economic powerhouse. His book is well researched and informative about India's current and future role in the global economy. If you are thinking of doing business in India, read this title.

Forsans, Nicolas and Nelson, Dean. *Doing Business in India*. Dorling Kindersley Pub., Inc., 2008. 72p. ISBN 978-0-7566-3708-8. $8.00.

Part of the Essential Managers series, this book provides information about India's rapidly changing market place, cultural do's, don'ts, and taboos, and the history and politics of the booming economy. These small books provide relevant facts and are a quick read before you begin your business adventure with India. (*Doing Business in China* by Jihong Sanderson is available from the same publisher. ISBN 978-0-7566-3707-1)

Haft, Jeremy. *All the Tea in China: How to Buy, Sell, and Make Money on the Mainland.* Portfolio, 2007. 224p. ISBN 1-591-841-59-3. $25.95.

Haft points out that China is buying goods and services from the United States at a much faster rate than we are importing from them. He elaborates on why this is and how U.S. manufacturers and other businesses can benefit. He also identifies the complexities of doing business with China as well as the opportunities. You will find practical advice on how to do business in China here. It is very important to know what actions are taken as a show of respect and what is offensive to the Chinese. Haft demonstrates how to avoid the pitfalls, provides an industry-by-industry guide to buying from, selling to, and competing with China.

Heberer, Thomas. *Doing Business in Rural China: Liangshan's New Ethnic Entrepreneurs.* University of Washington Press, 2007. 268p. ISBN 0-295-98729-4. $50.00.

Use these case studies to understand how to do business in China outside its major cities. Heberer also presents a large amount of economic data gleaned from his field work in this area. If you are thinking of doing business in this remote region of China, you should learn about the cultural, economic, and social climate of the area from this book.

Makar, Eugene M. *An American's Guide to Doing Business in India: a Practical Guide to Achieving Success in the Indian Market.* Adams Media Corporation, 2008. ISBN 1-59869-211-9. $14.95.

This title is one of the best books available for anyone planning to do business in India and is especially helpful for small businesses that only have a little experience in exporting/importing. U.S. exports to India have more than doubled over the last five years, and in one small book, Makar manages to cover every aspect of doing business for a country as large and complex as any you will find. He covers how to find joint venture partners and hiring local representation. From where to bank to what to wear, you will learn what makes India different and how to be successful there. His insights into conflicting cultural anomalies are especially helpful.

Manian, Ranjini. *Doing Business in India for Dummies.* Wiley Publishing Inc., 2007. 342p. ISBN 0-470-12769-4. $24.99

India, the world's largest democracy, is becoming a global economic power and emerging opportunities here are worth investigating. Manian covers the essential elements of opening and running a business in India, including political and economic issues, government regulations, cultural norms and etiquette, travel tips, tax ramifications, and more. This practical guide also covers basics like choosing a location, selecting your Indian employees, along with financing and marketing tips. Learn how to train and manage your Indian team as well as overcome communication challenges.

McGregor, James. *One Billion Customers: Lessons from the Front Lines of Doing Business in China.* S&S Free Press, 2005. 312p. ISBN: 0-74-32583-98. $15.00.

McGregor, the Wall Street Journal China bureau chief, provides a series of case studies of entrepreneurship during China's rise to capitalism. He paints a vivid and dark picture of the Chinese economy run by corrupt, old-style Communist officials, bribe-hungry bureaucrats, and cutthroat smugglers. As he describes China's true strengths and weaknesses, Western businessmen and investors should pay close attention. Because of 200 years of foreign domination and duplicity, China is still distrustful of outsiders, a fact that greatly influences business practices.

Pellman, Tom. *China Business Guide 2008.* 4th ed. China Economic Review Publishing, 2008. 703p. ISBN 9-881-71493-1. $40.00.

This essential tool for companies looking to enter or grow in the growing China market is compact and well-written. Presented by Pellman are an astounding number of facts, figures, overviews, foreign investment reports, analyses and expert reports, maps and data—all useful to those planning to do business in China, travel to China or set up a business permanently in this dynamic nation.

Plafker, Ted. *Doing Business in China: How to Profit in the World's Fastest Growing Market.* Grand Central Publishing, 2008. ISBN 0-446-69696-X. $16.99.

This user-friendly handbook offers tips and insights on the best opportunities in China, currently the world's fastest growing market. Plafker is a veteran correspondent who has been living in Beijing for eighteen years. He advises on all aspects of breaking into and expanding business opportunities in China. Find help here on selling and marketing techniques, rules and regulations, pitfalls to avoid, and cultural differences. Plafker looks at promising sectors such as automotive, biotech, financial services, retail, and media. He identifies basic maxims of selling and marketing that you need to know when doing business with China. He also identifies challenges like power and water shortages, ethical challenges, and the absolute control of the currency by the government.

Powell, Barnaby, and Mackinnon, Alex. *China Calling: a Foot in the Global Door.* Palgrave Macmillan, 2008. 256p. ISBN 0-230-21019-8. $45.00.

Find help here to develop a new worldview. Powell and Mackinnon review Chinese values and characteristics using Western strategic thinking to understand this new perspective. China's search for resources to fuel its growing economy is transforming Central Asia, Africa, and South America. Learn how China is adapting its traditional values and practices to target strategic investments worldwide and how your company can benefit. Learn and understand how China's very different approaches to problem solving permit an effective engagement with modern China as it seeks competitive advantage globally.

Sano, Yoshihiro, et al. *Doing Business with the New Japan: Succeeding in America's Richest International Market.* 2nd ed. Rowman & Littlefield Pub., Inc. 238p. ISBN 0-7425-5533-X. $24.95.

Japan is once again on the rise. This pragmatic guide for Westerners doing business in Japan explains the culture and negotiating techniques as well as provides advice on conducting productive meetings with Japanese clients. If you want to expand your product or services into Japan, learn from these experts.

Saxon, Mike. *An American's Guide to Doing Business in China: Negotiating Contracts and Agreements; Understanding Culture and Customs; Marketing Products and Services.* Adams Media Corporation, 2006. 275p. ISBN 1-59337-730-4. $14.95.

This rapidly growing economy undeniably has opportunities for many U.S. businesses and products. Learn about the very real political and cultural differences that making doing business in China extremely complex. Saxon explains all aspects of doing business there on a day-to-day basis. This practical guide will help any firm wanting to expand into the Chinese market.

Shen, Michael. *How to Do Business in China.* Dorrance Pub. Co., Inc., 2004. 146p. ISBN: 0-80-59644-36. $20.00.

This useful guidebook addresses how to start and run China operations, how to grow in that market, and how to manage traveling and living in China. Dr. Shen is a consultant for companies entering or growing in China today. Learn about the business, political, and cultural climate from an expert who has lived and worked in China.

Zinzius, Birgit. *Doing Business in the New China: a handbook and guide.* Praeger Pub., 2004. 237p. ISBN: 0-275-98031-6. $71.95.

Besides an introduction to the Chinese market, Zinzius analyzes the subtle nuances which will help Chinese investors, corporate managers, and entrepreneurs. This detailed and unbiased picture of today's China is based on fact and life-work experiences in China. Chapters discusses topics like the practice of "saving face," getting started with a Chinese company, management issues, and legal regulations, as well as culture-based influences on Chinese firms. Ways of Negotiating, To Do's and Taboos in China, and Cross-Cultural Management styles are also listed. Appendix 1 includes Recommended Web Sites, and a short list of Recommended Books is provided.

Online Resources

Asian Development Bank (ADB):http://www.adb.org/ (Accessed Spring 2009).

The work of the ADB and its member countries promotes economic growth, develops human resources, improves the status of women, and protects the environment, while serving its poverty reduction agenda. The section on the People's Republic of China provides an Annual Report, Country Economic Review, Asian Development Outlook (PDF), and Key Indicators (PDF). Many of the smaller member countries provide information through this site as well. News Releases, Publications, and Links are also provided to users.

AsiaOne: http://business.asiaone.com/Business/Business.html (Accessed Spring 2009).

You will find general news on Asia at this Web site, along with a special financial section. Some of information is concentrated on the investment sector, but general economic and industry news is included as well. Singapore's *Business Times* online edition is indexed here, as are the *Shipping Times* and *Computer Times*. The entire site is well organized and easy to use.

Austrade: http://www.austrade.gov.au (Accessed Spring 2009).

Austrade is the Australian Government's trade and investment development agency. It assists Australian businesses in succeeding in trade and investment internationally. It delivers consular, passport, and trade services in designated overseas locations. Find suggestions on help to determine where and when to visit, planning your trade visit, case studies, and export opportunities to work with Australian businesses.

Business in Asia: http://www.business-in-asia.com/ (Accessed Spring 2009).

This private site produced by Runckel and Associates has three locations in China and others in Vietnam, Cambodia, Singapore, and more. Some free useful information is provided on Asian countries as well as industries. Travel information for the region also available.

Chinabidding.com: http://www.chinabidding.com/pub/emain/index.htm (Accessed Spring 2009).

This interesting site especially targets companies wanting to sell to China. Many news stories relevant to import/export opportunities are provided. Procurement opportunities are listed daily. The Statistics and Analysis section provides current data on China's international trade activities and opportunities.

China Business Information Center: http://www.export.gov/china/ (Accessed Spring 2009).

This comprehensive resource from the U.S. Commercial Service will help small or medium-sized businesses begin or expand business into China. Seminars are provided for comprehensive guidance in entering the Chinese market. Experts are available to help and portray the realities and challenges inherent in doing business here. Take the self-assessment test to determine if you are China ready.

***China Business Review* (*CBR*): http://www.chinabusinessreview.com (Accessed Spring 2009).**

The only U.S. magazine providing in-depth analysis on China business for multinational companies, this 25-year old journal covers legal developments, politics, impending legislation, industrial-sector studies, and important investment information, plus Internet resources. Archival issues are available from 1997 to the present, and as with the current issue, some full-text material is available without a subscription.

China Economic Review: http://www.chinaeconomicreview.com (Accessed Spring 2009).

The leading English-language business journal about mainland China, this resource provides in-depth coverage of all aspects of trade and investment with the People's Republic. Analysis of business and financial news is given in articles about regional income, World Trade Organization (WTO) membership, economics, the stock market, and more. Back issues are available from 2000 for a fee. In addition, this Web site contains the largest China business index to be found on the Internet. A subscription is required to access full-text material.

China Today: http://www.chinatoday.com (Accessed Spring 2009).

Find here any kind of information on China or doing business with China. The Import & Export section is very useful as are the lists of suppliers, manufacturers, trade leads and more. Per the site, "China ranks (2nd in the world) with 8.8% of the world's exports in 2007." China travel information and cultural information is also available.

Global Sources: http://www.globalsources.com/ (Accessed Spring 2009).

Global Sources is a leading business-to-business media company and a primary facilitator of trade with Greater China. The core business facilitates trade from Greater China to the world by using a wide range of English-language media. Find here lists of products and companies manufacturing and selling them. Trade shows are also listed. The other business segment facilitates trade from the world to Greater China, and trade within China, using Chinese-language media. The company provides supplier information to volume buyers and integrated marketing services to suppliers. Be sure to check out the Research Reports tab. With the goal of providing the most effective ways possible to advertise, market and sell, Global Sources enables suppliers to sell to hard-to-reach buyers in over 230 countries. Find guides here on how to import from China. Use this site to begin your trade with China.

Japan Economic Foundation (JEF): http://www.jef.or.jp/index.html (Accessed Spring 2009).

JEF was established in July 1981 to deepen mutual understanding between Japan and other countries through activities aimed at promoting economic and technological exchanges. JEF provides information about Japan and arranges opportunities to exchange ideas with many countries in such fields as industry, government administration, academia, and politics in order to break down the barriers to mutual understanding. A highlight of this site is *Japan Spotlight*, a bimonthly publication that provides comprehensive information on Japan's business, trade, economic issues, current events, and politics. In addition, topics on Japanese culture and history are covered.

JGuide: Stanford Guide to Japan Information Resources: http://jguide.stanford.edu/ site/business_economics_133.html (Accessed Spring 2009).

Arranged by topic, this directory of resources offers links to information about Japanese society, business and economics, employment and study in Japan, among other categories. The Import & Export section is especially helpful. In addition, quick links to currency converters, local time in Japan, weather, and news are helpful.

National Portal of India: http://india.gov.in/?business=true#tabs (Accessed Spring 2009).

This large site covers issues concerning starting a business in India, the Indian economy, doing business with Indian companies, and more. If you want to do business with the government, want to be familiar with various Labour Acts, or simply want to know about India's trade relation with other countries, start here.

Nippon Keidanren (Japan Business Federation): http://www.keidanren.or.jp/ (Accessed Spring 2009).

Recognizing business and industry as essential contributors to society, the Japan Business Federation offers monthly white papers on this site on various topics for its more than 1600 members and its Internet audience. Find here current information on Japan's economic and political policies. Examples of topics covered are collaboration among industry/academia/government, aerospace industry in Japan, revitalizing family trade, green solutions for Japan, food safety, and serving an aging society.

People's Daily Online: http://english.peopledaily.com.cn/ (Accessed Spring 2009).

The Chinese People's Daily newspaper began publication in 1948 and has a current circulation of 3 million. The news reflects the views of the Chinese people and the People's Daily Online disseminates information on China to readers around the world. UNESCO places it among the world's top 10 and it is an authoritative and comprehensive source of current information on China. Basic facts about China are also readily available in the China at a Glance section.

The US-China Business Council: http://www.uschina.org/ (Accessed Spring 2009).

This organization provides information, help, and analysis for doing business in China. Full text of their journal *The China Business Review* includes industry trends, country information, economic data, and more, some free and some by subscription. Also find trade facts, legislation, export statistics, and more.

U.S.-China Chamber of Commerce: http://usccc.org (Accessed Spring 2009).

This large site provides information on many diverse topics such as Passports & Visas, Translation, Cross-Cultural Training, Small Business Assistance Center, Trade Mission and Trade Shows, just to name a few sections. Publications and news on recent and important elements of trading between the two countries are also highlighted.

Europe

Print Resources

Bosrock, Mary Murray. *European Business Customs & Manners: A Country-by-Country Guide.* Meadowbrook Press (S&S), 2006. 481p. ISBN 0-684-04001-8. $16.00.

This readable comprehensive guide is organized country by country and covers all the do's and don'ts of business etiquette. Bosrock covers an amazing array of information on situations businesspeople might encounter, including business attitudes and practices, meetings, negotiations, meals, punctuality, language, gestures, tipping, manners, and gifts. Learn how to avoid unrealistic expectations. This essential tool for anyone entering the international market helps you understand and respect the uniqueness of customers, clients, and employees. Success in business around the globe depends on cultural sensitivity.

Suder, Gabriele. *Doing Business in Europe.* Sage Publications, Inc., 2007. 368p. ISBN 1-4129-1847-2. $54.95.

Suder helps you understand the business ramifications of the European Union. Case studies provide real life illustrations of the cultural issues and other complexities of Europe's economic integration. Find out about the achievements and limits of regional integration in order to more effectively negotiate in the changing European environment. Learn how to play a part in raising business competitiveness within Europe.

Online Resources

Baltic Sea States: http://bibl.sh.se/baltic/(Accessed Spring 2009).

This Web directory for the region provides information on subjects like business and economy, the country and geography, environment, news, and society and law. Twelve countries are included. The site is searchable by keyword. This link directory is compiled and managed by the Library at Södertörns University.

Business Information Service for the Newly Independent States (BISNIS): http://www.bisnis.doc.gov/bisnis/new_bisnis.cfm (Accessed Spring 2009).

This unit of the U.S. Commercial Service is the primary market information center for U.S. companies exploring export and investment opportunities in Russia and Eurasia. Find strategies for doing business in this area of the world. Though now discontinued, start a search for information here through the links provided.

Business Portal for Central and Eastern Europe: http://www.ceemarket.com/ (Accessed Spring 2009).

This large site provides some free information on news, trends, economic climate, industries, cities, and countries in this region. Start at the Free Articles and Useful Links to find free, practical information.

Europa: http://europa.eu (Accessed Spring 2009).

This "gateway to the European Union" is a comprehensive site that arranges links by Activities, Institutions, Documents, and Services. Find news about the European Commission, as well as information on the Environment, External Trade, Foreign and Security Policy, Taxation, and Transportation, for example. The Documents section is an online library of the EU and related institutions. Services include consumer opinion polls (Flash Eurobarometer Reports), public procurement information, another library of information, and more. Find an Ombudsman to help you trade with the EU.

European Business Directory: http://www.bizeurope.com/(Accessed Spring 2009).

This large portal brings visitors and its members the latest leads, new company profiles, new distributor and importer contacts, and registered visitors can find export/import offers. Main sections include Find suppliers, Importers, Hotels,

Buy leads, New profiles, Keywords, Finance, and specific regions of the world. This is a good place to start if you are looking to trade with Europe and even China and India.

European Union (EU): http://www.eurunion.org (Accessed Spring 2009).

This EU Web site is designed to encourage international trade for small and medium businesses in the EU with other countries. The Guide to Cracking World Markets is extremely practical. It provides the Market Access Database, which aims to reduce obstacles to global trading. Find here the Exporters Guide to Import Formalities, a Statistical Database, and Studies (full text reports concerning market access for geographical areas or business sectors). Find help here in eliminating trade barriers. Find here a wealth of import information as well.

Eurostat: http://epp.eurostat.ec.europa.eu/portal/page/portal/eurostat/home (Accessed Spring 2009).

This large portal is sponsored by the European Commission. Listed along the left side of the home page are the general themes: General and Regional Statistics; Economy and Finance; Population and Social Conditions; Industry, Trade, and Services; Agriculture and Fisheries; External Trade; Transport; Environment and Energy; and Science and Technology. Elsewhere users will find tables on Employment, Demographic Changes, Environment, Economic Reform, and much more. Business and consumer surveys and Consumer Prices are also available. Much of the information is available free in PDF file downloads. This site is a good place to start for anyone looking to trade with Europe

North America

Print Resources

Becker, Thomas H. *Doing Business in the New Latin America: a Guide to Cultures, Practices, and Opportunities.* Praeger, 2004. 266p. ISBN 0-27-598132-0. $42.99.

Becker describes business as it is practiced and lived in Latin America today. Find here the practical knowledge needed to break into the new Latin American marketplace and convert the untapped profit potential into real opportunities especially for smaller firms. Because Mexico is Latin America's second-most populous country and is heavily urban, much of the information contained here relates directly to Mexico. Learn how to negotiate and sell to this new frontier of customers.

Canadian Almanac & Directory. annual. Federal Publications Inc. 1,732p. ISBN: 978-1-59237-220-1 (2009).

Highlights of this book include the Government Directory; Federal and Provincial/Territorial, Municipal Directory; Business and Finance section with Boards of Trade and Chambers of Commerce and Lobbyists; and Legal Directory. Within the more than 50,000 facts and figures are contact information for associations, radio and TV stations, magazines, commerce and finance organizations, tourism groups, and transportation companies.

Online Resources

Buyusa.gov: http://www.buyusa.gov/home/export.html (Accessed Spring 2009).

This simple-to-use government Web site offers to help businesses get into international sales through market research, trade events, introductions to buyers and distributors, and counseling for any and every step of the export process. One part of the Web site helps importers to the United States, and another helps exporters from the United States, and both parts cover products and services. Part of the Web site, AsiaNow promotes trade with 14 Asia-Pacific markets and provides single-point access to regional trade events, extensive services, and research covering Asian markets. Access Eastern Mediterranean provides U.S. companies with information on the region's markets and its 180 million consumers. The Americas and Showcase Europe provide information and services to those areas of the globe.

Canada Business Services for Entrepreneurs: http://www.canadabusiness.ca/ (Accessed Spring 2009).

Though aimed at Canadian businesses, you will find help and information here for exporting, importing, e-commerce, selling to the Canadian government, and more. The entire Exporting section is a wealth of information for small and medium-sized businesses, from writing the export plan to Business Trip Planning for Exporters. The links under E-Business will help you in many phases of starting or expanding your markets in Canada.

Canada Export Import: http://sbinfocanada.about.com (Accessed Spring 2009).

Developed to help small businesses, this well-organized site will help any company wanting to do business with Canada. Find and learn about creating an international marketing plan, business directories, steps to successful exporting, ways of marketing, financing, export permits, and more.

***Canadian Business*: http://www.canadianbusiness.com/entrepreneur/exporting/ index.jsp (Accessed Spring 2009).**

Articles in this journal deal with all aspects of business, management, international trade, and industry in Canada. Use it for news on economy, industries, and investments. Archived full-text articles from December 2001 are available for free through the search function.

Canada's Export E-business Portal: http://www.export.ca/default.asp (Accessed Spring 2009).

This large site aids exporters and importers. Non-Canadian information includes doing business in Canada, (buying from, selling to, and business forms). Another section of this thorough, well-organized site informs Canadians on business start-up and exporting/importing. Trade shows and trade events are also listed. Many of the links are sites available in French and English.

Doing Business with Canada: http://www.canadainternational.gc.ca/dbc/Export-to-canada-en.aspx (Accessed Spring 2009).

You will learn how to export to Canada, find companies to do business with, and how to establish a business in Canada at this large user-friendly site. The site is sponsored and maintained by the government of Canada and specializes in encouraging international business. On this site, you will find information on our programs and services, as well as our offices in over 140 cities worldwide. The site has been in existence since 2000 and is the result of a joint effort of 12 government departments, agencies, and crown corporations that provide various international business programs and services.

Foreign Affairs and International Trade Canada: http://www.tradecommissioner .gc.ca/ie-en/MarketReportsAndServices.jsp (Accessed Spring 2009).

This large Web site sponsored by ITCan, which has offices in every province, supports the development of trade with Canada by providing services to Canadian and non-Canadian businesses, developing policy, and attracting investment in the Canadian economy. It provides market and industry information, ideas on entering international markets, and advice on export financing as well as sponsoring international trade fairs and trade missions. Links to NAFTA information and podcasts on a variety of subjects are also available. Trade News and Events in Canada and elsewhere can also be located from their Web site.

Latin American Network Information Center (LANIC): http://www.lanic.utexas .edu/ (Accessed Spring 2009).

LANIC's objective is to provide Latin American users with databases and information services throughout the Internet world as well as provide information on and from Latin America. But users will also find lots of NAFTA resources as well as documents, publications, and news.

Mexico Information Center: http://www.mexico-trade.com (Accessed Spring 2009).

This one-stop information center for companies seeking to import from or export to Mexico provides current information, publications, and documents from worldwide sources. It lists business opportunities, trade shows, and more as well as regional and state information.

Strategis Canada: http://strategis.ic.gc.ca/ (Accessed Spring 2009).

This wonderful Canadian site provides a plethora of information for exporting, international trade facts and statistics, market research reports, industry analysis, and more. This useful site generally provides the same services as the U.S. Department of Commerce Commercial Service.

South America

Print Resources

Morrison, Terri and Conaway, Wayne A. *Kiss, Box, or Shake Hands: Latin America: How to Do Business in 18 Latin American Countries.* Adams Media Corporation, 2006. 210p. ISBN 1-59869-217-8. $14.95.

Each chapter of this book focuses on and profiles a country and follows the same format. Information provided includes business-related highlights; country background information like demographics, history, government, and language;

a cultural orientation; business practices; and protocols for things like gift-giving and personal space. The Know Before You Go tips are especially useful. Understanding the role that religion and the Church play in government and everyday life is essential for doing business in these countries.

Tuller, Lawrence W. *An American's Guide to Doing Business in Latin America: Negotiating Contracts and Agreements, Understanding Culture and Customs, Marketing Products and Services.* Adams Media Corporation, 2008. 264p. ISBN 1-59869-212-7. $14.95.

Learn how to determine market risk, find reliable Latin American partners, and use export trading companies to grow your business. Tuller provides up-to-date facts on the politics of 21 countries of Latin America and the United States' relations with various countries. Latin America has 500 million customers wanting to buy U.S. products and services. Discover ways to deal with the cultural differences.

Online Resources

Business in Mexico: http://www.mexconnect.com/mex_/business.html (Accessed Spring 2009).

Part of a large site with a great deal of information on Mexico, this section includes import/export guidelines for Mexico, Canada, and the United States, how to set up a business in Mexico, incorporating a Mexican company, taxes, and documents needed to ship products to Mexico. It contains very practical, useful business and legal data.

Hispanic Business Magazine: **http://www.hispanicbusiness.com (Accessed Spring 2009).**

This monthly publication covers successful Hispanic-owned businesses in the United States and Latin America. Our feature stories highlight significant trends in the U.S. Hispanic market and include profiles of successful entrepreneurs, analysis of economic trends, and news and data on such topics as government procurement, workplace diversity, politics, advertising, entertainment, and events. Columns and features follow political, economic, and social trends affecting Hispanic businesses. Consumer products and the tourism industry are highlighted also as well as tips for entrepreneurs, executives, and managers. This Web site has a searchable archive.

Latin American Network Information Center (LANIC): http://www.lanic.utexas .edu/ (Accessed Spring 2009).

LANIC's objective is to provide Latin American users with databases and information services throughout the Internet world as well as provide information on and from Latin America.

LatinFocus: http://www.latin-focus.com (Accessed Spring 2009).

An outstanding Web site from Spain, this source features economic and financial data by country. It is easy to find news, commentary, financial rates, economic forecasts, market analysis, and political risk assessments. There are good links to more sites such as Reuters, La Nacion, and Bloomberg.

Latin Trade Magazine: http://www.latintrade.com/ Accessed Spring 2009).

This combination print publication and Web site provides news, information, and Internet-based tools to promote import/export activities and achieve cost savings. Generally, it encourages international trade, working to bring buyers and sellers together. The site can be accessed in English, Spanish, and Portuguese.

Mercantil.com: http://www.mercantil.com (Accessed Spring 2009).

This commercial site is Chile's leading business portal. It provides companies and Web sites as well as business opportunity listings by industry or lists the companies in alphabetical order. Products and job opportunities are also identified. Press releases and some relevant news is provided.

Mexico Business Online: http://www.mexonline.com/data.htm (Accessed Spring 2009).

This very practical site explains how to open a Mexican bank account, how to start a business in Mexico, and how to obtain permits to work. Part of the larger MEXonline.com, the business section is short but very useful. The Mexico Business Directory enables users to find companies and professional contacts. The Real Estate and City Guides sections are also very useful.

Mexico Today: http://mexicochannel.net/business.htm (Accessed Spring 2009).

This collection of tables, graphs, maps, and brief texts in the Business Center enables reader to understand the magnitude, structure, and behavior of the Mexican economy and society in the global context. Especially under the heading Doing Business in Mexico, you will find information on setting up a business and on industries, public finance, trade balance, and aggregate economic information, along with a directory of exporters by industry. NAFTA information and other trade sites are very practical. Good links to other sites are provided.

UN Economic Commission for Latin America and the Caribbean: http://www.eclac.org (Accessed Spring 2009).

This organization strives to promote economic development throughout the region through cooperation and integration. Find here statistical information, publications, useful links, and some research and news relevant to the region.

Glossary

International trade, like other specialized fields, has its own distinctive vocabulary or jargon. Listed below and arranged alphabetically are some of the more commonly used terms and acronyms for guiding, regulating, and facilitating international trade. Lack of precise language and communications may impede communication, cause misunderstandings, and delay transactions. If you need more terms or more information, please check the U.S. Department of State's publication Language of Trade at http://www.4uth .gov.ua/usa/english/trade/language/glossac.htm

acceptance: agreement to purchase goods at a stated price and under stated terms.

African Development Bank Group (AfDB): fund established to foster economic and social development of the independent African nations and to promote their mutual economic cooperation.

air waybill: bill of lading or carrying agreement covering domestic and international portions of flights to ship goods to a specific destination.

anti-dumping duties: duty or tax that is intended to discourage importation and sale of foreign-made goods at prices substantially below domestic prices for the same items.

arbitrage: process of buying foreign exchange, stocks, bonds, and other commodities in one market and selling them immediately in another market for a profit.

Asian Development Bank (ADB): fund created to foster economic growth and cooperation in the region of Asia and the Far East and to accelerate economic development for the countries of the region.

ATA carnet: customs document enabling the holder to carry or send goods temporarily into certain foreign countries without paying duties or posting bonds.

balance of payments: summary of all economic transactions between one country and the rest of the world over a given period of time.

balance of trade: difference between a country's total imports and exports; if exports exceed imports, a favorable balance of trade is said to exist.

bank guarantee: assurance that the bank will pay an exporter up to a certain amount for goods shipped if the foreign purchaser defaults, an agreement that is obtained from a bank by said foreign purchaser.

barter: direct exchange of goods for other goods without the use of money; this means of trade is especially valuable in countries using currency that is not readily convertible.

boycott: to decline to do business with a country, business, or individual.

breadth: number of product lines offered for sale by a company.

business plan: detailed summary of a business including objectives and projects over a three- to five-year period.

buying agent: person or company that buys in a country for foreign importers.

CAFTA: the United States-Dominican Republic-Central America Free Trade Agreement (CAFTA) is one in a series of free trade agreements (FTAs) that the United States has entered into with its neighbors in the Western Hemisphere.

Caribbean Development Bank (CDB): fund that provides financing to foster economic development and integration in the Caribbean.

carnet: customs document that allows special categories of goods to be sent or carried across international borders without payment of duties or posting bonds.

cash against documents: term denoting that payment is made when the bill of lading is presented.

cash in advance (CIA): payment for goods in which the full price is paid before shipment is made.

cash with order (CWO): payment for goods in which cash is paid at the time of order and the transaction is binding for both the buyer and the seller.

certificate of inspection: document certifying that merchandise was in good condition immediately prior to shipment.

certificate of origin: document required by some foreign countries for tariff purposes certifying the country of origin of specified goods.

commercial attaché: commercial expert on the diplomatic staff of a country's embassy or consulate in a foreign country.

commercial invoice: seller's itemized list of goods shipped, with details, prices, descriptions, and costs; it is addressed to the buyer and represents a complete record of the business transaction between exporter and foreign importer.

confirmed letter of credit: document issued by a foreign bank with payment confirmed by a U.S. bank.

consignment: payment method option in which the buyer pays for goods after selling them.

consul: government official appointed to reside in a foreign country and charged with representing the interests of his country and its nationals.

contingency insurance: insurance taken out by the exporter complementary to insurance bought by the consignee abroad.

control of goods: identifies specific goods and technology that are controlled for export and exercised or identified through the transport document, and determines whether the buyer will be able to clear an inbound shipment without the transport document.

countertrade: deal in which seller is required to accept goods or other instruments of trade in partial or whole payment for its products.

cultural empathy: capacity of an individual for understanding cultural differences to an extent that allows the individual to see a situation from the standpoint of those in the other culture.

culture: sum of the knowledge, values, beliefs, and attitudes shared by a particular society or group of people.

currency fluctuations: changes in the value of one currency relative to another.

current ratio: the arithmetic ratio of current assets to current liabilities.

customs: duties levied by a country on imports and exports.

demographic characteristics: attributes such as income, age, occupation, etc. that best identify a target market.

depreciation: lessening in value of fixed assets, which usually provide the foundation for a tax deduction.

devaluation: official lowering of the value of one country's currency in terms of one or more foreign currencies.

doing business as (DBA): fictitious name used frequently by sole proprietors or partnerships to provide a name other than the owners or partners under which the business will operate.

dumping: sale of a commodity in a foreign market at less than fair value.

duty: tax levied by a customs authority on an import, export, or the use and consumption of goods.

e-commerce: a business methodology that addresses the needs of organizations, merchants, and consumers to cut costs while improving the quality of goods and services along with increasing speed of service delivery. E-commerce is associated with the buying and selling of information, products, and services via computer networks today and in the future.

economic environment: economic dimensions of the market environment, including population, income and wealth, and extent of economic development.

economic indicators: statistical measures associated with business cycles.

embargo: form of trade barrier that prohibits all trade.

entry strategy: company's strategy for how to do business in foreign markets and the plan for the marketing program to be used for a given product or market.

European Community (EC): an economic and political organization formed in 1967 from the consolidation of three western European treaty organizations: the European Economic Community, the European Coal and Steel Community, and the European Atomic Energy Community. The United Kingdom, Ireland, and Denmark joined in 1973; Greece in 1981; and Spain and Portugal in 1986.

European Union (EU): originally, an economic union consisting of Austria, Belgium, Denmark, Finland, France, Germany, Greece, Ireland, Italy, Luxembourg, the Netherlands, Portugal, Spain, Sweden, and the United Kingdom. Cyprus, the Czech Republic, Estonia, Hungary, Latvia, Lithuania, Malta, Poland, Slovakia, and Slovenia were added in 2004, and Bulgaria and Romania were added in 2007.

exchange rate: price of one country's currency in terms of another.

excise tax: domestic tax assessed on the manufacture, sale, or use of a commodity within a country and often refunded if the product is exported.

executive summary: part of a business plan that compellingly explains the opportunity, shows why it is timely, describes how the company plans to pursue it, outlines the owner's expectation of results, and includes a short sketch of the business.

expansive market selection: approach to selecting foreign markets that starts with the home or domestic market core as a base and expands on a market-by-market basis.

export: a good or service that is produced domestically and sold abroad.

export broker: person or company that brings together the exporter and importer for a fee and then withdraws from the transactions.

export development: process by which a business advances from not exporting to being a committed exporter.

export license: government document permitting the licensee to engage in the export of certain commodities and certain quantities to certain destinations.

export management company (EMC): company that acts as a complete vendor for a company's exporting needs, paying all expenses and receiving compensation for its services.

export merchant: producer or merchant who sells directly to a foreign purchaser with using an intermediary such as an export broker.

Export Packing List: an itemized list of the package contents.

export subsidy: direct or indirect financial contribution to the exporter by its government.

export trading company (ETC): business that also provides complete export service but also takes title to the company's exported goods and is usually formed under the Export Trading Company Act of 1982.

extinction pricing: price is set very low, close to direct cost, in order to eliminate existing competitors from foreign markets.

forecasting: analysis of past and current situations in order to anticipate the future.

foreign sales representative: agent who resides in a foreign country and acts on behalf of a U.S. firm, usually for a commission. Also called a sales agent or commission agent.

foreign trade zone (FTZ): U.S. term for a site sanctioned by the authorities in which imported goods are exempted from duties until withdrawn for domestic sale or use.

franchise: agreement by which a person permits the distribution of goods or services under his trademark, service mark, or trade name, during which time the franchiser retains control over others or renders significant assistance to others (from the FTC rules).

free trade area: economic integration schema whereby member countries abolish tariffs between themselves but each maintains its own tariffs for nonmember countries.

free trade zone (FTZ): area designated by the government of a country to which goods may be imported for processing and subsequent export on duty-free basis, without formal customs entry.

freight forwarder: independent firm handling export shipments for compensation.

free trade agreement (FTA): treaty such as NAFTA between two or more countries to establish a free trade area where commerce in goods and services can be conducted across their common borders, without tariffs or hindrances but (in contrast to a common market) capital or labor may not move freely.

General Agreement on Tariffs and Trade (GATT): was the outcome of the failure of negotiating governments to create the International Trade Organization (ITO). GATT was formed in 1947 and lasted until 1994, when it was replaced by the World Trade Organization (WTO).

globalization: the integration of national economies into the international economy through trade, direct foreign investment, capital flow, and the spread of technology.

global outlook: viewing the world as a single market consisting of a number of segments defined by the product(s) or services to be sold.

hard currency: currency expected to remain stable or increase in value in relation to other currencies.

harmonized system: the Harmonized Commodity Description and Coding System (HS) is an uniform international classification system that assigns identification numbers to specific products for all major trading countries.

high-context culture: a culture's tendency to cater toward in-groups, an in-group being a group that has similar experiences and expectations from which inferences are drawn. In a high-context culture, many things are left unsaid, letting the culture explain. High-context cultures are more common in the Eastern cultures than in Western and in countries with low racial diversity.

horizontal trade association: organization exporting a range of similar or identical products supplied by a number of producers.

import: to bring foreign merchandise into a country from another overseas country or territory.

import license: license required and issued by governments authorizing the entry of foreign goods into their countries.

Incoterms 2000: terms of sale indicating costs and responsibilities included in the price under a sales contract, last revised in the year 2000, and maintained by the International Chamber of Commerce.

indirect exporting: sale by the exporter to the buyer through an intermediary in the domestic market.

inspection certificate: document that may be required to prove that the goods ordered are in the shipment and in good condition.

insurance certificate: a negotiable document that needs to be endorsed before shipping documents are submitted to a bank for payment of goods.

intellectual property: patents, trademarks, service marks, copyrights, and trade secrets of a company are examples of intellectual property.

Inter-American Development Bank (IDB): fund that provides resources to finance development in Latin American countries and administers special funds.

International Chamber of Commerce (ICC): nongovernmental organization serving international trade and world business, it has members in 110 countries and was established in 1919.

internationalization: process, end result, and way of thinking in which a company becomes more involved in and committed to serving markets outside its home country.

interpreter: somebody who carries out oral translation from one language to another.

letter of credit (L/C): document issued by a bank per instructions by a buyer of goods, authorizing the seller to draw a specified sum of money under the stated terms.

low-context culture: a culture's lack of tendency to cater toward in-groups. An "in-group" is a discrete group having similar experiences and expectations, from which, in turn, inferences are drawn. Low-context cultures, such as Germany or the United States, make much less extensive use of such similar experiences and expectations to communicate.

management: responsible for the accomplishment of the mission of an organization, using planning, organizing, leading, and controlling behaviors.

market forecast: expected market demand.

market potential: amount of a product or service that could be absorbed by a market over a indefinite time period under optimum conditions of market development.

market research: the systematic development, interpretation, and communication of decision-oriented information for business owners or managers.

market survey: research method used to define the market parameters of a business.

most-favored-nation status: designation of a country's status in relation to a trading partner.

North American Free Trade Agreement (NAFTA): agreement that lowers trade barriers among the three countries (United States, Mexico, and Canada) from 1994 through 2009 in most categories of goods and services.

North American Industry Classification System (NAICS): the standard used by federal statistical agencies in classifying business establishments for the purpose of collecting, analyzing, and publishing statistical data related to the U.S. business economy.

non-tariff barriers: factors that inhibit international trade and are meant to discourage imports.

open insurance policy: marine insurance policy that applies to all shipments made by an exporter over a period of time rather than to one shipment only.

Organization for Economic Cooperation and Development (OECD): organization established in 1961 to promote the economic and social welfare of member nations and to stimulate efforts on behalf of developing nations.

overhead: all nonlabor expenses needed to operate a business.

packing list: information needed for transport including packing marks as well as the number and kinds of items that are being shipped.

packing marks: set of letters, numbers, and/or geometric symbols, sometimes followed by the name of the port of destination, placed on packages for identification purposes.

paying bank: bank nominated in the L/C to pay out against conforming documents. Exporters need to understand whether the paying bank is in their own country or that of their customer, the importer.

piggybacking: assigning of export marketing and distribution functions by one manufacturer to another.

political risk: possibility of losses incurred by war, government regulation, confiscation, currency inconvertibility, etc.; it is used in export financing and assessing market entry.

port of entry: port where foreign goods are admitted into the receiving country.

pro forma invoice: form of price quote prepared by exporter or seller prior to shipping merchandise informing the buyer of the kinds of goods sent, value, and important specifications such as size, quantity, and weight.

purchasing agent: individual or company that purchases goods in his/her own country on behalf of large foreign buyers.

quota: total quantity of goods of a specified kind that one country permits to be imported without restriction or imposition of additional duties. Most often imposed to protect a domestic market.

quotation: offer to sell goods at a certain price and under stated terms.

rate of exchange: basis upon which money of one country will be exchanged for that of another. Established based on demand, supply, and stability of the individual currencies.

reach: total number of people within a target market reached by a certain advertising campaign.

recourse: important concept in trade finance that indicates the paying party retains the right to the funds in the event that reimbursement from another party is not forthcoming.

return on investment (ROI): simple ratio of net profits to total assets.

revolving letter of credit: L/C that reinstates automatically in relation to time or value, value being cumulative or noncumulative.

Schedule B: U.S. Census Bureau publication based on the Harmonized Commodity Description and Coding System.

Shipper's Export Declaration: document that enables the Census Bureau to monitor exports for statistical purposes.

small and medium-sized enterprises (SMEs) term used to define businesses with fewer than 100 employees for small and less than 500 for medium-sized; globally, SMEs account for 99 percent of business numbers and 40–50 percent of GDP.

Standard Industrial Classification (SIC): numerical system developed by the U.S. government for the classification of commercial services and products that also classifies establishments by type of activity.

Standard International Trade Classification (SITC): standard numerical code system developed by the United Nations to classify commodities used in international trade.

strengths, weaknesses, opportunities, and threats (SWOT) analysis: a marketing and management tool used to evaluate a company's competitive position.

tariff: tax or duty on goods that a country imports and the rate at which imported goods are tax.

tariff quotas: setting a higher tariff rate on imported goods after a specified, controlled quantity of the item has entered the country at the usual tariff rate during a specified time period.

tariff schedule: a list or schedule of articles of merchandise with the rate of duty to be paid to the government of importation.

time management: control of the use of one's most valuable asset, time.

trade associations: industry group used for networking and valuable business contacts.

trade development program (TDP): program to promote economic development abroad and the sale of a nation's goods and services to developing countries.

trade mission: a group of individuals who are taken as a group to meet with prospective customers overseas in order to promote trade through the establishment of contracts and exposure to the commercial environment; it is often sponsored by federal, state, or local agencies.

trade show: stage-setting event in which firms present their products or services to prospective customers in a pre-formatted setting.

Uniform Offering Circular (UFOC): disclosure document containing required information supplied by the franchiser to the franchisee.

World Bank: fund that makes loans when private capital is unavailable at reasonable terms to finance productive investments in order to help develop its member nations.

World Trade Organization (WTO): organization created and named by the Uruguay Round in 1994 for the purpose of providing a set of rules for trade policies and a means for settling disputes among its 124 member nations.

Index

About the Author

SUSAN C. AWE is Associate Professor, and Director of Parish Memorial Library, University of New Mexico, Albuquerque. She is the author of *Entrepreneur's Information Sourcebook* (Libraries Unlimited, 2006), a regular reviewer for *American Reference Books Annual*, and a frequent contributor to such professional publications as *Library Journal* and *Booklist/Reference Books Bulletin*. She also edited *ARBA Guide to Subject Encyclopedias and Dictionaries*, 2nd ed. (Libraries Unlimited, 1997); contributed the "Business and Careers" chapter to *Reference Sources for Small and Medium-sized Libraries* (1999) and the "Current Events" chapter to *Topical Reference Books* (1991).